...thor

One of this century's most distinguished historians of religion, Christopher Dawson was born in England in 1889. Steeped in religious and social tradition, he first studied at Winchester, the most religious of the English public schools, and then at Trinity College, Oxford. His scholarly interests led him to devote himself to the study of the relation between religion and culture. He came to know the Bible thoroughly and through it "the fundamental unity of Catholic theology and Catholic life." The early reading of the lives of the great mystics and saints had greatly impressed him, as did also a later visit to Rome when he was nineteen. In 1914, at the age of twenty-four, he entered the Roman Catholic Church at St. Aloysius, Oxford.

A man of deep vision and historical acumen, Dawson is the author of numerous books on various aspects of religious history, culture, and civilization. Implicit in everything he has written is the theory, so eloquently and convincingly propounded, that without an understanding of religion it is impossible to understand the culture of a man or a race. Above all, Dawson is known for his vast erudition and sweeping grasp of universal history.

As the *Saturday Review of Literature* once remarked, "Mr. Dawson is the most exciting writer of our day . . . unequalled as a historian of culture. Unless we read him we are uninformed."

Religion and World History

A Selection from the Works of Christopher Dawson

Edited by James Oliver and Christina Scott
Foreword by R. C. Zaehner

IMAGE BOOKS

A DIVISION OF DOUBLEDAY & COMPANY, INC.
GARDEN CITY, NEW YORK
1975

Library of Congress Cataloging in Publication Data

Dawson, Christopher Henry, 1889–1970.
 Religion and world history.

 Bibliography
 Includes index.
 1. Religions. 2. Church history. 3. Civilization, Modern.
I. Title.
BL80.2.D35 1975   200'.9
ISBN 0-385-09551-1
Library of Congress Catalog Card Number 74-33612

Contents

Foreword

To be asked to write a foreword to *Religion and World History* is not only an honour and a pleasure, it is also a nostalgic experience, a return to what is indeed the recent past but which is yet a past that already seems to belong to another age. Certainly, as Christopher Dawson saw as clearly as anyone, the "modern age" can be dated from the three revolutions that broke upon the world towards the end of the eighteenth century—the industrial, the American, and the French—which among them brought to an end the dominance of Christian civilisation in the West. He was, however, lucky enough not to have lived to see not only what appears to be the final demise of the remnant of Christianity into a bog of secularisation and desacralisation but also the collapse of the values of its erstwhile enemies of the Enlightenment into the mechanised chaos and glorified violence of the apocalyptic age of terrified anxiety the reality of which even the most obtuse among us are now being forced to accept. He had, however, from the security of his faith and his deep embeddedness in the classical tradition of rationality and *areté* ("excellence"), foreseen it all, though perhaps even his fortitude might have flinched at the Gadarene rush to destruction that seems to have carried us all relentlessly away.

This posthumous collection of the essential writings of Christopher Dawson is a work of pietas in the best

sense of that word, for in it we are privileged to see
through the polished prose the essence of a man both
profoundly Christian and humane; in other words, a
well-rounded Catholic of the old school, open and
free from all sense of bigotry yet deeply anchored in
a Catholic tradition which, despite its authoritarianism
and hierarchical structure, owed quite as much to ancient Greece and Rome as it did to the more sombre
tradition bequeathed to us by the Hebrews. Christopher Dawson, as these essays will show, was very
much an heir to the Renaissance. Perhaps he stood at
the end of a dying tradition, but, with all its faults, it
was a noble tradition, and there is no nobility in the
modern world. Christopher Dawson was "noble" in
this sense; he valued and possessed what the Greeks
called *areté*.

"All men by their very nature long to *know*," Aristotle had said with a pardonable because generous ex-
aggeration. This was very true of Christopher Dawson,
whose thirst for knowledge seemed unquenchable.
Nor would he have disagreed with Aristotle in his co-
rollary to his initial thesis that one indication of this
human thirst for knowledge is an appreciation of the
senses, for Dawson, as a Catholic of the old school,
saw that sensuous beauty, so far from estranging us
from eternal Truth, re-presented that Truth in different forms to suit the taste of successive generations.
He could not, I think, have understood the modern
cult of what all previous civilisations would have
called simply ugliness. He disliked modernity because
it was ugly, brash, superficial, restless, irrational, and
therefore basically deranged. As a sane man he could
scarcely have found happiness in an already mad
world that is now increasingly *seen* to be mad.

His passion to know led him far afield, and in the
first part of this Anthology will be found some hitherto unpublished reflexions on various aspects of

Eastern religions. This, however, was a field in which he was as little at home as was Paul Tillich. One feels, too, that Dawson had little sympathy for them, and it is interesting that only one brief article on Buddhism is included in this book, and even this interprets it not in its own terms but in those of Christianity. But, then, Christopher Dawson was a European of the Europeans, a northern European, to be more precise, as deeply rooted in German thought as he was in English letters. But even German thought could go very wrong indeed. Dawson saw this, as is made very clear in his essay on Hegel, whose brooding genius he sees as being largely responsible for our present ills.

For good or for ill, European civilisation has been responsible for the Europeanisation (and now the Americanisation) of the entire world. Christopher Dawson saw this clearly, and in it he saw both terrible dangers and yet also a gleam of hope. In his view of the future he stands midway between the near-manic optimism of Teilhard de Chardin and the fully depressive pessimism of Georges Bernanos. As always, Dawson looks for the sane Aristotelian mean. What he wrote on the subject of our present crisis, which has indeed escalated to a terrifying degree since his death, seems to be absolutely true:

"The crisis of Europe is the crisis of the world. As Maritain has written: 'A new world is emerging from the chrysalis of history,' but it is only in and through Europe [he would later have added America] that this new world can realize itself. Europe has been led, as it were in spite of itself, to break down the barriers that divided peoples and cultures and to sow broadcast through the world the seeds of a new order. It is true that without spiritual leadership this movement may cause the enslavement of mankind to economic machinery and thus produce an inhuman and anti-spiritual order which is nothing but a kingdom of Anti-

christ. But it is equally capable of serving a higher
end. The material organization of the world by European ideas and Western science is a necessary preparation for that spiritual unification of humanity which
it is the mission of Christianity to accomplish."

Such hopefulness is indeed reminiscent of Teilhard,
but the possibility, indeed the probability, of total
totalitarian enslavement, homogenisation, and dehu-
manisation is far more squarely faced. This becomes
fully apparent in the Introduction to Part III of this
book, appropriately entitled "The Crisis of Civilisation" (not, it will be observed, "The Crisis of *Our* Civilisation"), for the crisis the world faces today is
unlike any that has overtaken us in the past simply because we are now one world, no part of which can go
it alone, as the tragic fate that overwhelmed both
Tibet and Czechoslovakia showed. And the bond of
unity is not a revitalized Catholic Church, as Teilhard
had fondly hoped, but a unity of relentless technoc-
racy either already achieved or eagerly pursued.

How much wiser, how much more prudent was
Christopher Dawson when he wrote in this chapter
(the best, perhaps, and certainly the most significant
in this book): "Today Christianity seems to many a
thing of the past, part of the vanishing order of the
old Europe, and the new powers that are shaping the
world are non-Christian or even anti-Christian." Indeed they are, and such unholy alliances between
naked power (*Realpolitik*, if you like) and "true" religion as that between former President Nixon and Dr.
Billy Graham only go to prove the utter subservience
of religion to the state.

Of course, in the new ecumenism Christians are
drawing together as they have never done before, but
that is scarcely surprising since, by the mere fact of
being "a thing of the past"—a "righteous remnant," if
you like—they have little choice but to stand or fall

together. How this happened is perhaps the main theme of this Anthology. To quote Dawson's own summing-up:

🖝 "First we have divided human life into two parts— the life of the individual and the life of the state—and have confined religion entirely to the former. This error was typical of bourgeois liberalism, and nowhere has it been more prevalent than in the English-speaking countries. But now men have gone further and reunited the divided world under the reign of impersonal material forces, so that the individual counts for nothing and religion is viewed as an illusion of the individual consciousness or a perversion of the individual craving for satisfaction.

"This is the typical error of Marx and Engels and of the totalitarian mass state in all its forms."

How old-fashioned this talk of "truth" and "error" sounds today when even the Catholic Church has abandoned its one-time certainties and presents a spectacle of confusion and disharmony against which she fought for nearly two millennia.

I do not think that Christopher Dawson ever underestimated the sickening power of Satan to destroy, corrupt, and distort all human ideals, including the Catholic ideal of wholeness and sanity-in-absurdity to which he adhered; but though the whole tone of his writing would suggest that his Catholicism, though deeply traditionalist, was always open to reasonable change, he could not but have deplored the total draining away of all sense of reverence from the life of the Church. Reverence, after all, is simply good manners as applied to God, and in the modern world, good manners have gone by the board along with all the other humanistic virtues we inherited from the Greeks. Perhaps it is for this reason that Christopher Dawson was more drawn to Confucianism than to any of the other Eastern religions. How well he would

have understood this song attributed to the Chinese
boy King Ch'êng, so utterly at variance with the brash
ethos of the modern young:

> Reverence, reverence!
> By Heaven all is seen;
> Its change is not easy to hold.
> Do not say it is high, high above,
> Going up and down about its own business.
> Day in, day out it watches us here.
> I, a little child,
> Am not wise or reverent.
> But as days pass, months go by,
> I learn from those that have bright splendour.
> O Radiance, O Light,
> Help these my strivings;
> Show me how to manifest the ways of power.

Christopher Dawson had reverence in all he wrote
and did; he had too, in his unobtrusive way, "bright
splendour." He wrote from within what were for him
divinely inspired values, and as such he was perhaps
the last and certainly one of the most distinguished
representatives of all that was most humane in English
Catholicism. It is doubtful whether he would have
welcomed the proliferation of religious studies as
taught today in some of the more recent universities,
since he might well have thought that learning about
religions, their phenomenology, sociology, psychology,
etc., was no substitute for what seems to be the irre-
versible decline of Christian belief. Yet without being
pretentious about a "theology of hope," his writings
display the much-neglected *virtue* of hope in what
seems to be a hopeless world. He liked to think that
"when ultimately a conflict takes place between the
new state and the Christian church" which would be
"far more severe in character than anything that has
been known before," Christianity would emerge triumphant, as it had from the fiercest persecutions of

the Roman Empire. What he failed to take into account was the continued vitality of the non-Christian world religions, the proper relationship of Christianity to these, and the role that they too might play, either in unison or in friendly rivalry, against the new totalitarian Leviathan. He was not alive to the now fashionable inter-faith "dialogue." Had he lived, it is open to doubt whether he would have been impressed, since he was surely wise enough to have pointed out that the non-Christian partners in the dialogue were as deeply infected (or even more so) by the blind worship of the mystery of science as were the Christians themselves.

Christopher Dawson may seem old-fashioned to our modern theological whizkids, but in the unlikely event of this planet surviving its present compulsive mania for self-destruction and the equally unlikely event of its returning to Aristotelian sanity, he will surely come back into his own as one of the last champions of *areté*—of "excellence", good sense, and dignity—in our present wasteland of vulgarity, unreason, and despair.

R. C. ZAEHNER

Christopher Dawson (1889–1970)
Chronology

1889   Born at Hay Castle, Herefordshire, on October 12. Only son of Lieutenant Colonel Henry Philip Dawson and Louisa Mary Bevan of Hartlington Hall, Burnsall, near Skipton, Yorkshire.

1900–4   Preparatory school, Bilton Grange, near Rugby.

1904–5   Winchester College; removed owing to illness.

1906–7   Attended private tutor at Bletsoe, Bedfordshire.

1907–8   Studied with private tutors at Oxford and in Germany.

1908–11   Trinity College, Oxford.

1911–12   In Sweden with Professor Gustav Cassel and in London working at the Conservative Central Office.

1912–13   At Oxford, School of Rural Economy.

1914   Received into the Roman Catholic Church at St. Aloysius Church, Oxford (January 5).

1915–16   At Oxford, teaching history in a school. His health incapacitated him from national service in the 1914–18 war.

1916   Married Valery Mills at Chipping Campden, Gloucestershire. Their family eventually included one son and two daughters.

1917–18   Worked for the Admiralty Intelligence Division in London.

1920–25   Began his writing career. His first published work appeared in 1920: an essay, "The Nature and Destiny of Man," which he contributed to a symposium entitled "God and the Supernatural." He also contributed articles to *The Sociological Review*.

1925–33 Assistant lecturer at Exeter University on
         the history of culture. Settled at Dawlish,
         near Exeter, Devonshire.

1928   *The Age of the Gods* (London: published
         by John Murray).

1929   *Progress and Religion* (London and New
         York: Sheed & Ward).

1930   *St. Augustine and His Age* (Sheed & Ward)
         (*A Monument to St. Augustine*).

1931   *Christianity and the New Age.* Essays in Or-
         der. (Sheed & Ward).

1932   *The Making of Europe* (Sheed & Ward).
         The Modern Dilemma. Essays in Order.
         (Sheed & Ward).

1932   Attended the Convegno Volta Conference
         in Rome on Europe and gave an address,
         "The Interracial Co-operation as a Factor in
         European Culture."

1933   On the death of his father, Dawson went to
         live in Yorkshire, at Hartlington Hall near
         Skipton.

1933   *Enquiries into Religion and Culture* (Sheed
         & Ward).

1934   Delivered the Forwood Lectures at Liver-
         pool University, *Mediaeval Religion and
         Other Essays* (Sheed & Ward).

1933   *The Spirit of the Oxford Movement* (Sheed
         & Ward).

1934   Lecture to the British Academy on Gibbon
         —The Annual Hertz Lecture on a Master-
         mind.
         During the 1930s he also contributed nu-
         merous articles to *The Dublin Review,* then
         edited by Algar Thorold; *The Criterion,* ed-
         ited by T. S. Eliot; *The Colosseum* edited
         by Bernard Wall; and *The Tablet,* edited by
         Douglas Woodruff.

1936   *Religion and the Modern State* (Sheed & Ward).

1938–39   Dawson left Yorkshire and went to live at Cambridge.

1939   *Beyond Politics* (Sheed & Ward).

1939   On the outbreak of war, Dawson went to live at Boars Hill, near Oxford.

1940   Became Vice-President of the Sword of the Spirit Movement, initiated by Cardinal Hinsley.

1940–44   Editor of *The Dublin Review*.

1943   *The Judgment of the Nations* (Sheed & Ward).

1947–48   Delivered the Gifford Lectures at Edinburgh University.

1948   *Religion and Culture* (Sheed & Ward).

1950   *Religion and the Rise of Western Culture* (Sheed & Ward).

1950   Lectured at Dublin University.

1951–52   Lectured in Spain.

1953   Left Oxford and returned to Devonshire, where he settled at Budleigh Salterton.

1952   *Understanding Europe* (Sheed & Ward).

1957   *The Dynamics of World History,* edited by John Mulloy (Sheed & Ward).

1958   Invited to be the first Stillman Guest Professor of Roman Catholic Studies at Harvard University.

1958–62   In residence at Harvard. While in the United States he lectured widely at various Catholic colleges and inaugurated a course of Christian culture at St. Mary's College, Notre Dame University. He was awarded an honorary degree at St. John's University, New York, and his wife was given an honorary LL.D. at Regis College by Cardinal Cushing.

1959   *The Movement of World Revolution* (Sheed & Ward).

1960   *The Historic Reality of Christian Culture* (New York: Harper & Row).

1961   *The Crisis of Western Education* (Sheed & Ward).

1962   Resigned Harvard professorship after a series of strokes and returned to England.

1962–70   At Budleigh Salterton, Devonshire.

1965   *The Dividing of Christendom* (Sheed & Ward).

1967   *The Formation of Christendom* (Sheed & Ward). (These comprised the two volumes of lectures delivered at Harvard, 1958–62.)

1970   Died on May 25 at Budleigh Salterton and was buried in Burnsall churchyard, near Skipton, Yorkshire.

        Posthumous publications:

1972   *The Gods of Revolution:* Introduction by Arnold Toynbee (London: Sidgwick & Jackson; New York: New York University Press).

1972   *The Dividing of Christendom* (English edition); Introduction by David Knowles (Sidgwick & Jackson).

1970   *Tradition and Inheritance: Reflections on the formative years;* Introduction by John J. Mulloy (St. Paul, Minn.: The Wanderer Press). Originally published in *The Wind and the Rain* (1949), London: A review edited by Neville Braybrooke.

Acknowledgments

THE GREATER PART of this selection from the writings of Christopher Dawson has never appeared in book form, and much of it is taken from unpublished manuscripts. The sources of all the material and the date of writing or publication are given in the Appendix.

Grateful acknowledgment is made to the editors of the various journals and publications in which these articles first appeared; to Sheed & Ward, New York, for permission to reprint extracts from *The Formation of Christendom* and *The Movement of World Revolution;* to New York University Press, New York, for permission to reprint extracts from *The Gods of Revolution;* Part One, Chapter 1, "A Definition of Religion," is reproduced by kind permission of the Caxton Publishing Company Limited, London, England; and the Epilogue, "The Future Life," is reproduced by kind permission of *The Spectator*, London.

One

The World Religions

"Civilisation is a road by which man travels, not a house for him to dwell in. His true city is elsewhere."
Religion and the Modern State (1935)

Introduction: Religion, Language, and Civilisation

IF OUR KNOWLEDGE of the past continues to advance as it has done in the last hundred years, we may be eventually able to write the History of Civilisation as we write that of a state or a nation today. Five, or even ten, thousand years are only a moment in the life of nature. Yet the whole course of human civilisation and all its works are only a matter of a few thousand years. And it is a continuous process, which is still in the course of development, so that when we study the growth of civilisation, we are living witnesses of the greatest of all the works of creation.

How was this miracle achieved? How did it come about that man alone among the countless forms of life that have existed on this planet has been able to separate himself from the other animals, to change his ways of life, and finally to transform the world in which he lives?

In the beginning was the word. Language is the gateway to the human world, which is also a moral world, and language is far older than civilisation. Its origins go back to the beginnings of human culture and consequently to the origins of humanity itself. The fact that it is possible to teach apes to ride bicycles, but impossible to teach them to talk, suggests that it is the use of language rather than the use of tools which is the essential characteristic of humanity. The word, not the sword or the spade, is the power that has created human culture. The invention of language

was the first step in the process that has led to civilisation, and none of man's subsequent inventions—agriculture and the domestication of animals, the use of
metals and the discovery of writing, the building of
the city and the state—important as these have been,
can be compared with this archetype and source of all
cultural activity.

Without language it would have been impossible for
man to free himself from the domination of instinct,
which determines the unchanging life of non-human
existence. For it is only by language that he can pass
on the memory of past experience to future generations and thus form the accumulation of knowledge
which is the condition of culture. Language is the organ of social tradition and the means of social communication, and these are the two main factors which
make human culture possible.

In reality a culture has far more resemblance to a
language than it has to a race. As a language is a peculiar way of communication, created by a group of
men inhabiting a common area to express its common
needs and ideas, so a culture is a particular way of
behaviour developed by a group of men to enable
them to live successfully in their particular circumstances and environment. Language is, of course, itself only a part of culture, but it is the aspect of
culture which is most sharply defined and most clearly
separate from non-cultural elements. Culture as a
whole is far more difficult to grasp, since it involves
many different factors, so that a highly developed culture is perhaps the most complex phenomenon that it
is possible to study. Even in the case of the simplest
known or conceivable culture, there are at least four
of these factors without which it cannot exist.

There are: (1) the sociological factor, or the principle of social organisation; (2) the geographical or
ecological factor, the adaptation of culture to its phys-

ical environment; (3) the economic factor, the relation between man's "way of life" and the way in which he "gains his living"; and (4) the moral factor, the regulation of human life in conformity with some system of values and standards of behaviour.

The civilisations, no less than the simpler cultural units, also involve a principle of moral order. We see this with exceptional clearness in the case of China—that is to say, Confucian China, which was preserved for more than two thousand years by what seemed to be a changeless norm based on the Confucian code of ethics and the Confucian standards of behaviour. But the same thing is true of the other world cultures of India and Islam, of Tibetan Buddhism, of Judaism, and finally of Christianity in the West.

For the world civilisations are the great beaten highways on which mankind has travelled through history, and in every case men believed that they were following a divinely appointed path. In the past they believed, and many of them believe today, that their civilisation is not merely a form of social organisation that has been developed through the centuries, but that it is also dependent on a transcendent divine order, which has been revealed in the inspired writings of the prophets and lawgivers who laid the foundations of their culture. All the great civilisations were originally, as the Moslems say, People of the Book. They all possess a corpus of sacred scriptures; each has its own sacred language and its sacred order of teachers, who are trained in the study or interpretation of the sacred writing and rites—Confucian scholars in China, Brahmins in India, Ulema in Islam, Jewish rabbis and Christian priests.

Thus there has been a close relation between the world civilisations and the world religions, which have endured for ages, which we must study if we are to understand the spiritual ideals that have inspired these great cultural unities which far transcend the national and political unities, which we are apt to regard as the ultimate social realities.

Nor has the advent of a world technological civilisation changed this. For it is a purely external order. It does not bring with it a new moral order. On the moral plane, therefore, influences of the old religious traditions still exist and mould man's ways of thought and behaviour.

A Definition of Religion

RELIGION IS THE WORD generally used to describe man's relation to divine or superhuman powers and the various organised systems of belief and worship in which these relations have been expressed. The belief in the existence of such relations is a general human conviction, common to all peoples and to all stages of culture, for though it has often been maintained in the past that various primitive peoples, such as the Kubu of Sumatra, the Andaman Islanders, or the natives of Tierra del Fuego, were entirely without any form of religion, the progress of ethnological knowledge has usually shown that these suppositions were groundless. It is true that it is often difficult to draw a clear distinction between religion and magic in primitive cultures, since magic often appears to be an alternative method of dealing with the same needs and situations with which religion is concerned. The two, however, are not mutually exclusive. Much that we call magic is simply the more specialised ritual techniques of primitive religion, while in other cases it represents such techniques which have become detached from religious beliefs or which have survived from an earlier phase of religion. The essential criterion of religion is the attitude of worship. When religious rites become detached from this attitude, they become magical techniques; when magical techniques are associated with the attitude of worship, they become religious rites.

The primary elements of religion are the act of worship and the object of worship. From the interaction of these two factors there arise the organised systems of thought and behaviour which are known as religions. The normal object of religious worship is a God, that is to say a superhuman being on whom man is dependent and who controls the world or some particular aspect of nature. But though God is the central and typical religious concept, there are many other forms of superhuman power which may be the objects of religious worship—spirits and ghosts, omens and portents, sacred men, sacred animals and sacred things—a whole world of sacred or supernatural powers with all of which religion is concerned. The various theories which have been constructed during the last two centuries to explain the nature and origin of religion have concentrated their attention on some particular element in this complex as the key to the solution of their problem. Thus Max Muller explained religion from the worship of the powers of nature and the development of Nature Myths. Tylor found the key in the belief in ghosts and the universal animation of nature by personal spirits. Durkheim found a sociological explanation in his theory of Totemism and the collective consciousness; while for Frazer, religion develops out of magic in consequence of the gradual recognition by primitive man that magical techniques are fallible and inadequate. Perhaps the broadest and most comprehensive theory is that known as Animism or Dynamism, which explains primitive religion in terms of an undifferentiated magical or supernatural power, an impersonal quality of divinity or sacredness which may become attached to particular persons or things and which manifests itself in any kind of abnormal experience or extraordinary event. Nearly two generations ago, however, Andrew Lang challenged the basic assumption of all these theories by arguing that the idea of a personal deity is not the final product of a complex religious evolution but that it is simple and primary, and is actually well represented among the most primitive peoples known to us. Since Lang's day this view has been supported by a great volume of evidence collected by W. Schmidt and his followers, and it is no longer possible to deny the existence of a belief in High Gods in low cultures. The fact is that it is no more possible to reduce primitive religion to a single element than that of civilised man. In both alike we find a great multiplicity of religious phenomena and a considerable variety of psychological attitudes. There is no simple unilinear process of religious evolution. There is, however, an intimate relation between the religion of a people and its culture or way of life, and recent advances in the understanding of religion have been largely due to the study of religious beliefs and practices in their dynamic relation to social institutions and economic functions.

But though the sociological interpretation of religion has proved of very great value, it must not be pressed too far. It is of the very nature of religion to transcend the social category, since it is essentially concerned with forces that are held to be superior to man—divine powers on which the life of society and the life of the individual are alike dependent. This sense of transcendence, of otherness, of divinity is characteristic of the religious attitude and makes the relation between religion and culture a two-sided one. The social way of life influences the approach to religion, but also religious beliefs influence social action. Already in primitive cultures we see the development of specialised social organs and techniques for religious ends—indeed, this development represents the earliest form of professional specialisation that is known to us. On the one hand, the development of a technique of communication with the divine led to the rise of a class of diviners, shamans, and prophets. On the other, the development of the technique of worship, and especially of sacrifice, led to the rise of the priesthood. These two classes have had a profound influence on the development of culture, and at least from the beginnings of the historic Sumerian and Egyptian civilisations about five thousand years ago, we can trace the continuous development of organised priesthoods and sacred corporations which were the guardians and the teachers of the religious traditions of their cultures. In this way there arose an organised body of religious knowledge, which was eventually embodied in religious literatures and codes of law.

The subsequent history of world religion is to be found in the development of these organised traditions and in their interaction and conflict with the teachings and criticisms of individual religious teachers who arose within the orbit of an existing religion. The most remarkable example of this religious and cultural continuity is that of Brahmanism, the tradition of the ancient—even prehistoric—sacred class of India, which has preserved the Vedic religious literature and ritual science intact for thousands of years. And out of this tradition there has arisen, by way of reaction and criticism, the world religion of Buddhism, as well as the no less ancient religion of Jainism. A continuous religious tradition of this kind tends to incorporate the whole structure of culture, so that religion and civilisation become fused in a social unity dominated and permeated by religious conceptions. Hence a world religion is not only a form of worship and a body of doctrine, it also involves a social ethic, a system of law, a cosmology, a sacred history, and a philosophy.

Down to recent times the whole civilised world was divided among five great religio-cultural traditions of this kind: the tradition of Christianity in Europe and America; the tradition of Islam in Western Asia and

North Africa; the Confucian and Taoist tradition in China and the Far East; the tradition of Brahmanism in India; and the Buddhist tradition, which has disappeared from its Indian homeland but maintains itself in wide areas of secondary diffusion in Southern, Central, and Eastern Asia. In addition to these, there are two great religions—Judaism and Zoroastrianism—which have survived as religions though they no longer possess any independent spheres of culture. All these seven world religions possess their own sacred books or inspired scriptures, which form the basis of their theological and ethical systems.

Some idea of the character and scale of these works may be gained from a survey of the material contained in the fifty volumes of the Sacred Books of the East, published in English at Oxford from 1876 to 1910. But these do not include the literature of the three Western religions (except for one work), and it is probable that the religious literature of Christianity alone exceeds in bulk all the literatures of the other six religions put together. The field of study is therefore a vast one, and it is only during the past century that the material for a comparative study of the different religious traditions has been made available. Until the nineteenth century, the study of religion was inevitably confined to a single tradition or at most to two traditions, so that every civilisation was a self-contained spiritual universe. But since the beginning of the nineteenth century, three fundamental changes have occurred. First, we have obtained access to the literature and thought of the other world religions: second, we have been able to study the religion and culture of uncivilised peoples, whose way of life and forms of thought are completely strange to us; and finally, archaeological discoveries have revealed the religions of extinct civilisations, some of which, notably those of Egypt and Mesopotamia, are of central importance for the history of world civilisation. These three new sources of information have transformed and renewed religious studies.

In addition to these new sources of information, the study of religion has also been influenced increasingly during the last half century by the study of psychology. Here the greatest contribution of the psychologists has undoubtedly been the discovery of the Unconscious and the demonstration of the immense importance of the unconscious mental processes on human thought and behaviour. Thus the very elements in religion which were ignored or depreciated or explained away by the earlier philosophic and rationalist students of religion have been put in the forefront of scientific study. In this way we have come to understand much more about these unexplored territories of the soul, which have been of such importance for religious experience—the world of dream and vision, the world of symbol and myth, and the unconscious forces of sublimation and repression that control the moral aspects of the personality.

No doubt the tendency of many psychologists has been to treat religion as the result of a delusional process of projection which can be explained away by scientific methods of analysis. But this is often due, as in the case of Freud, to an antecedent philosophical theory. And there are other psychologists, notably C. G. Jung, who fully realise the transcendent character of religious experience and who regard the process of symbol formation which is characteristic of religion as the key to the deepest levels of spiritual reality.

The combination of this intensive psychological study of the archetypes of religious symbolism with the extensive historical study of the world religions and the religions of earlier and more rudimentary phases of culture open the way to a new "phenomenological" science of religion, such as Professor van der Leeuw indicated in his important work *Religion in Essence and Manifestation.*

Such a science is concerned with religion in all its manifold forms and expressions as an autonomous field of human experience and existence which deserves to be studied and understood for its own sake without apologetic claims or philosophical judgments. It seeks to understand the religious fact or phenomenon as it appears to the religious man, and in order to do so it enlists the help of psychology and of all the specialised historical, anthropological, and philological sciences which provide the raw materials of its study.

Nevertheless, this phenomenological science of religion only deals with one side of the religious problem: it confines itself to the study of man's religious reactions. But since religion is essentially a dynamic relation between man and a non-human or superhuman Other, it can never dispense with a higher form of knowledge, which is concerned not with the human subject but with the divine object. This is the traditional function of theology, and theology must always retain its primacy and its autonomy, so long as religion is studied as a divine reality as well as a human experience. There is, however, no necessary conflict between the absolutism of pure theology and the relativism of religious phenomenology; indeed, the two disciplines are complementary and necessary to one another.

For it is obvious that if there is no theology—no knowledge of the object of religious experience, no knowledge of divine truth and divine creativeness— our attitude to religious phenomena will be different, and the religious phenomenon itself will tend to become dim and attenuated, as has in fact been the case with so many "philosophies of religion" and "histories of religion" in the past. The question of how such a form of religious knowledge or theological science is conceivable and attainable does not concern us here. We need only observe that all the higher forms of religion do in fact assume the existence of such a knowledge and base their teachings upon it. The conception of a word of God—a divine revelation; a divine law; and divine, eternal truths—are hardly less essential to religion than the concept of the divine object of worship itself.

Primitive Religion: Shamans and Divine Ancestors

RELIGION IS THE KEY OF HISTORY. We cannot understand the inner form of a society unless we understand its religion. We cannot understand its cultural achievements unless we understand the religious beliefs that lie behind them. In all ages the first creative works of a culture are due to a religious inspiration and dedicated to a religious end. The temples of the gods are the most enduring works of man. Religion stands at the threshold of all the great literatures of the world. Philosophy is its offspring and is a child which constantly returns to its parent.

And the same is true of social institutions. Kingship and law are religious institutions, and even today they have not entirely divested themselves of their numinous character, as we can see in the English coronation rite and in the formulas of our law courts.

All the institutions of family and marriage and kinship have a religious background and have been maintained and are still maintained by formidable religious sanctions. The earliest social differentiation and the one that has had the most potent influence on culture has been due to the specialised social classes and institutions, charged with the function of maintaining relations between society and the divine powers. The fact that this class has almost invariably been responsible in whole or in part for the education of the community and the preservation of sacred tradition and learning gives it an exceptional importance in the his-

tory of culture, and we must study the specific form it
takes in any particular culture or religion before we
can begin to understand it. The Sumerian and Egyptian temple priesthoods, the Brahmin caste in ancient
India, the clergy and the monastic orders in mediaeval
Christendom are not merely religious institutions, they
are also vital social organs in their respective cultures.
And the same is true of the Shamans, the medicine
men and witch doctors among primitive peoples,
although our current terminology often blurs the distinction between the sorcerer, whose function is non-
social or anti-social, and the priest, who is the recognised religious organ of the community—a confusion
which has been increased by the attempt to draw a
rigid and exclusive line of division between religion
and magic.

The more primitive a culture is, of course, the less
room there is for an explicit differentiation of social
functions, but on the other hand, the more directly is
its religion bound up with the elementary needs of
life, so that the social and economic way of life is more
clearly interpenetrated by and fused with religion
than is the case in the higher cultures.

Thus among the Australians there was no true
priesthood and the leadership in religion as in other
matters fell to the old men, who were the natural leaders of the tribe and the guardians of tradition. Nevertheless, they possessed a most elaborate and highly
organised system of religious rites to ensure the continuity of the life of the tribe and the maintenance of
its food supply—a regular liturgy, which in some instances, as described by Spencer and Gillen, occupied
the community almost continuously for three or four
months at a time. In this case the way of life of the
community is conceived as dependent on another and
a sacred world—the world of the divine totemic ancestors—from which the spirit comes and to which it

returns, and the totemic ceremonies provide the way of access and communion between the life of the tribe and the other world of the sacred *alcheringa* age.

It is difficult for a civilised man to understand either the religious significance or the cultural importance of such ceremonies. But to the primitive, the dance or mime is at once the highest form of social activity and the most powerful kind of religious action. Through it the community participates in a mystery which confers supernatural efficacy upon its action. How this may affect social life and change the course of historical events may be seen in the rise of the Ghost Dance religion among the Indians of the Plains at the end of the nineteenth century. Here we have a well-attested case of how a dance may become the medium by which the religious experience of an individual may be socialised and transmitted from one people to another with revolutionary political effects. Wovoka, an Indian of a little-known and unimportant tribe in Nevada, received in a vision a dance, the performance of which would bring back the spirits of their dead ancestors and the vanished herds of buffalo and the good times that were past. The dance cult spread like wildfire eastward across the mountains to the Indians of the Great Plains and finally stimulated the Sioux to their last desperate rising against the United States government.

The most remarkable thing about this movement was the extreme rapidity with which it communicated itself from people to people across half the continent, so that if it had not been defeated by a hopeless inequality of material power, the Ghost Dance might have changed not only the religion but also the social existence of the Indians of the Middle West in the course of a few years. Such revolutionary changes are in fact by no means rare in history. We have an example of it on the higher religious level and on a vast historical scale in the case of the rise of Islam. Here we see in full clearness and detail how a new religion may create a new culture. A single individual living in a cultural backwater originates a movement which in a comparatively short time sweeps across the world, destroying historic empires and civilisations and creating a new way of life which still moulds the thought and behaviour of millions, from Senegal to Borneo. And in this case there is no common geographical environment or racial inheritance to form a basis for the spiritual community. A common faith has imposed its stamp on the most diverse human material, so that the resultant product is even physically recognisable. The Arab of the desert, the West African Negro, the Malay pirate, the Persian philosopher, the Turkish soldier, the Indian merchant all speak the same religious language, profess the same theological dogmas, and possess the same moral values and the same social conventions. Just as Moslem architecture is different in every country but is everywhere unmistakably Moslem, so it is with this literature and speech and behaviour.

No doubt modern nationalism and secularism have altered all this, but they have done so only recently and superficially and incompletely. Islam still exists as a living culture as well as a world religion.

Thus Islam provides a classic example of how culture—the social way of life—may be transformed by a new view of life and a new religious doctrine, and how as a result social forms and institutions may be created which transcend racial and geographical limits and remain fixed for centuries. And on the other hand, we have countless examples—especially among primitive peoples—of religions which are so bound up with the culture of the community that they seem to be mere psychological reflections of the way of life of a particular people in a particular environment and to possess no religious significance apart from their social background. But however earthbound and socially conditioned these religions appear to be, they always look beyond society to some trans-social and super-human reality towards which their worship is directed.

And conversely, however universal and spiritual a religion may be, it can never escape the necessity of becoming incarnated in culture, and clothing itself in social institutions and traditions, if it is to exert a permanent influence on human life and behaviour.

For every historic religion, from the lowest to the highest, agrees on two fundamental points: first, in the belief in the existence of divine or supernatural powers whose nature is mysterious but which control the world and the life of man; and second, in the association of these powers with particular men, or things, or places or ceremonies, which act as channels of communication or means of access between the human and the divine worlds. Thus on the lowest levels of culture we find the Shaman, the fetish, the holy place, and the sacred dance, while on the higher level we have the prophet and priest, the image or sacred symbol, the temple, and the sacramental liturgy. Thus every great historic culture, viewed from within through the eyes of its members, represents a theogamy, a coming together of the divine and the human within the limits of a sacred tradition.

As a rule, the creative role in the formation of culture is assigned to divine or semi-divine mythical figures—culture heroes or divine ancestors—who have delivered to their descendants or followers not only the sacred myths and sacred rites of religion but the arts of life and the principles of social organisation.

Sometimes these figures are themselves the creators of man, like the totemic ancestors who, as the tribes of Central America believe, had in the beginning journeyed through their country, performing ceremonies and leaving spirit children behind them. Sometimes they are heroic human figures which have become the centres of a cycle of myths; while the great historic cultures for the most part look back to the personality of some historical prophet or lawgiver as the source of sacred tradition or the mediator of divine revelation. And there seems to be no reason why we should exclude a priori the possibility of such figures arising in very primitive cultures, in the same way that Wovoka arose among the Paviotso in the nineteenth century. We must never forget that existing or recorded primitive culture is, no less than any higher civilisation, the result of a long process of historical change and development, in the course of which there may have been periods of advance and regression in thought as well as in action. And though primitive culture is more communal and anonymous than the higher civilisation, it is never so communal as to exclude the creative action and influence of individual personalities. Hence the mythical figure of the first man, the culture hero, the firebearer, the teacher of the arts of life and the rites of religion, is the archetype of the many forgotten or half-remembered figures which have played a decisive role in the formation or transformation of culture. In classical and oriental archaeology the progress of modern research has discovered again and again a solid bedrock of historical truth underlying the myths and legends that tradition has preserved, and in the same way behind primitive culture there is a lost world of history which is still more deeply submerged beneath the surface of consciousness.

In this twilight world history and religion are inextricably interwoven and confused, as we can see in the legends of our own past, where lost gods like Bran and Pwyll appear side by side with half-remembered historical figures like Arthur and Maxim Wledig and with the creatures of poetic legend. In fact, culture is like a palimpsest in which the new characters never entirely efface the old, or a patchwork in which fragments of different age and material are brought together in a single social pattern.

To the outside observer the most striking feature of primitive culture is its extreme conservatism. Society follows the same path of custom and convention with the irrational persistence of animal life.

But in reality all living culture is intensely dynamic. It is dominated by the necessity of maintaining the common life, and it is possible to ward off the forces of evil and death and gain life and good fortune and prosperity only by a continuous effort of individual and social discipline. Hence the ascetic element is prominent in primitive culture and in both primitive and advanced religions. The law of life is the law of sacrifice and discipline. If the hunter is to capture his prey, if the warrior is to overcome his enemies, if the cultivator is to receive the fruits of the earth, he must give as well as take. And he does not think of this giving in terms of manure, or drill, or athletic exercise, he views it in religious terms as sacrifice and penance and ritual acts paid to the powers above. This is the meaning of the fertility rites of the peasant culture, of the ascetic practices of the Indians of the Plains and the cult of the animal guardians among primitive hunters, all of which are keys to the understanding of their respective cultures.

So too the initiation rites, which hold so large a place in every form of culture, represent an intensive effort of social discipline directed towards the incorporation of the individual into the community under the sanction of religious powers. These are not merely ordeals of social fitness to prepare the candidate for adult life as a full member of the community, they are even more an initiation into sacred mysteries, which confer new powers upon him. In some cases these initiations involve supernormal psychological experiences, so that a youth's future social career may depend on the nature of his visionary experience. "Your young men shall see visions and your old men shall dream dreams." This is no more than the common experience of many an uncivilised people, and it shows how, even in lower forms of culture, religion tends to transcend the social way of life and seeks to open a path of direct access to the world above.

Thus while a culture is essentially an organised way of life, it is never conceived as a purely man-made order. The social way of life is founded on a religious law of life, and this law in turn depends on non-human powers towards which man looks with hope and fear, powers which can be known in some fashion but which remain essentially mysterious, since they are superhuman and supernatural.

Primitive Religion:
Mother Goddess and Fertility Cults

THE VITAL CHANGE in primitive culture is not that from
magic to religion, for as we have seen, religion lies at
the root of the whole development, but from Shamanism to Priesthood. When the latter stage is reached,
man's relation to the supernatural powers that govern
his existence is no longer dependent on the unregu-
lated transports of the Shaman, but becomes a social
function controlled by a regular order.

Even the most anomalous and individualistic aspects of Shamanism acquire social significance when
they are transferred to the hands of a priestly corporation. For example, the history of the Delphic oracle
shows how the office of the diviner, when adminis-
tered by an able priesthood, may become of transcendent social importance for a whole civilisation.
Nor is this a unique phenomenon, for the Long Ju-Ju
of Aro, the famous oracle of the Cross River, played
a very similar part among the barbarous Ibo peoples
of Southern Nigeria.

But it is in the case of these functions which are pre-
eminently social, that is, the rites which deal with the
physical welfare of the people and the safeguarding of
their means of sustenance, that the socialisation of religion has the most important results on the development of culture. As far back as Palaeolithic times, the
evidence of the cave paintings suggests that one of
the most important social functions was the attainment
of success in hunting by magical practices, which were

intended to give man control over the beasts, which were the chief source of his food supply. But it is probable that this hunting magic was associated with the individualistic type of Shamanism which is still found among the most backward peoples of North America, for example, the tribes of the Mackenzie basin, among whom the social unit is the small and unorganised band of hunters. A higher stage of organisation is reached when a society becomes subdivided into a number of different groups, each of which has its own sacred rites, and is united by ceremonial or religious bonds. And just as the Shaman, or even the individual hunter, in a simpler phase of society has his own guardian spirit, usually in animal form, so now each group possesses a sacred bond with some particular species of animal or plant. A number of different conceptions may enter into this totemic relationship. Indeed, the term totemism has been so loosely used that it is often made to cover all kinds of different ideas, from the belief in animal guardian spirits and the worship of animal gods, to the use of semi-heraldic tribal emblems.

The root of true totemism, however, seems to be found in the conception of the totem as a food giver, and in the rites for the conservation and increase of the means of subsistence. As among the hunting peoples of North America and Siberia, the buffalo and the bear are sacred animals, so in Australia every object which supplies the native with food, whether the wichetty grub, the grass seed, or the kangaroo, becomes the totem of a group. This aspect of totemism is seen most clearly in the ceremonies for the multiplication of the totemic animal or plant, known among the Arunta as Intichiuma, for example, in the case of the wild grass totem. Here the magic rites have entirely lost their individualistic character. The head of the totem performs the rites which cause the growth of the wild grass seed, or the multiplication of the wild bees not for his own profit, since he is forbidden to partake of them except in a solemn ritual manner, but for the welfare of the people as a whole. He is in fact a true priest, a social functionary, who performs a sacrament, not for himself but for the community.

Moreover, insofar as these ceremonies take the form of a mimicry or imitation of the processes of nature, they afford an opportunity for men to acquire a knowledge and control over nature which is substantial and real, not merely an illusion of magical art. When, for example, the Australian native collects the grass seed and blows a little of it in all directions in order to make it grow plentifully, it is easy to see in the ceremony the germ of a development which might eventually lead to the discovery of agriculture. And in the same way, when the Arctic peoples of Siberia rear a tame bear cub—"the common bear," as it is called—which is at last ceremonially killed in order to ensure a food supply of bear's meat for the year, we seem to be witnessing an early stage in the domestication of animals. It is true that the Australians have never attained to the agricultural stage, nevertheless, their peculiarly stereotyped culture seems to represent, as it were, a fossilised survival of a stage of culture intermediate between that of the mere food-gatherers and that of the primitive agriculturalists. The actual invention of agriculture may well have been a unique discovery which was diffused from a single centre of origin, but we have good reason to suppose that it arose in connection with a cult of natural fertility and as a result of the ritual imitation of the processes of nature.

One of the oldest and most universal forms of religion consists of the worship of the Mother Goddess, the goddess of the earth and of all that lives and grows. The divine figure appears all over the world in connection with the beginnings of the higher civilisation

in Mesopotamia and Syria, in the Aegean and As
Minor, in prehistoric Europe, and even in West Afric
and in the New World. The rude, female figures, whic
represent idols of the goddess or fertility charms, hav
been discovered by the spade of the archaeologist i
the earliest deposits of the prehistoric cultures, whil
in the higher civilisations the same figure reigns in th
great temple cities of Babylonia and Asia Minor, a
she still does in modern India today.

And among many primitive peoples at the presen
day this deity is still worshipped, as we see in the fol
lowing utterance recorded by K. T. Preuss, among th
Kagaba Indians of French Guiana: "The mother of ou
songs, the mother of all our seed, bore us in the begin
ning of things, and she is the mother of all types o
men, the mother of all nations. She is the mother o
the Thunder, the mother of the streams, the mothe
of the trees and all things. She is the mother of th
world and of the older brothers, the stone people. Sh
is the mother of the fruits of the earth and of al
things. She is the mother of our younger brothers, th
French, and the strangers. She is the mother of ou
dance paraphernalia, of all our temples, and she i
the only mother we possess. She alone is the mothe
of the fire and the sun and the Milky Way. She is th
mother of the rain, and the only mother we possess
And she has left us a token in all the temples—a toker
in the form of songs and dances."

But the fertility cult finds its most characteristic ex
pression in those symbolic representations of the di
vine marriage of the Great Mother, and of the deatl
and resurrection of her divine child or lover, the goc
of vegetation, which formed the mysteries of so many
ancient Asian cults, such as those of Ishtar and Tam
muz, of Attis and Cybele, and of Astarte and Adonis
And it is easy to see how the drama of the death and
resurrection of the powers of nature would become in-

separably bound up with symbolical representations such as the opening of the furrows, the sowing and watering of the seed, and the reaping of the sacred corn sheaves. We may well believe that some such symbolic representation or imitation of the processes of nature may have actually given rise to a knowledge of agriculture, and that its practical utilisation followed on its first performance as a sacred ritual art intended to promote the increase of the natural products of the soil. In the same way, the keeping of sacred animals, such as the bull and the cow, which were the symbols or the incarnation of the divine fecundity, may have led, in Western Asia, to the discovery of the art of the domestication and breeding of animals. For all these arts of husbandry were, to the men of the ancient world, no mere matters of practical economy, but sacred mysteries, the secret of which lay at the very heart of their religions.

But whatever may be the final conclusions regarding the religious origins of agriculture and the domestication of animals, there can be no doubt that the earliest forms of the higher civilisation were characterised by the development of the priesthood as an organised social order. The transition from Shamanism to priesthood approximately corresponds with the transition from the lower to the higher type of culture.

It is unfortunately impossible to study this process of evolution in the cultures of the Old World, for the decisive step had already been taken before the beginnings of history. In America, however, where the whole sequence of cultures is more recent than in Eurasia, it is still possible to find examples of very primitive types of agricultural societies, and even of the transitional phase between the culture of the hunter and that of the peasant. In every case there seems to be a very close association between the prac-

tice of agriculture and the development of ritual cere
monies and priestly organisation. For while th
diffusion of ritualism is wider than that of agriculture
its highest development is to be found in the early
centres of agricultural civilisation, and it steadily in
creases in intensity as it radiates outwards from these
centres.

The most remarkable of all these societies is that o
the Pueblo Indians of Arizona and New Mexico, since
in spite of changes of population, their cultural tradi
tion has survived almost intact from prehistoric times
in fact, it is essentially of the same type as the early
Neolithic peasant cultures of the Old World, especially
the so-called Painted Pottery cultures, and it seems to
carry us back to the first beginnings of the higher civilisation such as underlie the earliest historic cultures
of Sumer and Egypt. The whole life of the people centres in the rites concerned with the cultivation of the
maize, and its fertilisation by warmth and moisture.
In spite of the comparatively small size of these communities, they possess a large number of different
priesthoods and religious confraternities, each of
which has its specific function and ceremonials.
Among the Hopi there are the snake priests, the
priests of the sun and the calendar, the Horner Priests,
who perform the great annual ceremonies of the New
Fire, and many more. And in all these ceremonies
the corn maidens and the rude symbols which represent Alosaka, the power of germination, or Talatumsi,
the earth mother, or "the elder sister of the dawn,"
play a leading part.

Now when a ceremonial cycle of this type, based
upon the agricultural year, has once been established,
it is capable of being developed into a vast ritual order which embraces the whole social and intellectual
life of society. This is what we find in the higher civilisations of Central America, such as those of the Maya

and the Aztec peoples. In the case of the former, the development of the ritual cycle led to that amazing progress in astronomical and chronological science which is embodied in the great Maya calendar, with its ingenious system of interlocking cycles, and its simultaneous use of the Venus year of 584 days, as well as the solar and lunar periods. This calendar is, as Wissler says, "not a dating device," but a ceremonial order that "provides the religious programme for each day in the year or a complete cycle of never-ending services." The ritual order was at once the reflection and fulfilment of the cosmic order, since it co-ordinated the order of the heavens with that of the seasons, and by its ceaseless round of sacrifice and prayer assisted the powers of nature to function.

The same system was inherited by the later Aztec culture of Mexico which, however, in spite of its military power, stood on a far lower level of civilisation than that of the old Maya city-states. Spinden aptly compared the relation between the two peoples to that between the Greek and Roman cultures, while the older Toltec culture of the Mexican highlands occupies the same relative position between the other two as was held by the Etruscans in the ancient world. Here the sacrificial aspect of ritual became of overwhelming importance, and expressed itself in a continual series of human sacrifices, usually accompanied by dramatic representations in which the victim impersonated the god. The fertility and rejuvenation of nature could only be secured by a copious expenditure of human blood, and the warlike character of the Aztec culture was due to the necessity of providing an annual supply of captives for the sacrificial rites.

Thus in both of these instances, as well as in the South American cultures, the civilisation was essentially a development of the ritual order, and when, as in the case of the Maya culture, the ritual was broken

or its custodian, the priesthood, declined, the whol
civilisation fell into decay.

This ritual character of the archaic civilisation i
most clearly seen in the American cultures, for, as
have said, it is only in America that the early stage
of higher culture survived into historical times. Nev
ertheless, there are plentiful traces of the existence o
the same type of culture in the Old World. Each o
the archaic civilisations was a ritual civilisation, and
its character depended on the type of ritual that wa
predominant. Thus in ancient China the calenda
seems to have possessed a ritual significance no les:
than among the Maya. The Emperor, the Son o.
Heaven, was the lord of the sacred calendar, and th
whole state cultus was based on the idea of the ritua
co-ordination of the social order with the cosmic order
as manifested in the way of heaven. Even the sacrec
palace—the Ming T'ang—was arranged in accordanc
with this idea, as the House of the Calendar, and the
Emperor moved from chamber to chamber according
to the month of the year, changing his dress, his food,
his ornaments, and even his music so as to harmonise
with the changes of the seasons. In India, on the other
hand, the emphasis of the ritual was placed on the
sacrifice, and there the cosmic order was conceived
as bound up with and actually dependent upon the
sacrificial ritual.

In the case of India and China, however, we can
only trace the vestiges of this early phase of civilisation surviving under the forms of a higher type of culture. In Western Asia, on the other hand, we can follow the development of the archaic ritual civilisations
back to a far earlier period, and see how the religion
of the Mother Goddess presided over their origins.
For the first development of the higher culture in the
Near East, the beginnings of agriculture and irrigation
and the rise of city life were profoundly religious in

their conception. Men did not learn to control the
forces of nature to make the earth fruitful, and to raise
flocks and herds, as a practical task of economic organisation in which they relied on their own enterprise and hard work. They viewed it rather as a religious rite by which they co-operated as priests and
hierophants in the great cosmic mystery of the fertilisation and growth of nature. The mystical drama, an-
nually renewed, of the Mother Goddess, and her dying and reviving son and spouse was, at the same time,
the economic cycle of ploughing, and seed time and
harvest, by which the people lived. And the King was
not so much the organising ruler of a political community, as the priest and religious head of his people,
who represented the god himself and stood between
the goddess and her people, as the minister and interpreter of the divine will.

But it is only in highly conservative regions like
Asia Minor that we can see this primitive religion in
comparative simplicity. In Mesopotamia, at the very
dawn of history in the fourth millennium B.C., it had
already developed a highly specialised theology and
temple ritual. The god and goddess of each city had
acquired special characteristics and personalities, and
had taken their place in a Sumerian pantheon. But
Sumerian civilisation still remained entirely religious
in character. The god and the goddess were the acknowledged rulers of their city; the King was but their
high priest and steward. The temple, the house of the
god, was the centre of the life of the community, for
the god was the chief landowner, trader, and banker,
and kept a great staff of servants and administrators.
The whole city territory was, moreover, the territory
of the god, and the Sumerians spoke not of the boundaries of the city of Kish or the city of Lagash, but of
the boundaries of the god Enlil or the god Ningirshu.
All that the King did for his city was undertaken at

the command of the god and for the god. And the
remains of the ancient literature that have come down
to us prove that this is not merely the phraseology of
the state religion; it represents a profound popular belief in the interdependence and communion of the
city and its divinity.

In the case of Egypt also we find a no less intensely
religious spirit impregnating the archaic culture. The
Egyptian religion is, however, less homogeneous than
that of Mesopotamia or of Asia Minor. In the first
place, there is the worship of the animal gods of the
nomes, which is the primitive religion of the natives
of the Nile Valley; second, there is the cult of Osiris,
which is essentially similar to that of the Asiatic nature
gods, Tammuz and Adonis, of whom we have just
spoken, and which was perhaps introduced into the
Delta in predynastic times from Syria or Palestine; finally, there is the religion of the sun god, which became the official cult of the Pharaohs, and inspired the
main development of the archaic Egyptian civilisation.

Never perhaps before or since has a high civilisation
attained to the centralisation and unification that char-
acterise the Egyptian state in the age of the Pyramid
Builders. It was more than state socialism, for it
meant the entire absorption of the whole life of the
individual in a cause outside himself. The whole vast
bureaucratic and economic organisation of the Empire was directed to a single end: the glorification of
the sun god and his child, the god King.

It is indeed one of the most remarkable spectacles
in history to see all the resources of a great culture and
a powerful state organised, not for war and conquest,
not for the enrichment of a dominant class, but simply
to provide the sepulchre and to endow the chantries
and tomb-temples of the dead Kings. And yet it was
this very concentration on death and the afterlife that
gave Egyptian civilisation its amazing stability. The

Sun and the Nile, Re and Osiris, the Pyramid and the
Mummy—as long as those remained it seemed that
Egypt must stand fast, her life bound up in the unend-
ing round of prayer and ritual observance. All the
great development of Egyptian art and learning grew
up in the service of this central religious idea, and
when, in the age of final decadence, foreign powers
took possession of the sacred kingdom, Libyans and
Persians, Greeks and Romans all found it necessary to
"take the gifts of Horus" and to disguise their upstart
imperialism under the forms of the ancient solar theocracy, in order that the machinery of Egyptian civilisation should continue to function.

4

The Rise of the World Religions:
Confucius and the Tao

IT IS DIFFICULT TO EXAGGERATE the debt that the world owes to the archaic ritual cultures, for they laid the foundations on which the whole later development of civilisation has been built. To them we owe the invention of writing and of the calendar; the discovery of the use of metals; architecture and engineering; and almost all the arts and crafts of daily life, as they are practised down to the present day in both the Near and the Far East. We can measure their achievement in some degree by their monuments—the pyramids and sun temples of Egypt, the canals and temple towers of Babylonia, and the Maya and Toltec remains in America—which are unsurpassed in majesty of form and power of execution by the works of modern man in spite of his vastly increased control over matter.

But while they realised an enormous material progress—relatively the greatest perhaps that the world has ever seen—this progress was strictly limited. Each culture was bound up with an absolutely fixed ritual form from which it could not be separated. When once it had realised its potentialities, and embodied its ritual order in a complete social and material form, it became stationary and unprogressive.

We see the consequences of this in the great civilisations of the Near East which were not permanently affected by barbarian invasions. The very features of the Egyptian culture which we have noted as evidence of its strength and permanence are also the measure of its limitations. From the point of view of material civilisation, the Egyptians were the equals or even the superiors of the Greeks and Romans who had conquered them. But it was an entirely conservative civilisation, bound up with the religious forms of the distant past. Even her conquerors had to fall in with these forms, in order to rule the country. The old temple services still went on, the old sacred state still persisted. Only Ptolemy or Caesar had stepped into the shoes of the Pharaoh. Nothing is more curious than to see, on the wall of the later Egyptian temples, the figures of Tiberius or Ptolemy, depicted in Egyptian dress with the high white crown of the Pharaohs on their heads, in the act of adoring Isis and Osiris or the crocodile-headed god Sebek, and to read their European names followed by the old divine titles, "Son of the Sun, lord of both lands, beloved of Ptah and Isis." The whole of Egypt had become a great archaeological museum, and if her culture survived, it was like the survival of a mummy, not that of a living being.

The same process would no doubt have occurred in the case of the other ancient civilisations, had they been allowed to follow their own line of development without external interference. In the majority of cases, however, the tradition of the archaic culture did not survive intact.

From the third millennium B.C. onwards, the societies of the higher culture were exposed to a series of invasions of more warlike but less civilised peoples, such as the peoples of Indo-European stock, which gradually led to the formation of new nations and cultures. The invaders, however, brought no impulse towards a higher material civilisation. They came as destroyers rather than creators, like the barbarians who conquered the Roman Empire, or the Turkish invaders of the Near East. And, as in these cases, they

owed their progress in civilisation almost entirely to
the elements of culture that they took over from the
conquered peoples.

Nevertheless, in the first millennium B.C. a cultural
change of the most profound significance passed over
the world, a change that was not confined to any one
people or culture, but which made itself felt almost
simultaneously from India to the Mediterranean and
from China to Persia. It was, however, a change of
thought rather than a revolution of material culture.
It was due to the first appearance of new spiritual
forces, which have been active in the world ever
since and which still influence the minds of men today. The teachings of the Hebrew prophets and the
Greek philosophers, of Buddha and the authors of the
Upanishads, of Confucius and Lao Tzu, are not the
half-comprehended relics of a vanished world, like
the religious literature of Egypt and Babylonia; they
are of perennial significance and value. They have the
same importance in the intellectual and spiritual life
of mankind that the material achievements of the Archaic Civilisation possess in the sphere of material culture. Like the latter, they have laid a permanent
foundation on which all later ages have built and on
which our own intellectual and religious tradition is
based.

So great is the originality and power of the age
which saw the rise of the world religions that it is easy
to underestimate its own debt to the past. What link
can there be between the Hellenic vision of an intelligible universe or the ethical humanism of Confucius
and the bloody rites and barbarous myths of the old
pagan culture?

Nevertheless, just as the culture of the new peoples
was based on the tradition of the Archaic Civilisation
that they had conquered, so also they had inherited

much of the intellectual and religious conceptions of the older world. But the dual character of the new cultures tended to produce a spirit of criticism and reflection which had been absent in the earlier stage of civilisation. Men could no longer accept the existing state of society and human life as a manifestation of the divine powers. The destruction of the old theocratic order had left its mark on the popular consciousness, and everywhere we find a tendency to idealise the memory of the vanished order as a golden age when the gods had ruled mankind before the coming of injustice and strife. In contrast to this idealisation of the past, the present appeared as an age in which the divine order was no longer observed, and evil and wrong-doing ruled supreme. And thus there arose a sense of moral dualism, an opposition between that which is and that which ought to be, between the way of man and the way of the gods. Men compared the world they knew with an ideal social and moral order and passed judgment upon it accordingly.

In this way, the central belief that underlies the archaic culture—the conception of a sacred order which governs alike the way of nature and the life of man—continued to exercise a vital influence on the mind of the new age, but it was at the same time remoulded and transformed. The idea which the previous age had expressed in a ritual form became moralised and spiritualised. The sacred order was no longer a ceremonial system, but a moral law of justice and truth.

Thus the ancient conception of a sacred ritual order was everywhere the starting point from which the new religious development proceeded. The connection is to be seen most clearly, perhaps, in the case of China, where the older type of culture had survived with less breach of continuity than elsewhere. Here the new moral teaching of Confucius was essentially connected

with the old idea of a ritual order. Its importance in
his eyes consisted not in the ethical ideals themselves,
but in their application to the traditional rites.

The religion of China is perhaps the most difficult of
all the great oriental religious traditions for the European mind to understand. This difficulty is not due,
as in the case of Indian religion, to the abstractedness
of its metaphysical or theophysical doctrines. On the
contrary, no people has shown a more practical and
utilitarian spirit in religious matters than the Chinese,
and nowhere has the social and moral aspect of religion been more insisted upon. The difficulty is rather
that the official religion of China at least is so exclusively practical in its teaching that it hardly seems to
be a religion in our sense of the word at all.

And yet it has been more powerful in its influence
on society and on the daily life and habits of the people than any religion we know. In other civilisations
religion may control thought almost entirely, or the
priesthood may possess a strong hold on society and
education, but there always remains a residuum of
secular knowledge and a distinction between the religious and secular spheres of life. But in China the
Confucian moral teaching and the influence of Confucian learning so permeated society that they became
a second nature to the Chinese people, a psychic discipline that was no longer felt as something external
but that moulded every thought and feeling from
within. The word for religion is the same as that for
education, and the whole literary tradition of Chinese
civilisation has been in the hands of the Confucian
learned class.

Hence in order to understand the religion of China
one must enter thoroughly into the spirit of Chinese
culture. We can only understand it fully when we understand the history of the Chinese people, and since
Chinese history, especially in its social and cultural

aspects, is necessarily a closed book for most of us, it is no wonder that the study of Chinese religion is neglected or misunderstood by the majority of educated Europeans.

For China is not like any other nationality that forms part of some larger whole and that shares elements in its civilisation with other peoples. It is like a complete world, as rich as the world we know in art and literature and history, but always different, unexpected, and new; to know China is, as it were, to double one's knowledge of humanity.

Thus the history of Chinese civilisation is peculiarly interesting for the student of comparative religion. We see the same forces at work as in the other regions that we have studied, but the results are utterly different. In China, just as in Southern and Western Asia and in the Aegean, the period from the sixth to the fourth centuries B.C. saw the rise of a number of great personalities who were the authors of a great religious movement. Confucius above all had the same importance for the future of Chinese religious thought as Zoroaster had for that of Persia, Buddha for that of India, and the Hebrew prophets and the Hellenic philosophers for Israel and Greece.

There is, however, a striking difference between the developments in China and those elsewhere. All the other founders of the world religions and even the great philosophies were innovators and reformers who made an abrupt break with the nature religions of the older type of culture, whether by open revolt and denunciation or by more gradual reform. In China, on the other hand, the greatest reformers were the greatest conservatives. There was no break, at least no open and conscious break, with the old religious tradition of the people. So that while from one point of view the culture of China is the most rationalist of all the great civilisations, it has preserved a

direct continuity of religious rites and customs that go
back to an extremely primitive stage of culture.

But the early religion of China, while belonging to
the same general type as that of the other archaic cultures, differs from that of ancient Egypt or Babylonia
by reason of its greater simplicity. There was no elaborate pantheon of deities, each with its own personality and its own images and temples. So great is this
simplicity that at first sight the religion of the ancient
Chinese seems to be monotheistic, owing to the universal character and overwhelming importance of the
chief deity—the sky god. This deity, who was known
as the Lord of Heaven, Sublime Heaven, or simply as
Heaven, was the supreme ruler of heaven and earth.
He directed the course of the sun and the stars and the
succession of the seasons as well as the fortunes of
man. Above all, it was by virtue of his authority that
kings reigned, and a peculiarly close relation existed
between the Lord of Heaven and his earthly counterpart and representative, the Son of Heaven.

The early nature religion never developed a brilliant poetical mythology, like that of the Greeks or
the Hindus, nor did it produce an organised pantheon
like that of the Babylonians. On the other hand, in the
sphere of ritual and ceremony, it was extraordinarily
fertile and creative. The culture of ancient China is
perhaps the most perfect example of that type of a
ritual social order that was more or less characteristic
of all the archaic civilisations. In China even more
than in Mesopotamia or India, the whole social order
rested on a religious basis, and there was an exact co-
ordination of social function and religious ritual.
There was none of the individualism and self-interest
that so often formed the motive of the Vedic sacrificial
rites in India. The whole spirit of the cultus was impersonal and altruistic, and even the Emperor must
subordinate his private feelings and interests to the

common good; for he was not only the vice-regent of Heaven by reason of his celestial mandate, it was also his office to be the link between Heaven and Earth and to co-ordinate the social order with the Way of Heaven. Thus every act of his life had a sacred ritual character, and contributed to the maintenance of the order of the universe, the regular succession of the seasons, and the due proportion of sun and rain.

The same spirit pervaded the whole ritual order of Chinese society. The ruling idea of ancient Chinese religion is to preserve an exact and constantly renewed conformity of man's public and personal acts with the movement of the cosmic cycle of the heavens and the seasons. It was man's duty to harmonise his conduct with the universal rhythms and thereby to assist nature in its work.

This theory of the sacred rites and of the co-ordination of human actions with the cosmic order was no doubt implicit in Chinese civilisation from the first. Its explicit development and its systematic application to ethics was, however, much more recent, and probably took place during the same period that saw the dawn of a rudimentary type of philosophical reflection elsewhere—from the eighth to the sixth centuries B.C. It was apparently the work of a literary class—the scribes who were attached to the Imperial Chancery and whose duty it was to draw up official documents and to record the order of the rites and ceremonies of the state cult. These scribes were known as Jou ("the literary men with whiskers," according to Wieger), and they held a very important place in Chinese life. They were the specialists in the state ceremonial and ritual technique that played such an enormous part in ancient China, where every act of social and political life had its appropriate ritual formula.

During the decline of the Chou dynasty from the

sixth to the fourth centuries B.C., each of the states of which China was composed had its own school of these ritual lawyers and archivists, without whose advice no important action could be undertaken.

It was in this milieu that Confucianism appeared. Confucius was the organiser and teacher of one of these schools—that of the little state of Lu, the rulers of which traced their pedigree to the earliest ages, and it is through the tradition of this school that almost all our knowledge of the ancient history of China is derived.

Confucius was himself a member of the class of Jou and prided himself not on his originality but on his conservatism and his fidelity to the traditions of his order. "I transmit, I do not invent," he said. He did not profess to teach a philosophy; he merely expounded and commented on the ancient books of the scribes, the Book of Odes, the Book of History, the manual of divination and the local annals, and above all the correct method of performing the Rites.

It is essential to bear these conditions in mind when we attempt to estimate the work of Confucius. We know Confucius as the founder of a world religion, one whom the Chinese regarded as the teacher of mankind, "the Perfect Saint," and "the Equal of God," and we naturally approached the Confucian writings in the expectation of finding in them profound philosophical or religious doctrines like those of Buddha.

Hence the ordinary reader is apt to be thoroughly disillusioned when he finds in the sayings of the Master a number of minute rules of deportment and etiquette and a collection of moral platitudes, such as "The superior man follows the line of duty"; "The wise man is slow to speak and quick to act."

In reality the teaching of Confucius was not mere abstract moralising. Its importance consists not so much in the ethical ideals themselves as in their appli-

cation to an already existing religious teaching. The
Rites have the same importance for Confucianism that
the Law possesses for Judaism, and it is no more possible to understand the ethical teaching of Confucius
without them than it would be to separate the Law
and the Prophets in the religion of Israel. The common
English translation of the great Confucian virtue Li—
"propriety"—is entirely misleading. It signifies not a
conventional correctness of behaviour but an interior
conformity of the individual mind to the universal order, which governs not only the life of society but the
whole course of nature. The Rites are the external
manifestations of this eternal order in the lives of men.

The true greatness and originality of Confucius
consist in his giving these ritual practices an ethical
content. Instead of regarding the rites as magically
efficacious or of being satisfied with a purely external
form of observance, he demanded a moral adhesion
of the whole man. His procedure was the reverse of
that which has usually been followed by the religious
reformers of the West. They swept away the traditional rites or only permitted them to remain insofar
as they were in accordance with new spiritual ideals,
while Confucius deliberately conformed the inner
spirit to the outer form.

This combination of exact ceremonial observance
and moral idealism is of the essence of Confucianism
and lies at the root of the classical civilisation of
China. It would, however, be a great mistake to regard
it as universally accepted by Chinese thinkers. From
the very beginning there existed another current of
thought that criticised the Confucian ideals as strongly
as any representative of modern Western civilisation
has done. This was the Taoist tradition, which goes
back to the half-mythical figure of Lao Tzu—the Old
Philosopher—who is said to have been an elder contemporary of Confucius himself. The Taoists placed

their ideal of conduct not in the observance of rites
and ceremonies and in a painstaking obedience to
moral precepts but in a mystical quietism by which
man conformed himself to the divine order of nature.
Hence their criticism of the artificial character of Confucian ethics, their hostility to the niceties of ceremonial etiquette, and their ridicule of the Confucian
cult of the precedents of antiquity. They compared
the efforts of the disciples of Confucius to restore the
ancient usages to an attempt to dress up a monkey in
the robes of one of the princes of antiquity. The
monkey remains a monkey, and the fine robes only
accentuate its absurdity. Above all, they condemn the
futile optimism of the pedants who attempt to restore
the golden age by merely external means.

The traditions preserved in the classical works on
which the Confucians relied are mere dead words—
"the dregs and leavings of the ancients." True knowledge is to be found only in the direct intuition of transcendent reality, which is acquired not by learning
but by mystical contemplation. Rational and sensible
knowledge can only show us the external movement
of the world, the succession of the seasons, the
changes of birth and death, of growth and decay. But
behind this visible, ever-changing movement of the
universe there is a higher transcendent principle,
which itself unchanging, is the source of all change,
itself beyond existence is the source of all that exists.
Lao Tzu writes, "There is something undefined and
yet complete, which precedes the birth of Heaven and
Earth. O immovable, O formless, which alone is without changing, which penetrates all things without al-
teration. It may be considered the Mother of the Universe." And the most important of his followers—
Chuang Tzu, who flourished in the fourth century and
is perhaps the greatest writer that China has ever produced—exclaims, "O my master, my master! Thou who

destroyest all things without being cruel, Thou who doest good to the thousand generations without being kind; Thou who wert before the ages and who art not old; Thou coverest the heavens, Thou bearest the earth, Thou art the creator of all forms without skill! To know Thee thus is divine joy."

There is no doubt that the mystical profundity of writers like Chuang Tzu, their love of nature and above all their sense of humour, make a far greater appeal to the ordinary European reader than the formal and prosaic style of Mencius and the Confucian scholars.

In spite of the hostility between the two schools of thought, which became accentuated after the fourth century B.C., they have far more in common than we should at first suspect. The Confucians believed no less than the Taoists in the existence of a universal order to which man must conform himself in order to fulfil his true destiny. The Taoists like the Confucians regarded this order as manifested in the course of nature, above all in the stars, and in music, and both agreed in their use of divination by means of the tortoise shell, and the sacred diagrams of the Book of Changes, through which they believed that the way of Heaven was made known to men. They differed only in the application of their fundamental idea, for while the Confucians strove to conform themselves to the cosmic order by an active moral discipline and by the observance of ceremonial rites, the Taoists sought the same end by mystical contemplation and the practise of magic and alchemy.

Moreover, the Taoists, no less than the Confucians, could claim to carry on the tradition of the early Chinese religion. We have seen how the scholars, the Jou, were the successors of the scribes attached to the Imperial Chancery, and in the same way the Taoists represent the tradition of another class of learned officials, the college of augurs and diviners who were attached to the Third Ministry, the department of religious affairs. It was their business to ascertain the will of Heaven by the use of the sacred diagrams that are preserved in the Book of Changes, the most sacred of all the Chinese classical books, and on the basis of these practises a regular system of philosophy was gradually worked out, resting on the theory of the two cosmic principles—Yin and Yang—negative and positive—whose alternation constituted the Way of Heaven, the Tao or rhythm of the universe.

The two traditions ultimately took shape in the developed philosophies of classical Confucianism and Taoism, each of which represents one side of the ancient tradition of Chinese culture and one aspect of the Chinese soul. As one might suppose, Taoism appealed to the more imaginative side of the Chinese character, and its legends and ideals have always been the favourite themes of poetry and art.

Confucius himself adopted an attitude of reserve towards the supernatural. "Treat supernatural beings with respect," he says, "but keep aloof from them," and the Analects relate that there were four subjects on which the Master would refuse to speak: prodigies, "arbitrary acts of power," acts of rebellion, and the apparitions of spirits. This does not, however, imply, as modern writers have often supposed, that the sage was sceptical or hostile to supernatural religion. No doubt he believed in the appearance of spirits just as he did in acts of rebellion. Both of them were, however, anomalous—they fell outside the regular ceremonial and social order, and consequently they were to be avoided by the wise citizen. If spirits appeared it was because they were not properly fed; in other words, the ancestral sacrifices had been neglected, and so their appearance testified to a neglect of duty on the part of the living.

In the course of time, however, the attitude of the scholars towards religion underwent a considerable change. From the time of Sunn-tzu in the third century B.C., their teaching grew more and more rationalistic, and the belief in the personal character of the Heavenly Sovereign, Shang-Ti, whose overruling providence governed all things—a belief that was still dominant in the Confucian age—gave way to the idea of an impersonal natural force that left little room for religious feelings. Thus the official cult became an empty form, though the great sacrifices to Heaven continued to be offered according to the old tradition right down to the revolution, and the Chinese people turned elsewhere to find satisfaction for their religious instinct.

This was the cause of the extraordinary development of Buddhism in China, which began during the time of the later Han Dynasty and reached its apogee in the age of division and foreign conquest that followed the breakup of the Empire in the fourth and fifth centuries A.D. The whole of China was covered with Buddhist monasteries and temples, and even the sovereigns of the different states became fervent devotees of the new faith.

5

Mysticism in India

THE SAME CONCEPTION of a universal order is also of fundamental importance in the religious development of India and Persia. It appears in the Rigveda, the most ancient of the sacred books of India, under the name of Rta or Rita—the same word that is found in Old Persian as Arta, and as Asha in the Zend-Avesta. It is usually translated as Order or Right, but it is difficult to find any equivalent for it in modern English, since it is at once cosmic, ritual, and moral. It is seen primarily in the ordered course of nature, the succession of the seasons, and the movement of the heavens. The year is the wheel of Rita, the wheel with twelve spokes. The sun is "the clear and visible face of Rita," and the rivers follow the sacred Rita in their unceasing flow. But its ethical aspect is even more important. It is usually associated in the Rigveda with Varuna, the righteous god who watches over justice and punishes sin. He is "the foundation of Rita," "the guardian of Holy Rita," and the just man prays that he may help "to increase Varuna's spring of Rita," an expression that is almost identical with that used in the Avesta, which speaks of "swelling the spring of Asha." Finally, Rita, like the Latin *ritus*, is pre-eminently applied to the ritual order of the sacrifice. The sacrificial fire is "the shoot of Rita, born in the Rita," and it carries the offerings to the gods by way of Rita.

Varuna is associated with Mitra—"the friend," the Mithras of the Persians—also a sky god, probably a rain god. In early Persian religion he is the guardian of compacts, lord of the oath.

Beyond a number of nature gods, there are two very important deities, especially associated with the Brahmin priestly class. These are Agni, the sacrificial fire, and Soma, the sacred drink. Agni mediated between gods and men, associated with Varuna as the guardian of ritual order, the Rita of sacrifice. As yet there were no temples or images, and sacrifices were in the open air, but there was already a highly organised priesthood whose services were in great request among the chieftans and nobles, since nothing important could be undertaken without the ceremonies of which they were the masters.

Their influence continues to grow throughout the early period of Indian history, and indeed it determines the course of the religious development that converted the straightforward nature worship of the Vedic period in Brahmanism.

At first sight we should have expected the religion of the Rig-Veda to develop into an ethical monotheism, with Varuna as the central figure. He seems to have all the requisite qualities for such a position. If a reforming movement like that of the Hebrew prophets had arisen among the worshippers of Varuna, the religion of India might have become as strictly monotheistic as that of the Jews. Why was not this the case?

As a matter of fact, the evolution of Indian religion followed a totally different path. The thinkers and reformers entirely neglected Varuna and concentrated on the ritual element of their religion. They worked out a regular philosophy of ritual, which caused the sacrifice to overshadow the gods to whom it was originally offered. It is the sacrifice that makes the sun rise and keeps the course of nature true. The gods themselves are dependent on sacrifice and can do nothing without it. The ultimate force in the world is the sacrificial or priestly formula of the Brahmins. This is Brahma, an impersonal abstract deity, "a new deity but an old word," an abstract principle or essence rather than a god. The personal, naturalistic gods of the Veda are absorbed and subordinated to this new idea of the divine. "All the gods are only one single Being under different names," says the later Vedic teaching. This is the foundation of the later religious and philosophical development that was to be of such immense importance in India.

The great change in the character of Indian religion is due to an entire change of spirit: from external activity to contemplation and reflection; from interest in the outer world to concentration on the inner reality of things. "All is guided by Mind, is based on Mind. The World is guided by Mind. The foundation is Mind. Brahma is Mind." (Ait. Upanishad. III, v. 3.)

This is due to the rise of a new class, the ascetics or hermits, who withdrew from society into the forest to study the esoteric side of their religion; the inner meaning of the rites and legends; as well as to practise austerities and penance, which were believed to give them supernatural powers.

This new development is usually ascribed to the influence of native Indian culture. It certainly seems non-Aryan: The Indian ascetic in his original form is very similar to the Shaman or medicine man of primitive religion. It becomes, however, the most characteristic feature of Indian religion right up to the present day, the muni, the sannyasi, the sadhu, the yogi. In Brahmanism the monastic ideal is incorporated into the earlier Aryan religious system by becoming one of the four stages through which the Brahmin was supposed to pass during his life: (1) the student; (2) the householder (married); (3) the anchorite or forest dweller; (4) the wanderer (bhikshu).

In Buddhism and Jainism, monasticism is even more

important—the Buddhist church or sangha is simply a
monastic order. The Brahmin ascetic differs from the
Christian monk in that his ideal is intellectual rather
than moral. He tries to win salvation by *knowledge*. In
the Brahmanas this knowledge is still primarily knowledge of ritual, though it is an esoteric mystical knowledge.

A higher stage is reached in the sacred writings
known as the Upanishads, which are the foundation of
the higher religion of India. Their date is uncertain,
but they are closely connected with the Brahmanas.
They are earlier than Buddhism, that is, previous to
500 B.C. The Upanishads are also known as the
Vedanta—the *end* of the Vedas. They must have
been due to a new movement of thought, inspired by
the desire to attain absolute reality; not merely to get
behind the material appearance of things, but to get
beyond the personal gods of the earlier religion, and
even to get beyond the sacred rites as interpreted
by the Brahmanas; so as to reach the one absolute essence that alone is true, that alone *is*.

Now, this ultimate reality is Brahma, a word that is
already in general use in the Brahmanas to describe
the highest principle of the universe. The original
meaning is prayer—that is, the essence of the power
of the Brahmins or priests. But it has acquired a metaphysical meaning somewhat similar to that of the
Logos—the divine Word in Christianity.

But there is another word to describe this ultimate
reality, which is of even greater importance in the
Upanishads. This word is Atman—originally breath,
like anima, etc., then soul. Finally Self.

This Self or soul lies behind everything that exists.
It is "the web and warp with which the universe is
woven." Above all, it is the self of our finite selves, the
soul of our souls, for the human self and the ultimate
self are in a sense identical. This is shown in the fa-

mous dialogue between the teacher and his disciple in the Chandogya Upanishad (VI, pp. 66–67).

The whole religion of the Upanishads consists in the effort to attain the realisation of this absolute unity. All the good works of the older religion, the worship of the gods, sacrifice, knowledge of the rites, and even asceticism, are worthless in comparison. That is to say, they can only procure relative goods—prosperity in this world and a happy afterlife—the Way of the Fathers. It is only by the realisation of the unity of the Atman—the supreme unification of the soul with the Absolute—that man attains to liberation. He has shed his body, as a snake sloughs its skin, and he will never be reborn in bodily form.

This marks the first appearance in literature of the idea of reincarnation and karma, or the law of retribution, which determines a man's future fate, ideas that were to govern the whole future development of Indian thought. There is no sign of a belief in reincarnation in the Rig Veda and probably not in the Brahmanas either. It was not a part of the original Aryan religion, and there can be little doubt that its origin is to be found in the belief of the aboriginal population. But it was in the Upanishads that it first received a philosophical treatment and was completed by the ideas of karma, retribution and deliverance.

The essential point is that the man who is ignorant of ultimate reality, who still nourishes desires, is still fettered by his past works. He returns again from the other world to this world of action. But for the man who knows Brahmin, who no longer cherishes desires, there is no return. He is one with the Absolute.

This doctrine of unity—of non-dualism, as the Hindus call it—is the fundamental teaching of the Upanishads and indeed of all the later religion of India. As de la Vallée Poussin said, "It was the great discovery which has remained for at least twenty-five centuries the capital and most cherished truth of the Indian people."

Some Western critics regard the religion of the Upanishads as hardly a religion at all, since it resulted in the rejection of an ethical theism in the interests of an intellectualist pantheism. Moreover, the Western admirers of Indian thought, like Schopenhauer and Deussen, only accentuate this view of the doctrine of the Upanishads, since they regard it as a pure philosophic monism, like that of modern Western metaphysicians. Nevertheless, the pantheistic expressions in the Upanishads are somewhat misleading. Vedantism is in reality a supertheism, rather than a pantheism in our common sense of the word. Western pantheism is a kind of religious democracy in which all things are equally god; the non-dualism of the Vedanta, on the other hand, is a religious absolutism in which only God exists. There may seem little difference between the statement that everything that exists is divine, and the statement that nothing but the divine exists. From the religious point of view, however, there is all the difference in the world.

It is well put in a verse attributed to Sankara, the great mediaeval interpreter of the Upanishads:

> Though difference be none, I am of Thee
> Not Thou, O Lord, of me;
> For of the sea is verily the wave,
> Not of the wave the sea.

God is the One Reality. Apart from Him nothing exists. In comparison with Him nothing is real. The Universe only exists insofar as it is rooted and grounded in His Being. He is the Self of our selves, the Soul of our souls, as St. Augustine says. So far the Upanishads do not differ from the teaching of Christian theologians. The one vital distinction consists in the fact that Indian religion ignores the idea of creation. Either it

teaches that the external universe is an illusion—Maya
—which melts like a dream when the soul awakes to
true knowledge, or alternatively the world is the self-
manifestation of the Divine Mind, a conditioned embodiment of the absolute reality. In either case there
is a full recognition of the absolute transcendence of
the Divine Nature.

Thus the whole tendency of the Upanishads is profoundly religious. They teach a way of spiritual deliverance—of salvation—not merely a philosophical
theory of knowledge. Here again the Westerner is apt
to be misled by preconceived ideas and to suppose
that the Upanishads are rational and philosophic because they lay such stress on the importance of knowledge. We must, however, realise that the saving knowledge of which the Upanishads speak is not knowledge
in our sense of the word at all. It is a superrational intuition of pure being, which transcends all logical categories and in which even the distinction of subject
and object disappears.

From the rational point of view, all our knowledge
of Brahmin and the Self is a negative knowledge. It
can only be described by the words *Neti, Neti*—not
so, not so. And this is closely similar to the doctrine
of the *Via Negativa* of the Christian mystics, as when St.
Thomas Aquinas writes, "We know God by negations,"
and when Suso describes the Deity as an Eternal
Nothing.

And the ethical aspect of the Upanishads must be
understood in the same way. The religion of the
Upanishads is not indifferent to the moral issue, in
the sense that a metaphysical theory may be. On the
contrary, it has a very high moral ideal, but it is that
of the mystic, not that of the practical man. It is an
ethic of absolute renunciation and detachment—the
flight of the Alone to the Alone.

It is easy to draw a parallel between the doctrine of

the Upanishads and that of the Christian mystics. It is not an intellectualist denial of moral values, but a mystical transcending of them—the attainment of a state of absolute perfection in which all relative distinctions pass away. Hence it is clear that the Upanishads must be judged from the point of view of mysticism rather than of metaphysics, and that in their essential meaning they are thoroughly religious documents.

Nevertheless, it must be admitted that they are the most intellectualist of all forms of mysticism, and that they are exposed to the characteristic dangers of this type of thought. There is always the tendency towards rationalisation, even in the case of so antirational a doctrine as that of the Upanishads. The theory of knowledge is apt to be mistaken for the knowledge itself, and that which was a spiritual experience becomes an intellectual formula. Even so intellectualist a thinker as Plato, who was in complete agreement with the Indians with regard to the value of the pure intuition of reality, realised this danger and refused to put his central teaching in writing lest it should be bad for men. "It is not capable of expression like other branches of study," says he, "but as a result of long intercourse and a common life spent on the thing, a light is suddenly kindled, as from a leaping spark, which when it reaches the soul finds nourishment for itself therein."

And in India itself the attempt to express the inexpressible and to attain deliverance by the way of knowledge seem to have led ultimately to rationalism and to the denial of the objective reality of the absolute being, which was the essence of the teaching of the Upanishads. The following period was marked by the rise of a series of movements that were hostile to Brahmin orthodoxy and that tended towards a completely non-theistic conception of religion. Such were

the Sankhya philosophy, the religion of Jainism and
above all the Buddhist movement.

It was in Buddhism that the ascetic ideal found its
highest expression, and Buddhism is also the most complete and thoroughgoing example of the new disciplines of salvation. The thinkers of the Upanishads were
primarily interested in their speculations concerning
Brahma and the true nature of being; deliverance was
a secondary question. To the Buddhist, on the other
hand, the problem of deliverance was the one vital
issue.

The Buddha expressly condemned all attempts to
enquire into or to define the nature of the supreme
goal. Salvation was to be found not in metaphysical
knowledge, but in the strenuous moral endeavour
which destroys desire, the root of all suffering and of
physical existence itself.

Thus Buddhism arose as a movement of reaction to
the intellectualism of the Upanishads and the philosophical schools. It reasserted the moral element of the
conception of Rita—order—which had been subordinated to its ritual and cosmological aspects ever since
the days of the Rigveda. It stands in the same opposition to the Upanishads as Confucianism did to Taoism
—as a moral discipline against a mystical cosmology
and a metaphysical doctrine of Being. Like Confucianism, it claimed to be the "doctrine of the Mean," which
alone can afford a true form of behaviour for the guidance of the sage. It is, indeed, more exclusively ethical
in its content than Confucianism itself, since its moral
teaching was not engrafted on the old ritual tradition.

Early Buddhist doctrine is marked by a severely
practical and rational spirit, which is very unlike that
of the Brahmanas or the Upanishads. It demands no
extremes of asceticism, it promises no revelation of
divine mysteries. Everything is brought down to a few
very simple truths—suffering and the cause of suffer-

ing; the extinction of suffering and the way to the extinction of suffering. These are the Four Noble Truths on which the Way is founded. There is no knowledge beyond these truths and no reality outside this way. The whole of religion, the whole of philosophy, and the whole of human life are reduced to the interior way of moral and mental discipline, by which the nothingness of existence is realised and the extinction of desire and passion is attained.

How is it possible to reconcile this extremity of introversion and negation with the existence of culture and the order of social life? We have the undoubted record of history, engraved for all time on rocks and pillars, that it was actually accepted conscientiously and intelligently as a principle of government by the greatest ruler India has ever known—Asoka, the founder of the Maurya Empire, who became a convert to Buddhism c. 260 B.C.

And even apart from that, the records of Buddhist monasteries prove that the moral law of the Buddha has justified itself through the ages as a positive social force that has exercised an even greater influence on the civilisation of Southern, Eastern and Central Asia than orthodox Brahmanism has done.

Nor is it difficult to see why this should have been the case, since any effective spiritual discipline that is inspired by high moral ideals must inevitably be a powerful social force. The problem is rather how a religious doctrine which is so lacking in positive theological beliefs and so negative and pessimistic in its attitude to human life can provide the motive power for effective moral action.

The answer seems to be that Buddhism contains a much larger element of positive religion than its philosophy seems to suggest. In the first place, even though the Buddhist discipline of salvation is a *via negativa*, it remains a discipline of salvation—a re-

ligious absolute; and even though it admits no worship of gods and no divine order of nature, the way of
salvation is itself divine; inasmuch as it is the way to
an absolute good which transcends human life and
human knowledge.

However negative are the terms of definition, the
goal, spiritual perfection, is a transcendent religious
object capable of inspiring religious emotion and
moral action.

And in the second place, the figure of the Buddha—
the Enlightened One who has pity on men and
opens to them a pathway of deliverance from evil—is
an object of religious devotion and religious worship.
Buddha may not be a god in the theological sense,
but he is a much higher and more spiritual figure than
the gods of the Indian pantheon who are the official
objects of prayer and sacrifice. Buddhism never denied the gods—there were gods and demigods, devils
and goblins, dragons and vampires—there was room
and to spare for all of them in the infinite series of
worlds and heavens and hells in which Indian cosmology ran riot. But all these beings, good and bad,
high and low, pitiful and terrible, were alike bound to
the wheel of existence and to the law of retribution
from which the Buddha alone had found the way of
salvation and release.

The delightful story in the Dialogues of the Buddha
concerning the monk who indulged in cosmological
enquiries shows the fundamental scepticism of the
Buddhists towards the mythology they had transcended. The monk, who desired to know where the
world ends, made a tour of enquiry among the gods
and the successive heavens, and the gods replied: "We
do not know, O monk, where the world ends. But
there is Brahma, the great Brahma, the creator of all
things, he will know the answer." So when the monk at
last found himself in the presence of Brahma, he asked

him where the world ends. And Brahma answered: "I am the great Brahma, the supreme one, the mighty, the all-seeing, the ruler, the lord of all, the creator, the chief of all, appointing to each his place, the father of all that are or that are to be." "I do not ask you, friend," said the monk, "whether you are indeed all that you say. But I ask you where the four elements cease, leaving no trace behind." Then the great Brahma took the monk by the arm and led him aside and said, "These gods my servants hold me to be such that there is nothing I cannot see, understand, realise. Therefore I gave no answer in their presence. But I do not really know where the world ends. Go you now, return to the Lord, ask him the question, and accept the answer according as he shall make reply." (*Dialogues of the Buddha*, tr. Rhys Davids, I, 280.)

And the answer of the Buddha was always the same as that of the mediaeval Christian monk. A man must not busy himself in vain questions that do not concern him. Let him concern himself with the way of perfection and the salvation of his soul, for these are the only things that matter.

But if the Buddha is the saviour and the gateway to eternal deliverance, he is for all practical purposes God; and with the rise of the Mahayana system in the first centuries of the Christian era, Buddhism formally accepted this conclusion and worshipped the Buddha under divine titles similar to those which the great Brahma had claimed for himself in the story I have just quoted: "The Father of the World, the Self-Born, the Healer, the Protector of All Creatures." Thus the Mahayana, which dominates the historic development of Buddhism in China and Central Asia, has become as theistic or more theistic than Brahmanism itself, being inspired by a passionate personal devotion to the Saviour Gods who were the Buddhas. Thus the primitive Buddhist discipline of salvation has been trans-

formed into a way of devotion directed to the worship
of the Buddha and the salvation of man and all other
creatures. The sober self-discipline of the old Buddhist
monasticism has given place to an ethic of self-
sacrifice and universal love which finds expression in
the Bodhicharyavatara of Santideva, a poem which expresses all that is noblest and purest in Buddhist spirituality.

This transformation of Buddhism appears to have
taken place in the Kushan empire, which extended
from the Oxus to the Jumna and which formed the main
channel through which the new religion was diffused
in Turkestan and China. It is therefore, possible, even
probable, that it represents a fusion of Indian and Iranian religious influences, such as one would expect in
a culture of mixed origins. But we also find a similar
transformation taking place in Hinduism at the same
time, if, as many scholars believe, the Bhagavad Gita
dates from this period. For in the Gita we see the
same transformation of the way of knowledge into the
way of devotion and the same transition from an impersonal metaphysical doctrine to a personal theistic
faith. Moreover, the god of the Gita, like the Buddha
of the Mahayana, is a Saviour God who manifests
himself on earth for the salvation of man.

But this personal devotion to a divine saviour is
united alike in the Gita and in the Mahayana with the
ideal of spiritual perfection, the exercise of virtue, and
the cultivation of the interior life. In the Mahayana
this represents the continuity of the old Buddhist tradition, whereas in the Gita it is expressed in yoga terminology. But in addition to these two elements the
Gita adds a third principle, which is the *raison d'être*
of the poem and which has been of immense importance for the religious life of India. This is the doctrine
that a man can win salvation only by pursuing the
duties of his state and caste in a spirit of disinterested

devotion. The warrior need not become a monk or a hermit in order to be a saint; the true path of perfection is the performance of a man's social duty without attachment to the fruits of his action. In this way the metaphysical absolutism of the Upanishads and the monastic ideal of individual perfection are reconciled with cultural values and with the claims of the social order.

Nevertheless, this reconciliation is not complete, nor is it altogether satisfying from the moral point of view, since it involves the uncritical acceptance of the whole ritual and social law as embodied in the caste system. Moreover, it is not inspired by the moral doctrine and example of a great historical teacher like Buddha; it is worked into a mythical episode in the heroic epic, which is rather as though Plato had put the arguments of the Phaedo into the mouth of one of the Homeric heroes and incorporated them in the *Iliad*.

Hence the Gita, in spite of its immense popularity and influence, has not changed the religious ideal of India. Arjuna, the happy warrior, the hero of the Gita, who attains salvation by the performance of his duty in battle, has never displaced the figure of the world-renouncing ascetic and contemplative as the pattern of Indian sanctity.

And the same is true of Buddhism, where the new Mahayana ideal of devotion to the salvation of others did not displace the older way of moral asceticism and individual self-perfection as the dominant religious motive. Indeed, in the development of Northern Buddhism, the Dhyana (Zen) school of contemplation or mystical intuition which has been so important in mediaeval China and modern Japan approximates to the antimonian quietism of the Taoists, and this represents a deviation from primitive Buddhism in the opposite direction from that of the moral activism of the Bodhisatva ideal.

6

Zoroaster in Persia

IN SPITE OF CERTAIN RESEMBLANCES between the religion of the Eastern Indo-European peoples and those of the West, notably the cult of the sacred fire, the religions of the Aryans of India and Persia possess a number of peculiarities that they do not share with the other Indo-European peoples, and it is highly probable that these were developed in Iran itself after the occupation of that region by the Aryans. For there is no reason to suppose that the early population of Persia was originally Indo-European. In the extreme south-west, in Elam, we know that there existed a very ancient civilisation, and that a non-Indo-European agglutinative language was spoken. To the south-east, in Baluchistan, the remnants of a Dravidian-speaking people exist to this day, while the prehistoric remains at Nal prove a connection with the Indus Valley, where there existed in the third millennium B.C. an advanced civilisation of a similar type to that of the ancient Sumerians and Elamites.

It is difficult to say how much of the resemblances between the Iranians and the Indo-Aryans is due to their common racial origin, how much to the common culture that they shared before the Aryan invasion of India, and how much to the common elements that may have existed in the pre-Aryan cultures of Persia and north-western India. But if all these influences were common to the two peoples, how are we to explain the striking divergence in their historical development? To some extent, no doubt, these may be accounted for by the differences of climate and natural environment between the Iranian plateau and the steaming lowlands of the Ganges Valley—for it was not until the Aryans had reached the Ganges that the specifically Indian development of their culture took place. But it was the development of the world religions themselves that did more than anything else to cause the divergence between the two cultures, and this development was due not to the influence of blind natural forces, but to the conscious work of great historic or semi-historic personalities. On the one hand, we have Buddha and the anonymous thinkers of the period of the Upanishads; on the other, the single figure of Zoroaster, the prophet of Iran. It is difficult to conceive a more complete contradiction than is presented by the two resultant attitudes to life. For the Buddhist, on the one hand, the "Aryan law" is a law of renunciation and apathia, life is evil, the body is a source of suffering, and the supreme goal of effort is the dreamless peace of Nirvana. For the Zoroastrian, on the other hand, the material world is "the holy creation of God"; death is the supreme evil. The duty of the Aryan is "to make the world advance" by husbandry and righteousness, and his reward is eternal life in "the House of Song" and to share in the victory of Ahura, when the servants of the Lie are finally defeated in the day of the Great Consummation. And yet both these profoundly irreconcilable views of life agree in that they are both alike reactions from a common type of polytheism and nature worship. Zoroastrianism is no more representative of the primitive religion of the Aryans than is Buddhism of the religion of the Upanishads. It represents the moralisation of an older nature religion of the same type as that which existed in India during the Vedic period.

It is true that we have no evidence of the earlier

stage of Iranian religion, such as the Rig Veda supplies us with in the case of India. The whole sacred literature of ancient Persia is posterior to the Zoroastrian reform, and the oldest portion of that literature consists of the utterances of Zoroaster himself, or at least of the prophet and reformer who went by that name. These hymns, which are known as the Gathas, are comparable from the linguistic point of view to those of the Rig Veda, and must be considerably earlier in date than the other portions of the Avesta, such as the Vendidad and the Yashts, which differ both in dialect and metrical forms from the older elements. Nevertheless, it is from these later texts, together with a few scattered passages in Greek authors, that our only knowledge of the older pre-Zoroastrian religion of the Aryans of Persia is derived.

By the period of the later Avesta, Zoroastrianism had incorporated practices and beliefs which belonged to the old Aryan nature religion and dated back to the age of Indo-Iranian unity, long before the days of Zoroaster and his reform. It had in fact become the national religion of Persia. But when we turn to the older portion of the Avesta—the Gathas—we enter an entirely different atmosphere. The religion of Zoroaster is not the religion of a warlike aristocracy, such as we find in the Rig Veda, nor is it, like that of the later Avesta, the religion of a national kingdom. On the contrary, Zoroaster is the prophet of the poor and the humble, whose only refuge against the oppression of the powerful is in Ahura Mazdah, and the Gathas are inspired throughout by the need of defending the cause of the cattle and the husbandmen against the men of violence, the "followers of the Lie." It is essentially a religion of the peasant, not of the warrior, and the dualism of the earlier Avesta is primarily a social dualism between the men of peace, who "cause the world to advance" by piety and good husbandry and

he men of violence, who "destroy the life of the ox
with shouts of joy"—"the liars who destroy life, and are
determined to deprive the matron and the master of
that heritage." But this social dualism is at the same
time a religious one, for the husbandmen, the followers of Right (Asha), are the servants of Ahura, while
the men of violence are the worshippers of the Daeva
and the servants of the Lie.

Moreover, Zoroaster is not the national champion of
the Iranians against a foreign enemy. On the contrary,
he complains like Jeremiah of his unpopularity and
isolation. "To what land shall I flee, whither betake
myself? From the nobles and the priesthood they
sever me, nor are the people pleased with me, nor the
rulers of the land that follow the Lie. I know therefore I am without success. Few cattle are mine and
I have but few folk. I cry to Thee, see Thou to it, O
Lord, granting me help, as friend giveth to friend."
(Ys. 46.1–2.)

It seems on the whole, then, more probable that the
opposition described in the Gathas was a social rather
than a national one. We have seen that Iranian culture
was itself probably of mixed origin and was composed
of two distinct elements: a very ancient type of settled peasant civilisation on the one hand, and on the
other, the warlike tribal culture of the pastoral Aryan
peoples. Now it is easy to understand how in such a
culture, a social opposition may have existed between
the ruling aristocracy, which had inherited the ideals
of warrior tribesmen, and the subject agricultural population. Indeed, such a conflict is implicit in the contrast of warrior lord and peasant serf.

Now about this period, in other parts of the world,
there were arising champions of the poor and the oppressed who gave voice for the first time in history to
the wrongs of the subject classes and to a criticism of
the rulers and the rich. Such were Hesiod in Greece,

and Amos and Isaiah in Israel, and it is when viewed from a similar point of view that the utterances of Zoroaster become most fully intelligible, as the forces of the spiritual world are brought in to redress the balance against the injustice and evil of the present life. For whatever the issue of the earthly struggle, the followers of Asha are assured of victory in the Last Day, when the world is judged by fire, and the servants of the Lie are condemned to eternal torment, while the souls of the righteous shall be happy forever in the heavenly kingdom, "the Pasture of Right."

Thus there is no ultimate dualism, for the victory of Asha is assured. Only the regeneration of the world must be worked out slowly and painfully in daily warfare with the powers of evil. The saints are they who "cause the world to advance," by Right, by husbandry, and by good works. This is "the Road of Good Thought, built by Asha on which the souls of the Future Deliverers shall pass to their reward." (Ys. 34.13.) Thus every good act increases the dominion of Ahura and hastens the coming of the kingdom—in the words of the later Avesta, "He who relieves the poor, maketh Ahura King." Consequently, the Zoroastrians' hope of a world to come in no sense implies a spirit of other-worldliness or any contempt of the present life or of material concerns. The prophet himself sometimes shows a naïve anxiety about his material interests, as when he writes, "This I ask, tell me truly, Ahura —whether I shall indeed, O Right, earn that reward even ten mares with a stallion and a camel which was promised to me, O Mazdah, as well as through Thee the future gift of Welfare and Immortality" (in the world to come). (Ys. 44.18.)

In the same way, the spiritual powers possessed a very close relation to the concrete forces of the natural world. Each of them is linked with some particular province of nature or some category of objects. Thus

Asamaiti—Piety—is the Genius of the Earth; Asha—
Right—is the spirit of the Fire. This gives Zoroastrianism a peculiar interest for the students of comparative religion. For on the one hand, it stands out
even among the other world religions of the new
period by reason of its uncompromising monotheism
and its high ethical teaching, while on the other, its
view of the world still has much in common with the
simple animistic conceptions of the old nature religion. The other world religions (with the possible
exception of Confucianism) tended to turn away from
social life and material activity in order to seek a
purely spiritual kingdom, and even, like the Buddhists, despised the body and all earthly existence as
essentially evil. Zoroastrianism alone preserved the
spirit of the agricultural religion of the archaic culture,
which had regarded the earth and the life of nature
as holy, and looked upon the work of tillage and husbandry as sacred rites. Throughout history the followers of Zoroaster have remained faithful to the teaching that is inculcated so persistently in the Avesta.

It is true that this eminently sane and practical ideal
of conduct is obscured by an elaborate growth of
magical conceptions and ritual practices that often appear absurd and revolting to the modern mind. The
slightest contact with a corpse involves a state of un-
cleanness, which must be counteracted by a rigid
method of purification and ritual quarantine. Nevertheless, these practices in spite of their crudity, are
often of real hygienic value, and it has been truly said
that the Zoroastrian attitude towards the spirit of
death and disease—the Nosu—is much the same as that
of the modern educated European towards bacteria
and infection. For instance, it is taught in the Vendidad that wet matter is a greater conductor of unclean-
ness than dry matter, and that metal can be cleansed
of infection more easily than wood. This practical

and utilitarian spirit is, however, only one side of the
Zoroastrian religion. It survives in its full strength
among the existing remnant of the followers of
Zoroaster, the Parsis of Bombay and the Guebres of
north-western Persia, but it has had little influence on
the outside world.

It is the more spiritual elements of Persian religion
—its eschatology, its dualistic theory of the eternal
conflict of the forces of light and the forces of darkness, and its teachings with regard to guardian angels,
etc.—that have been of most importance for the history
of religion. In the early centuries of the Christian era,
above all, Iranian culture and Iranian religion made
their influence felt in all directions. It is to be seen
in the spread of the worship of Mithras in the Roman
Empire; in the rise of new syncretistic types of religion, such as Manicheanism and some of the Gnostic
sects; and even in the transformation that the Buddhist religion underwent in Northern India and Central Asia during this period.

It is, however, a very difficult problem to decide
how far Zoroastrian influence affected the earlier development of religion in Western Asia. There are
obvious resemblances between the religion of the
Avesta, on the one hand, and both Judaism and early
Christianity, on the other, and the changes that took
place in later Judaism, with its increased emphasis on
eschatological and apocalyptic teachings, suggest an
even closer parallelism. There has been a widespread
tendency, especially among German writers, to attrib-
ute the new developments mainly to Zoroastrian influence, and even to regard the idea of the redemption of the world by a supernatural deliverer and of
the Last Judgment as actually of Zoroastrian origin.

Now it is true that the Jews were in contact with
Persian influences from the sixth century onwards,
and it may well be from this source that they derived

the new beliefs in angels and demons that appear in the books of Daniel and Tobit. In the latter case Persian influence is certain, since the evil spirit Asmodeus bears the name of a Zoroastrian demon, Aeshama Daeva. On the other hand, the Jewish belief in the coming of the Kingdom of God and the Messianic deliverer is deeply rooted in the whole tradition of the religion of Israel, and there is no need to invoke foreign influences to explain its subsequent development. It has even been maintained that the resemblance between the two religions points to an influence of Judaism on Zoroastrianism, rather than vice versa. But though this view is not impossible, it is purely hypothetical, and the uncertainties of the date of the Gathas and of the Zoroastrian reform itself make it difficult to affirm anything definite about the historical circumstances of its origin. Consequently, it is safest to assume a completely independent origin for the monotheism of Israel and that of Iran, and to confine the question of mutual influence to a secondary stage.

7

Development of Greek Thought

OF ALL THE NEW MOVEMENTS of thought that arose in the first millennium B.C., that of the Greeks must always appear to us the most original and creative and the most fruitful in its influence on social progress. Nevertheless, "the Greek miracle" no longer stands out in isolation from the rest of history, as it did in the days of Renan. We know that Athene, the genius of Hellenic culture, was not a daughter of the Olympians, nor did she spring fully armed from the head of Zeus, as the Greeks believed. She belonged to the old pre-Hellenic culture of the Aegean world and had ruled her land in the Mycenean age before the coming of the younger gods.

For in Greece, no less than India or Persia, the existence of an ancient culture tradition, inherited from the ages before the Indo-European invasions, was an indispensable condition for the rise of the new civilisation. It is true that owing to the natural conditions of the Aegean world, this tradition survived in a more sporadic and irregular way than elsewhere. It was not embodied in an organised priesthood, as in India, or in a political order, as in China. The Greeks themselves possessed a strong sense of this loss of continuity and of the discord that existed between the old and the new orders—a sense that finds expression in the legends of the dethronement of Chronos and the older gods by Zeus and his Olympians. The memory of the archaic culture survived in the tradition of a

Golden Age before the coming of war and strife, when men lived in familiar friendship with the powers of the earth, "reaping the labours of their hands in quietness together with many good things, being rich in flocks and dear to the blessed gods."

The new mythology of the Olympian deities was of far less importance for the religious man than the due performance of the sacred rites, whose origins were deeply rooted in the archaic past. The theology of the Greeks was a thing of yesterday, as Herodotus remarks, but their religious practices were of immemorial antiquity. Men might believe what they would concerning the nature of the gods, so long as they maintained an exact and scrupulous performance of the rites, for that alone could ensure the safety of the city and the fertility of the soil. The law of sacrifice was "the ancient and best law" on which the whole social order depended.

Nevertheless, the conditions of the new age in Greece as well as in the East led men to turn their minds to ethical problems and to seek a moral principle in the order of the universe. In Hesiod, we find the same sense of social injustice—the oppression of the poor by the "bribe-swallowing" kings, which inspired the utterances of Zoroaster and the Hebrew prophets, and the same appeal from the unrighteousness of men to the righteousness of God. The law of the natural order—of Hesiod's Works and Days—is also the Law of Dike—Eternal Right—the all-seeing daughter of Zeus. When men follow justice the city blooms, the earth bears rich harvests, and children and flocks increase; but for the unjust all nature is hostile, the people waste away from famine, and a whole city may reap the evil fruit of one man's ill deeds.

This belief in a moral order was, however, still inextricably bound up with ritual conceptions. Moral evil was often hardly distinguishable from ritual impurity. The sense of sin as a mysterious curse that a man might unwittingly incur lay heavy on the mind of ancient Greece, and even in the historical period, both states and individuals resorted to the magical powers of professional wonder-workers and seers to obtain the catharsis or purification of which they felt the need so deeply.

It forms the theme of the greatest masterpieces of Greek literature. In fact, the mind of the Attic trage-dians was dominated by a desire to justify the moral order of the world by finding an answer to this prob-lem. In their hands the primitive legends of the inef-faceable stain of ritual impurity and the nemesis that follows the infringement of a tabu gradually acquired moral significance as the expression of a higher law that guides the affairs of men to a spiritual consumma-tion—an inscrutable power that directs all human things in righteousness in its silent path.

This, however, represents the highest achievement of Greek culture in the period of its maturity. In the earlier period, the thirst for purification led men to turn to professional seers, the "night-walkers, Magians, priests of Bacchus and priestesses of the wine vat, mystery-mongers" of whom Heraclitus speaks, and they seem to represent a backward and primitive element in Greek religion. Nevertheless, they also con-tributed to the development of the new thought. The Shaman becomes a prophet, and from the tradition of the old wonder-workers and seers there emerges a new type of religious life and teaching. The mysteries of the old vegetation religion became transformed from magical practices intended to secure the fertility of nature into the instruments of spiritual catharsis. They were transformed from the life of nature to the soul of man. This change occurred in the case of the great Eleusinian mysteries at Athens and also more widely in the mysteries of the orgiastic culture of the

Thracian vegetation god Dionysius, whose worship had spread throughout the Greek world at an early period. And it is in connection with this latter cult that there first appears in the sixth century the purely religious movement of the Orphic confraternities, though this remained outside the mainstream of the Hellenic development, in spite of the deep influence it exercised on Greek thought.

The new movement that found expression in the oriental cultures in the world religions was represented in the West above all by Greek philosophy. For the spirit of enquiry that led in China to the theories of the two cosmic principles and five agents, and in India to the cosmological speculations of the Brahmins and to the developed Sankhya philosophy, found its highest development in the Greek world. Nevertheless, like the Orphic mysticism, it stood outside the native religious development and had no roots in the culture of mainland Greece. It arose in the cosmopolitan cities of Western Asia Minor and spread thence to the new colonial societies of Italy and Sicily. Thus it undoubtedly owed something to the influence of the great oriental cultures with which the Ionians came in contact through their commercial relations with Lydia and Egypt—a debt which is recognised by Greek tradition in the stories of the travels of Thales and Pythagoras and their study of the wisdom of the Egyptians. From the beginning, however, Ionian philosophy is marked by a spirit of free enquiry and true scientific curiosity that is utterly unlike the strict traditionalism of oriental thought. They regarded the world as a living whole—a cosmic process—and they sought to explain its nature and the cause of its changes not by a mythical cosmogony, like Hesiod or the Orphic rites, but by the evolution of some primary element that is the fundamental substance of all that exists. Nevertheless, it is easy to exaggerate the rational

and scientific elements in these conceptions. The Ionian philosophers were materialists only in the sense
in which the writers of the Brahmanas were, and both
were so only because they had inherited the old undifferentiated view of reality that was common to the
nature religions. It was only at a later period when the
distinction between matter and spirit had become a
commonplace of philosophy that Plato could condemn
the Ionian cosmogony as mechanical and atheistic.
In reality the physical monism of the Ionian philosophers was only a development of conceptions that
were already implicit in primitive religion.

Thus when Thales or Anaximenes attempts to find
the ultimate principle of the universe in water or air,
he is following the same path that the writers of the
Upanishads followed in their premature efforts to
identify Brahmin with Breath or Space. And as the
latter prepared the way for the deeper and more
metaphysical solution of the Atman theory, so also the
crude speculations of the early Ionian thinkers are the
first landmarks in the Hellenic search for a transcendent principle of reality. Moreover, in Greece, no less
than in the East, this search was determined by the
conception of a sacred order that was at once cosmic
and moral. If the powers of nature were divine, as the
beliefs of the old religion taught, there was nevertheless a higher principle beyond them, whose laws even
the gods were powerless to disobey since it was older
than they and had allotted to each one his destined
place and office. "Even the Sun," says Heraclitus, "will
not overstep his measures, for if he does, the Erinyes,
the handmaids of Justice, will find him out."

But the full potentialities of this idea were first realised in the teachings of the Pythagorean school, which
arose in southern Italy in the latter part of the sixth
century. Unlike the earlier Ionian philosophers of
the school of Miletus, the Pythagorean doctrine was

not simply an enquiry into the nature of things, it was also a way of salvation, a method of spiritual catharsis similar to that of the Orphic confraternities that flourished at the same time and in the same region. It is in fact difficult to draw a sharp line between the two movements. Both of them taught the doctrine of the transmigration of souls, and the Pythagoreans laid no less emphasis than the Orphics on purely ritual rules connected with diet, clothing, and behaviour as necessary means for the attainment of purification and deliverance. The true originality and importance of Pythagoreanism is not, however, to be found in these doctrines and practices, which were no doubt taken over from the older Orphic movement, but in its teaching regarding the cosmic order and its theory of science as a means of spiritual purification. The very name of Cosmos, which signifies the ordered march of nature, is a Pythagorean term and shows the essential contribution that the new movement made to Greek thought.

"What is the most just of things? The act of sacrifice. What is the most wise? Number. What is the most beautiful? Harmony." In these three articles of the Pythagorean catechism we see the primitive conception of a sacred ritual order in the process of giving birth to a new view of reality to which the whole later tradition of European science owes its origin and apart from which modern European science could never have existed. The Pythagoreans sought the ultimate basis of nature, not in some fundamental substance from which all things were derived according to the theories of the old Ionian physicists, but in the principle of number. They divined an element of numerical proportion and harmony underlying the whole of nature and manifested in the harmonic intervals of the octave and in the relative proportion of geometric figures. It is true that they developed this principle into a fantastic system of numerical mysticism according to which things *are* numbers, and every number and figure has a transcendental and esoteric significance. Nevertheless, it is in fact only by the study of the numerical and quantitative relation of things that a genuine scientific knowledge of nature is possible, and the systematic cultivation of arithmetic, geometry, and music that was carried on by the Pythagorean schools in the fifth and fourth centuries laid the foundations on which science has built ever since.

The primitive Pythagoreanism of the sixth century must of course have been a very different thing from the highly developed philosophy of science that Archytas taught at Tarentum at the beginning of the fourth century, but we can hardly doubt that the fundamental idea of an order that governs the course of nature by the law of number and harmony belongs to the original tradition of Pythagoreanism. Indeed, this conception dominates the whole development of Greek thought from the close of the sixth century onwards and influences thinkers who were otherwise independent of the Pythagorean movement. It is already completely developed in the writings of Heraclitus (c. 500 B.C.), who would have to be regarded as its author if it were not a part of the original Pythagorean teaching. To Heraclitus it is the one principle of reality in the ever-changing flow of appearances. To know it is to know "the Way of God," "the thought by which all things are steered through all." "This cosmos," he writes, using the Pythagorean term, "which is the name for all, no one of the gods or men has made; but it was ever, is now, and ever shall be, an ever-living fire, with measures kindling, and with measures going out." But though Heraclitus identifies this order with fire, after the manner of the Ionians, he does so in no materialistic sense. It is also divine wisdom, "the thought by which all things are steered through all things." It is the source of spiritual enlightenment and of moral order, "for all human laws are fed by the one divine law." It is in short God, One, Eternal, and Omnipotent—a God who is "willing and unwilling to be called by the name of Zeus," because it infinitely transcends human conceptions, "for the wisest man is an ape compared to God, just as the most beautiful ape is ugly compared to man." Thus Heraclitus is a prophet and a religious reformer no less than a philosopher and a cosmologist. He pours scorn alike upon the vain fables of the poets and the superstition and idolatry of the popular cult. The only true catharsis is that of wisdom, the logos of the inspired teacher. "The mysteries practised among men are unholy mysteries." They vainly purify themselves by defiling themselves with blood, like men who step into mud to wash themselves. But "justice shall overtake the artificers of lies and the false witnesses," since there await men when they die such things as they do not dream of.

This stern, almost puritanic, spirit of hostility to popular superstition had already made its appearance in the writings of an earlier Ionian thinker, Xenophanes of Colophon, whose criticism of the men who make gods in their own image, "deeming that the gods are begotten as they are, and have clothes like theirs and voice and form," marks an epoch in the history of Greek religious thought. Against the lying fables of the poets he sets up a new conception of divinity, "one god, the greatest among gods and men, neither in form like unto mortals nor in thought." No doubt he identifies this deity with the physical universe, but he is not therefore to be regarded as an atheist. Greek religion—both popular and philosophic—was essentially cosmological in character, and the movement of religious reform went hand in hand with the new doctrines concerning the nature of the cosmos.

Thus in Greece, no less than in China and India, the realisation of the unity of the cosmic order inevitably led to the recognition of a higher reality that transcends all change and limitation. As in India the writers of the Upanishads developed the conception of Brahmin from a quasi-physical world substance into the absolute Atman, so in Greece Parmenides replaced the cosmic whole of Xenophanes by the metaphysical concept of pure Being. It is impossible for anything to be and not to be. That which is, alone is, and beside it there is nothing. It abides forever by itself apart from all change and becoming—like a perfect sphere, absolutely simple and sufficient to itself, at once the one being and the one object of thought. This extreme monism seems to leave no room for the many-coloured world of human experience, and to lead to a view of the illusory nature of the world of appearances, not far removed from the Vedantic doctrine of Maya. But it was inevitable that some attempt should be made to avoid this extreme conclusion, and with Empedocles, the great Sicilian prophet and philosopher, the Parmenidean doctrine of Being is fused with the Orphic and Pythagorean doctrines of the soul and its wanderings to form a new synthesis of a distinctively religious character.

With Parmenides he holds there is no coming into being and no perishing: That which is will always be, and that which is not can never come into existence. Nevertheless, there is a process of cyclic change, governed by the alternate sway of the forces of Strife and Law by which the One is divided into the Many, and the Many return again to the One.

Now this cycle of becoming is also the cycle of rebirth in which the soul pays forfeit for its sin. The spirit that has followed strife or polluted its hands with blood, is driven forth for thrice three thousand years through all the circle of mortal births, changing one toilsome way of life for another. "Such a one," cries the prophet, "am I, an exile and a wanderer from the gods, for that I put my trust in insensate strife." "I have been a bush and a bird and a boy and a girl and a dumb fish in the sea."

It is only by a strict discipline of moral and ritual purification that the soul can recover its lost estate. Nothing could be more unlike the commonly accepted conception of the Greek attitude to life than this dualistic doctrine of purification and release. It seems to belong rather to the world-denying asceticism of the oriental religions. Indeed, the closest parallel to it is to be found, centuries later, in the Manichean doctrine of the two world principles of Light and Darkness, and the cosmic drama of their intermixture and separation. It proves that the same forces that led to the turning away of the oriental mind from human life and temporal existence were already at work in the Hellenic world, and that the later religious development of Stoicism and Neoplatonism were not wholly due to external influences but were deeply rooted in the culture of the classical period.

It is true that there existed another current of thought, of a purely humanist character, that tended towards the secularisation of Greek culture, but this tendency also has its representatives in the oriental civilisations—in the materialists or Carvakas of India, and in the sophists and professors of politics who acted as advisers to the Chinese princes and tyrants in the period of war and confusion that preceded the rise of the empire. In Greece, however, the absence of political unity and the wide distribution of political power were especially favourable to freedom of thought and discussion. In the democratic world of Periclean Athens, where power and influence de-

pended on persuasive speech and every citizen had
a voice in the management of public affairs, it was
easy to believe that man was the measure of all
things, and that the most fundamental religious moral
truths were merely matters of opinion. Perhaps for
the first time in the history of the world, a state of
society existed in which nothing was too sacred to be
discussed and criticised, and every institution and belief was submitted to the test of reason. Nevertheless,
it was in the midst of this universal questioning and
strife of tongues that the Greek vision of an intelligible
order, which pervades all things and which is the
source and end of the whole material world, found
its highest expression.

It is already foreshadowed in Anaxagoras' doctrine
of eternal mind as ordering the movement of the universe; it was freed by Socrates from the externalism
and materialism of the old Ionian physicist tradition,
and with Plato it appears in the final and classical
form that was henceforth to dominate the mind of
the ancient world.

For it was in the philosophy of Plato that the theory
of a transcendent reality attained its classical expression in the West. The vision of Eternity that had so
long absorbed the mind of the East, at last burst on
the Greek world with dazzling power. With Plato,
the Western mind turns away from the many-coloured
changing world of experience to that other world of
eternal forms.

Nevertheless, the Platonic mysticism differs from
that of the oriental religions in that it is essentially a
mysticism of the intelligence that seeks illumination
not so much by asceticism and ecstasy as by the discipline of scientific knowledge. Yet the object of the
higher sciences was not in the view of Plato—or indeed of the Greek world in general—a utilitarian one.
Geometry leads the mind away from the corruptible

and perishing to the contemplation of true being and eternal order. To the man who follows this path there will be revealed a common bond binding together every geometrical diagram, every related group of numbers, every combination of the musical scale, and the single related movement of the revolutions of all the heavenly bodies into a single intelligible harmony, and so will he be brought to the shore of that vast sea of beauty where the transcendent reality of the absolute beauty is at last revealed to him.

8

The Etruscans and the Rise of Rome

THE LEADING CHARACTERISTIC of the early history of
Italy was its lack of cultural unity. It was a meeting
place and battleground of competing cultures rather
than the centre of a strong independent tradition.

Owing to its geographical character, Italy never
possessed the possibility of internal cultural unity, until the Roman engineers had succeeded in supplying
the country with a system of artificial communications
more perfect than anything the world had known before the nineteenth century. Every district was divided from its neighbour by mountain and forest, and
nowhere was there sufficient open plateau or lowland
to give room for the formation of a homogenous and
independent culture. And yet while Italy is thus divided from herself within, she is more open to influences from without than any other Mediterranean
land. She lies across the Mediterranean, like a greater
Crete, open to every influence from North Africa and
Spain, from the Aegean and the Levant; while on the
north she is equally open to central Europe and the
Danube lands, for the Alps are more a spectacular
frontier than a real barrier, and especially on the east
from the Trentino to the Carso the long and easy
descent into Lombardy and Venetia irresistibly attracts
invaders from the outer lands.

Thus throughout the ages, with the exception of the
central period of Rome's greatness, internal separatism
and the meeting of foreign cultures have been the

dominant notes of Italian history. On her soil Sabellians and Celts have met Greeks and Etruscans, Goths and Lombards and Normans have struggled with Byzantines and Arabs—up to modern times she has been the battlefield of Spain and France and Austria. Only in one vital period did a power arise in Italy that was capable of transmuting the weakness of her situation into strength, of uniting Italy and with her the whole Mediterranean basin, and of making her the bridge by which the civilisation of the Levant passed over to the barbarous West.

The real turning point in the history of Italian culture was due to none of the inland peoples, but to a new wave of influence from the higher civilisation of the eastern Mediterranean, which reached Italy through the Etruscans. This strange people, utterly different in language, in civilisation, and probably also in race to all those who surrounded them, were a problem to the ancient world and remain a problem to us to-day. They were a sea-people of pirates and traders, who established themselves on the coast of Tuscany at least as early as the later part of the ninth century, and thence extended their power gradually over middle Italy from the Po to the Bay of Naples. There can be little doubt that they are the same as the Tursha, who attacked Egypt in company with the other "peoples of the sea" at the end of the thirteenth century. They are mentioned in company with the Shardana, and their later culture, for example, their rock-cut tombs, have considerable resemblances with that of Sardinia. But whereas the latter culture dates back to the beginnings of the Bronze Age about 2000 B.C., our earliest archaeological evidence for the Etruscans belongs to the ninth century. Whence then did they come? Herodotus states that they came to Italy from Lydia, and he also mentions "Tyrsenian Pelasgians" being driven out of Attica and settling in Lemnos until its conquest by Miltiades in the fifth century, and in fact an inscription of Etruscan type has been found in that island.

The name of the people, Tyrsani, Tyrreni, or Tursanna, is perhaps derived from the town of Tursa or Turra in Lydia, but since that name is simply a form of the Aegean or Lydian word for acropolis or stronghold, Tursis or Turris, the Tursenna might equally well mean "the people of the strongholds," a derivation that agrees well enough with the form of their early settlements in Italy. On the whole it seems almost certain that they were a pre-Greek Aegean people, like the Carians, and that they were driven out of their earlier homes during the age of the Dorian invasion and the Greek settlement of Asia Minor. But the view has also been maintained that their settlement in Italy dates from a far earlier period, and that the archaeological remains that are usually held to date the coming of the Etruscans to Italy really only mark the awakening of trade between them and the peoples of the eastern Mediterranean.

There is reason to think that the Etruscans were in touch with central Italy, before their actual settlement in the country, and it is probably from this source that the Aegean element in the geometrical ornament of the early Villanovan period was derived. They came, no doubt, like the earlier Prospectors, in search of metal, especially of the iron and copper of Elba, and it is noteworthy that their earliest permanent settlement, Vetulonia, lies on the mainland opposite that island. From this point they gradually extended their settlement until they occupied middle Italy from the Tiber to the Arno. Their cities lay for the most part strung out along the Tuscan coast—not by the sea, like the Greek cities of the south, but from four to twenty miles inland, but the four cities of Umbria lay by themselves in the interior, with Volsinii

as a link between the two groups. These made up the
famous confederation of twelve cities. Only at a later
period was the Etruscan power extended to Campania,
and (about the end of the sixth century) to Bologna
and the Valley of the Po, but their occupation of Elba
and Corsica was probably early.

From the first the Etruscans appear as a city-
dwelling people, and it is their essential importance
that they were the initiators of town life and, in fact,
of the city-state among the Italic people of central
Italy. All the rites connected with the foundation and
organisation of the city, as practised by the Latins in
historical times, were attributed to the Etruscans, and
were carried out according to the prescriptions of
their ritual books. The Etruscan city was not a mere
clan stronghold, it was the centre of an extensive territory and the dwelling-place of an aristocracy,
whose tombs bear witness to a high degree of wealth
and material culture. It lay high upon an isolated hill-
top, like Orvieto and Volterra, or on a ridge between
two streams like Veii, and in some cases it possessed
an arx or capitol separated from the town itself. Nothing is more characteristic of the early Etruscan culture
than the luxury and elaboration of their private life—
that "Capuan luxury" that was afterwards proverbial.
Their typical arts are the arts of luxury—jewelry and
bronze ornament, especially the famous Etruscan mirrors. Women took a far more prominent place in social life than they did in the Hellenic world, and in the
tomb paintings we see the wife taking part by the side
of her husband in the banquet and watching the dancing and the flute-playing. Outside the walls lay the
necropoli with their tombs hewn out of the rock, and
surmounted in southern Etruria by great round bar-
rows. Indeed, the city of the dead was of far more
enduring character than that of the living, and bears
witness to that almost Egyptian sense of preoccupation

with the afterlife that overshadows the whole course of Etruscan culture and differentiates it so strongly from that of the Greeks.

The writers of the nineteenth century, led by Mommsen, who had an almost personal antipathy to the Etruscans, were apt to deny all originality to the Etruscans' culture and art. It is true that in the seventh century the Etruscans were still passive recipients of that strange denationalised and stereotyped artistic tradition that dominated the Levant in the centuries between the fall of Minoan civilisation and the rise of Hellenism, as the Byzantine tradition did in the early Middle Ages—a syncretistic survival of the traditions of Egypt and Mesopotamia, of Crete and Asia Minor. Even at that date, however, two of the most characteristic arts of the Etruscans, their jewelry and their metalwork, had attained the highest perfection. In the following century the Etruscans came into full contact with the living stream of Hellenic culture. In spite of piracy and wars with the Italian Greeks, Etruria became in artistic matters a province of the Hellenic world. Its tombs are full of masterpieces of Greek art—vases, gems, and bronzes. Greek workmen painted the sepulchral frescoes, and moulded the terra-cotta revetments of its temples. Nor was the share of the Etruscans in this merely passive. Like the Lydians, they were not simply barbarian pupils of the Greeks, they were also co-heirs in a common Aegean culture tradition. Their three-celled temple of wood or brick with its terra-cotta revetments remained to the last a perfectly distinct type. Their wall-paintings and sculpture, in spite of their dependence on Greek models in subject and execution, acquired the imprint of their peculiar character, and as we see it in the terra-cotta Apollo of Veii, or the bronze Capitoline wolf, they were capable of producing by the end of the sixth century works of real originality and power.

It was from Etruria, as Roman tradition truly tells, that the first images of the gods came to Rome. Vulca of Veii, perhaps the very artist of the Apollo, is said to have made the terra-cotta image of Jove for the sixth-century temple of Jove on the Capitol and that of Hercules in the Forum Boarium. In later Roman history and legend the Etruscans have acquired a sinister reputation as a people of sombre superstition from whom the Romans learned the gladiatorial show and the penalty of crucifixion, and whose greatest originality lay in the elaboration of the science of augury. But it is only fair to remember that they were the first to introduce into Italy the city-state and the higher civilisation of the eastern Mediterranean, and that it was they who laid the foundations on which the great Roman development was founded.

The Etruscans were not, however, the only representatives of the higher civilisation, for southern Italy and Sicily lay within the sphere of direct Hellenic influence. From the latter part of the eighth century, the Greeks began to settle thickly on the southern shore of the peninsula and the eastern coast of Sicily, while farther north the oldest of all the Greek colonies, Cumae on the Bay of Naples, lay on the verge of the Etruscan sphere of influence and formed the channel through which Hellenic trade and culture reached not only the rich Plain of Campania, but also the Latin country and the Valley of the Tiber.

This then was the situation at the dawn of Roman history. On the one hand, a primitive Italic population of shepherds and peasants, divided into numerous independent tribal communities; on the other, the prosperous and warlike trading cities of Etruria, some of which possessed territories as wide as the whole of

Latium. It was inevitable that the higher culture
should dominate and influence the lower, and this
process of permeation by the higher culture began
at such an early stage that it is very difficult for us to
go back behind the Graeco-Etruscan period and behind the civilisation of the city-state and to divine the
social life of the primitive Latin community. Here we
have no Homer to help us, as in the prehistoric age
of Greece. We are dealing with a people without art
or letters, without cities or temples.

The Roman city and its culture were due to the
fusion of these two alien and opposite elements—the
Etruscan city-state and the Latin peasant community.
From the one side came all the institutions of city life
—the symmetrical division of the community into
three tribes and thirty curiae, like the tribes and
phratries of the Greek city-state; the magistracy, with
its insignia, such as the curiale chair, the purple toga,
the ivory sceptre, and the rods and axes of the lictors.
Etruscan also were the triumphal procession and the
public games, which were traditionally ascribed to
the first Etruscan king, and which as we see from the
tomb paintings of Tarquinii and Chiusi played such a
large part in Etruscan life. Even more important was
the introduction of writing and the alphabet, which
came to the Latins not from the Greeks directly, but
through the Etruscans, even if the latter derived their
knowledge of them from the Greeks of Cumae, and
did not, as some authorities now believe, already
possess them before their coming to Italy.

On the material side Rome owes to the Etruscans
its actual foundation as a city together with the drainage and laying out of the Forum and the foundation
of the acropolis, with its city temple on the Capitol.
The Servian wall and the Cloaca Maxima, which used
to be ascribed to the Etruscan kings, are much later,
but on the other hand, the great drainage tunnel of

the Alban Lake is probably of this period, and it may well explain the Roman tradition of how the Etruscan lords forced their Latin subjects to labour for long years on their great drainage works and tunnels.

The same opposite currents are visible in the Roman religion, which remained to the very last extraordinarily primitive in character, so that the official cult of the Roman state at the time of its greatness, still preserved almost intact—petrified but not changed —the animistic religion of an earlier age.

But it is very difficult to say how much in this religion is native Italian and how much is of Etruscan origin. From the Etruscans were derived, no doubt, the first temples and images, and the Roman city temple on the Capitol, which was built by the Etruscan kings and was dedicated like the city temples of the other Etruscan cities to the triad—Jupiter, Juno, and Minerva. The Latin communities as a rule worshipped a nature goddess or mother goddess of the type with which we are so familiar, such as the Junos of Lanuvium and Falerii, the Fortuna of Praeneste, the Mater Matuta of Satricum, and above all, the Diana of Aricia. But at Rome the presiding deity, the father and protector of the community, was Mars, who was in origin not a war god, but a vegetation deity. He was the vague power that presides over the spring and the rising crops, but no less was he the god to be invoked, by the dancing warrior priests, when the war parties were sent out on their annual raid. To the primitive mind, there was nothing incongruous in the association of the spring and vegetation and the spirit of war; both were the expressions of the vital power on which the life of the community depended, but it was natural in later times, when Rome was more and more a great military power, that the father god of the city should be conceived as a war-god pure and simple. We do not know whether he was originally an Italian or

an Etruscan god. The Etruscans worshipped him as
Maristuran, Mars, the Lord, just as they worshipped
the mother goddess as Turan, the Lady, and he also
takes the foremost part in the Umbrian rituals of the
Gubbio inscription. The practice of augury, however, which played a part of enormous importance in
the life of the Roman community, was undoubtedly
an Etruscan institution, and goes back in part to the
elaborate science of divination and magic, which originated in ancient Babylonia. Before any important
public art could be performed, it was necessary for
the college of augurs to ascertain the will of the gods
and obtain their consent by observing the entrails of
the sacrificed victim or the flight of birds, or the light-
ning.

Nevertheless, the Roman religion as a whole bears
the strong imprint of a primitive peasant culture. The
religion of the community is in many respects the
counterpart and expansion of the religion of the peasant household, with the Rex in place of the Pater-
familias, the Flamens of his sons, and the Vestals of
his daughters. The house cults of Janus and Vesta, the
doorway and the hearth, remain the centre of the
public no less than of the private cult; the guardian
ship of the state hearth and its sacred fire retained
to the last its solemn symbolic significance in the life
of the Roman state. And as the individual farm had
its shrine of the Lares and its consecrated boundary
stone, Rome had its shrine of the Public Lares below
the north-east corner of the old Palatine City, and
celebrated the feast of the Terminalia at the Stone of
Jupiter Terminus on the Capitol. So, too, the simple
lustration of the private dwelling and the fields becomes the solemn public Amburbium and Ambarvalia.
And even more primitive types of worship survived
throughout Roman history in the war dance of the
Salii, and the running of the blood-smeared wolf-

priests from the wolf's den—the Lupercal—on the Palatine, round the bounds of the earliest city.

The primitive conditions of Latin peasants live on in the prescriptions of Roman ritual; the use of bronze in place of iron, of the flint knife in sacrifice, and the primitive pottery made, as in the Bronze Age, without the potter's wheel. So, too, in the worship of Vesta, where the extinguished fire could only be rekindled by the primitive method of friction, and the offerings had to consist of cakes not made from wheat, but from spelt, the earliest grain food of the Italic peoples. In later times the Romans prided themselves of being *religiosissimi hominum*, "the most scrupulous of mortals," and though this had degenerated in the later republican period into a hard legalistic formalism, in its origins it rested on a very intense and real primitive religious sense. The gods of the Roman religion were not the heroic figures of the post-Homeric Greek mythology, but vague classes of spirits—Lares, Penates, Semones, Carmentes, the tutelary Genii and Junones of living men and women, and the Manes and Lemures of the dead. They did not worship a personal deity with a name, so much as invoke the vague circumambient powers by whatever names might bind them. Every process of nature, and every vital act in the life of the farm, the family, and the community had its corresponding tutelary spirit, which had to be sedulously placated. But these spirits and powers multiply and melt into one another endlessly, so that we get extraordinary composite cult titles, like the Tursa Cerfia Cerfi Martii of the Umbrian inscriptions, and the catalogues of numina, classified according to every conceivable function of the Roman Indigitamenta.

Thus any individual characterisation was impossible, and the rite became more important than the god or spirit for whose sake it was performed. Many of the most important festivals of the Roman year—such as the Lupercalia, the Fordicidia, the Parilia, the Poplifugium, and the Regifugium—are practically without a presiding deity, and in the case of others, which have a definite god, such as the Robigalia, the Consualia and Opiconsiva, the character of the deity is to say the least highly indefinite. Moreover, it was of the greatest importance to keep the true or binding name a secret, lest the protecting deities should be called away—"exaugurated"—by the priests of a hostile community.

This strange formal and ritualistic cult, so utterly different from the imaginative religion of the Greeks, which always pictured the gods in human form and as human personalities, left a deep imprint on the Roman character. All ancient religions were a religion of the state, but nowhere else was it so inseparably bound up with the life of the state as at Rome.

9

The Mission of Israel

THE RELIGION OF ISRAEL is of unique interest for the study of the world religions. If the achievement of Greek culture has been regarded as a miracle, how much more that of Israel! All the other world religions were linked with some great world culture. Even Greece had inherited the tradition of a whole civilisation—that of the ancient Aegean culture. The achievement of Israel was based on practically no material foundation. It was the work of a people who occupied a territory no larger than Wales, and one that was neither rich nor highly civilised. Nevertheless, it had a wider sphere of influence than any other religion in the world and has affected the development of civilisation, at least indirectly, over the greater part of the earth.

In spite of these unique characteristics, the rise of Israel is at the same time one more example of the invasion of a settled agricultural civilisation by a warlike pastoral people. Indeed, there is no other instance in which the opposition of these two elements is so striking. The whole history of Israel and the whole of their sacred literature bear witness to the struggle that went on between these two forces in the life of the people and show how hard it was for the invaders to preserve their own traditions against the influence of native civilisation of Canaan and the higher material culture and political power of the surrounding peoples.

What distinguishes Israel from among all the other peoples of the Near East was the national tradition of their origin. The true founder of Israel was not a king or a leader in war, but Moses, the inspired prophet and law-giver, and their birth as a nation dates not from their conquest of Palestine, but from the solemn covenant of Sinai, by which Israel was consecrated to their national god Yahweh, and accepted his sovereignty and his law through the mediation of Moses.

Now there is nothing peculiar in the fact that the people of Israel should have owned allegiance to a single god. That was more or less the normal state of things among all the Semitic peoples. There was Asshur, the god of the Assyrians; Chamosh, the god of Moab; Moloch, the god of Edom; the great Baal of Tyre, and many more. But these were in some cases heads of a whole pantheon of lesser deities, and in almost all were accompanied by a female companion or consort, such as Ishtar or the Ashtoroth of the Bible, for the sexual element entered deeply into Syrian religion, and the more civilised was the people, the stronger was the emphasis on that aspect of religion. The god of Israel, on the other hand, tolerated no companion. He was a jealous god, who hated the licentious cults of the native agricultural populations of Canaan. "Hear, O Israel, the Lord Thy God is One God." That was the foundation of the whole tradition of Jewish religion, and it is difficult to believe that it does not date back to the very origins, to the religion of Moses, instead of being, as so many critics have argued, a product of the later prophetic movement.

For Yahweh was from the first a god of war and the desert. The whole traditional history of Israel down to the age of the Prophets consists of the story of these wars of the Lord. The god of Israel—Yahweh of the Hosts, as he was called—was the leader of his people in war; the ark that was the sign of his presence was carried at the head of their armies, and it was he who gave victory to Israel over the nations who possessed the land of Canaan. And just as Israel was the enemy of the native populations, Yahweh was the enemy of the old gods—the gods of the land— the Baals and the Ashtoroth of the native religion of Syria.

Yet it was inevitable that the warlike pastoral tribes of Israel should absorb the culture and the religious practices of the more civilised agricultural population that they had conquered; since agriculture was bound up with the religious cultus of the mother goddess and the vegetation god, a pastoral people who adopted agriculture would naturally adopt at the same time the worship of the lords of the earth and the harvest on which the prosperity of their crops depended. The worship of Yahweh was not abandoned, since he remained the leader of the people in war. But the worship of Baal and Ashtoroth at the local high places was superadded to it, and would necessarily tend to take the foremost place in times of peace among the agricultural classes.

We see this in the days of Solomon, when the united kingdom attained the highest point of material prosperity. On the one hand, Solomon was the builder of the Temple and the palaces that made Jerusalem the sacred city of Judaism; on the other hand, his friendship with the neighbouring powers and his marriage to foreign princesses led him to neglect the worship of Yahweh and go after strange gods.

So too under the house of Omri, when the kingdom of Israel was most flourishing, the alliance with Tyre and the royal marriage to Jezebel led to the worship of the Tyrian Baal becoming general in the northern kingdom. And in each case the forces of opposition and revolt were the anti-foreign party, which remained faithful to the old national tradition and to the worship of the God of Sinai. This is most striking in the second instance, when the opposition to Ahab and Jezebel was led by the prophets Elijah and Elisha. The great story of the flight of Elijah into the desert, his despair at the apostasy of his people, and his meeting with Yahweh at Horeb typify the way in which the religion of Israel drew its strength from the desert where it had its origins.

Thus the history of Israel shows how a lower and more barbaric material culture may become the vehicle of a higher religious tradition. For Yahweh was not only a war god, he was also the god of righteousness and truth; his law was an ethical law that inculcated not merely ritual purity but social justice and a high moral ideal. The intolerant and uncompromising spirit of an Elijah or an Elisha is of the very essence of the Jewish tradition. This alone made it possible for a minority to defy the forces of material power. Hitherto the efficacy or truth of a religion' had been regarded as necessarily resulting in material prosperity or power. The real forces that dominated the world were divinised and worshipped whether they were good or bad. Now for the first time we see this idea reversed. The servants of Yahweh are named the poor, his enemies are the kings of the earth. Victory comes not from the arm of the flesh, but exclusively from the hand of Yahweh, who needs no human allies.

Hence it was that alone among the great religions of the world, the religion of Israel owed nothing to the greatness of its material power. The period that saw the destruction of Israel as a nation witnessed also the rise of Judaism as a world religion. From the ninth century B.C. the whole political situation in the Near East was altered by the appearance of a new factor: the imperial power of Assyria. Assyria was the first of a long succession of world powers with which Israel came into conflict—Babylon, Persia, the Graeco-

Macedonian Empire, and finally Rome—and its relations with Assyria determined the course of development both for the people and its religion. Successful resistance to the superior military power proved to be impossible; complete submission would have been equivalent to a denial of the belief in the sovereignty of Yahweh. Nevertheless, each policy was followed for a time and led to the complete extinction of the northern kingdom and the grave peril of Judah. The true solution—the one that gave Judaism its unique character—was that found by the prophets: the acceptance of material defeat and temporary disaster together with the preservation of faith in the power of Yahweh and of hope in an ultimate salvation. For while the prophets prophesied disaster to Israel and denounced the wrath of Yahweh on his unfaithful people, they taught that Assyria herself was but an instrument in the hand of the God of Israel, which would be broken when that purpose was accomplished.

Thus in the eyes of the prophets, Yahweh is no tribal god, but a world ruler, and the course of history —at least insofar as it concerns the fate of Israel—is but the working out of his purpose.

This universalism is already apparent in the earliest of the prophetic writers—Amos—who prophesied in the northern kingdom about 760 B.C. His warnings are directed not only to Israel, but also to all surrounding peoples. He denounced the anger of Yahweh not only against the enemies of Israel, but also against all who had done wrong—even when the outraged party was an Edomite. And in the case of Israel his denunciations are directed especially against moral evils— above all, the oppression of the poor and the luxury and injustice of the ruling classes.

Thus the prophetic movement tended on the one hand to a more universal view of the nature and power of Yahweh—a true religious monotheism—and on the other towards the moral and religious purification of the people. It was too late to produce much fruit in the northern kingdom, which was finally destroyed by Assyria in 722, ten years after the fall of its northern neighbour Damascus. In the southern kingdom, however, it bore fruit in a reforming movement that finally culminated when the power of Assyria was on the wane in the reforms of Josiah. The occasion of these reforms was the discovery of the Book of the Law in the Temple, probably in the year 622. The King entirely went over to the side of the reforming party. Not only was the Temple purged of the polytheistic Babylonian cults that had been introduced during the period of Assyrian supremacy, but also the native cults of the Baals were suppressed and the high places were desecrated. For the first time in the history of Judaea, the exclusive worship of Yahweh and the strict observance of the Mosaic sacred law was enforced by the royal power.

This religious reformation was not, however, the beginning of a national revival. Babylon stepped into the place of Assyria, and Judaea shared the fate of the northern kingdom, within a generation of the reform of Josiah. But thanks to the work of the prophets, the Jewish people did not lose their national consciousness, as the northern kingdom had done. The fall of the old kingdom was the prelude to the birth of a new people and of Judaism as a world religion.

That events should have taken this course was largely due to the work of the two great prophets of the age, Jeremiah and Ezekiel, the former at Jerusalem, the latter among the captive people in Babylonia. Jeremiah is perhaps the most remarkable figure in Jewish history. Indeed, he is the first man in the history of the world whom we know as a living personality, as one who has revealed his inner character and the crises of his personal experience. His writings show the crises of despondency through which he passed—the contrast of his conviction of his divine vocation, and his despair at the hostility and obstinacy of his people. For he had to set himself against the whole current of national patriotism. He preached the necessity of submission to the world power of Babylon and the hopelessness of resistance. Naturally, he was intensely unpopular, and he narrowly escaped with his life at the time of the siege of Jerusalem.

Ezekiel, among the captives in Babylonia, while condemning the apostacy of Judaea even more vehemently than Jeremiah, also prophesied the restoration of the faithful remnant and drew an ideal picture of the new order of things—a purely theocratic order in which the whole people should live for the service of Yahweh. The captivity was to be like a second return of the people of Israel into the desert, and a second time they would enter the promised land and renew the Mosaic covenant. And this program actually bore fruit in the period that followed the fall of the Babylonian Empire, when the new Persian power at least permitted the return of the exiles and the rebuilding of the Temple.

The religion of Judaism had emerged as a true monotheism inspired by a strong ethical feeling and connected with the ideal of an ultimate social and moral revolution: the kingdom of God on earth.

This conception of the sovereignty of one God over all the earth revealed through the historic mission of a single people was the essential idea of the reformed Judaism. The religious exclusivism of the warrior people from the desert had given place to a new spirit of universalism of which Israel was to be the messenger to the nations.

10

Islamic Mysticism

OF ALL TYPES OF MYSTICISM, that of Islam is the richest
perhaps in the quantity and certainly in the quality of
its literature. In the West, apart from a few outstanding exceptions, mysticism and literature have followed separate paths, and the man of letters often
knows nothing of works which from the religious point
of view are spiritual classics. In the East, however,
this is not so. Mysticism and letters go hand in hand
in all the Moslem countries—among the Persians,
above all, but also among the Arabs and Turks. The
greatest poets have devoted themselves to give literary expression to spiritual experience and to fuse
poetical and mystical ecstasy in a single flame. A short
time ago only the great mystical poets of Persia—
'Attar, Jalalu'ddin Rumi, Hafiz, and Jami—were well
known in the West, and it was usual to regard Moslem
mysticism as predominantly Persian, but since we have
had access to the works of the great Arab mystics,
such as Ibnu'l 'Arabi and Ibnu'l Farid, it is at last possible to have some idea of the wealth and variety of
Sufi literature.

It is in their prose writings that the Arabic mystics
are seen to most advantage. The genius of the language
and the race lend themselves to the vivid portrayal
of individual character and the eloquent expression of
personal emotion, and there are many passages in the
lives of the Sufi saints which are of unsurpassed beauty
and religious significance.

Thus it is related of Rabi'a, the saintly freed-woman of Basra, that at night she would go to the house-top and pray as follows: "O my Lord, the stars are shining and the eyes of men are closed, and the kings have shut their doors and every lover is alone with his beloved, and here am I alone with Thee."

Again she would say: "O my Lord, whatever share of this world Thou dost bestow on me, bestow it on Thine enemies, and whatever share of the next world Thou dost give me, give it to Thy friends; Thou art enough for me."

Even more remarkable are the prayers of al-Hallaj, the great Martyr of Sufism, who suffered at Bagdad in A.D. 922.

His disciple Ibrahim ibn Fatik relates:

When Husayn ibn Mansur al-Hallaj was brought to be crucified, and saw the cross and the nails, he laughed so greatly that tears flowed from his eyes. . . . And when he had finished he uttered a prayer of which I remember only these words: "O Lord, I beseech Thee to make me thankful for the grace that Thou hast bestowed upon me in concealing from the eyes of other men what Thou hast revealed to me of the splendours of Thy radiant countenance which is without a form, and in making it lawful for me to behold the mysteries of Thy inmost conscience which thou hast made unlawful to other men.

And these Thy servants who are gathered to slay me, in zeal for Thy religion and in desire to win Thy favour, pardon them and have mercy upon them; for verily if Thou hadst revealed to them that which Thou hast revealed to me, they would not have done what they have done; and if Thou hadst hidden from me that which Thou hast hidden from them, I should not have suffered this tribulation. Glory unto Thee in whatsoever Thou doest, and glory unto Thee in whatsoever Thou willest.

What strikes us in these passages is not, however, their literary beauty so much as the extraordinary

Christian spirit they manifest. Nothing could be more
unlike the harsh legalism and militant intolerance
which we are accustomed to regard as characteristic
of the religion of Islam. And this brings us to the fundamental problem of Sufism. Is it a genuinely Islamic
movement? Or is it a foreign importation which has
no real roots in the religion of the Prophet?

Now the religion of the Koran undoubtedly provides a certain foundation for mysticism. Its first principles are the same as those which the Epistle to the
Hebrews lays down as the first conditions of Faith—
namely, the belief that God is, and that He is a Re-
warder of those that seek Him. Mohammed himself
was a visionary with a profound sense of the reality
of God, and of the transitory and dependent nature
of created things. He lived in a continual meditation
of the Four Last Things, and he taught his followers
to do the same. But apart from this, nothing could be
less mystical than his religious teaching. It was a religion of fear rather than of love, and the goal of its
striving was not the vision of God, but the sensible
delights of the shady gardens of Paradise. And this
was not simply due to a lack of spirituality; it had a
positive theological basis. Man's reward was propor-
tionate to his nature. God was so exalted above creation that any idea of human communion with the
Divinity savoured of presumption. The duty of man
was not the transformation of his interior life, but the
objective establishment of the reign of God on earth
by the sword and submission to the law of Islam.

Thus the religion of Mohammed has more in common with Mahdism than with mysticism. It is a militant puritanism of the same type as the modern Wah-
habite movement. But it was never a purely external
system. Its puritanism was not only that of the warrior,
it was also that of the unworldly ascetic who spends
his time in prayer and fasting and his goods in alms-

giving. From the first there existed in Islam, side by side with the externalism and legalism of the canonists and theologians, a tradition of interior religion, an "Islam of the heart," which showed itself in simple and unworldly piety.

This latent conflict between the Religion of the Saint and the Religion of the Prophet came to a crisis in the case of al-Hallaj, whose life and death mark the turning-point of the whole Sufi movement.

The early Sufis, with the exception of Rabi'a, had concentrated their attention on the negative aspect of the mystical way. Al-Hallaj also emphasized this negative process, but he went beyond it and sought to realise the positive aspect of the mystical union. To him the mystery of creation was not, as to Mohammed, the divine Will—the sheer decree of divine Omnipotence; it was the divine Love, the Essence of the divine Essence in which man was called to participate. Hence the mystical union does not consist in that pure intuition of the divine unity, which is the goal of later Sufism; it is a personal adhesion to the divine *fiat*, which makes the soul of the mystic the organ of the Divine Spirit and causes it to participate in the life of God.

This ideal of mystical conformity with the divine Will was personified in the person of Jesus, who even in the Koran appears as the typical representative of the outpouring of the Spirit, and of "those who have near access to God." Al-Hallaj, however, goes further and regards Jesus as the type of deified humanity—the second Adam in whom the divine vocation of the human race is realised.

The martyrdom of al-Hallaj is the culmination of the Christian tendencies which were already latent in the earlier Sufi movement. Al-Hallaj founded his ideal of mystical sanctity on the Koranic tradition of Jesus, and this imitation of the Koranic Christ led him on to

a literal conformity with the real Christ in His Passion
and death.

Many different causes contributed to bring about
the death of al-Hallaj: the hostility of the theologians
and canon lawyers, the scribes and Pharisees of Islam;
the distrust of the government for his activity as a
propagandist; and the disapproval of many of the Sufi
leaders themselves; but behind them all there lay a
conviction of the incompatibility of the Hallajian doctrine of mystical sanctification with Islamic orthodoxy
—the conflict between the Religion of Law and the
Religion of the Spirit. And consequently the condemnation of al-Hallaj was not an isolated episode. It was
the decisive refusal of the dynamic and transforming
power of sanctity. The rejection of al-Hallaj forced
Sufism aside towards intellectualism and monism, and
ultimately led to its absorption by the forces of an
alien syncretism which were then beginning to in-
vade the world of Islam.

By far the most important representative of this
movement of syncretism in orthodox Islam is Ibnu'l
'Arabi, the great Spanish mystic, born in 1165 at
Murcia, who is known as "The Great Shaykh," par
excellence, since he was the first to organise it in a
system of speculative thought dominated by a monism
as absolute and as unflinching as that of the Vedanta.
Being is one, whether it be pure and unmanifested or
contingent and manifested. Pure Being is not God,
since it cannot be known and is beyond existence; nor
is Contingent Being God, since, though it is ultimately
identical with Him, it has no independent subsistence,
but is restricted to its particular mode of being. Creation is therefore necessary as the medium through
which God realises Himself. The contradiction of the
two forms of Being is resolved and transcended in
man—not, indeed, in the rational man who only participates in the Universal Soul, but in the perfect or

spiritual man who is the expression of the Universal Intelligence.

The whole system resembles a gnostic or neoplatonic version of Christianity rather than an orthodox interpretation of Islam, and it is remarkable that it can ever have been regarded as tolerable in orthodox circles. Nevertheless, from the thirteenth century onwards, Ibnu'l 'Arabi has been accepted as the great doctor mysticus of Islam, and has set his seal on the later development of Sufism. And this reception of his doctrine involves a vital change in the character of Moslem mysticism. It marks the triumph of an intellectualised theosophy over the experimental mysticism which the earlier Sufis had drawn from their life of prayer.

The movement, which began as an extreme development of orthodox Islamic pietism, ended in a pantheistic universalism which transcended alike religious dogma and moral law. In fact, Sufism in its extreme development may be regarded as the most perfect and consistent type of a universalist or undenominational religion which has ever been achieved. In Sufism we see undenominationalism carried out consistently and unflinchingly as a religious movement and not as a secularising one, and consequently it leads to a purely religious conclusion, to spiritual ecstasy. But it is a sterile ecstasy, which no longer fructifies the social life of the Islamic community, as it did in the days of Hasan of Basra, and Rabi'a and al-Hallaj, but which allows the vital sources of spiritual energy to waste away in a nihilistic quietism. It is remarkable that three writers who differ so widely in their general outlook as Gobineau, Lammens, and Massignon, should all agree in their unfavourable verdict on the social and moral effects of the later Sufism. To Gobineau it is this quietism, this "passive disposition of spirit which surrounds with a nimbus of inert sentiment all conceptions of God, of man, and of the universe . . . that is the running sore of all oriental countries." To Massignon it is the divorce between social life and mysticism and the degeneration of the latter into a kind of "supernatural opium smoking" which is "far more profoundly than all the military and economic factors, the true cause of the present disintegration of the Moslem community" for the salvation of which the early ascetics and mystics had struggled and suffered. It is no doubt due to a confused sense of these dangers that there has been so widespread a reaction against Sufism in modern Islam.

Yet the mystical tradition has entered so deeply into the mind of Islam that its disappearance would leave the religious life of the Moslem world disastrously impoverished. For with all its faults and weaknesses, the Sufi movement remains one of the great witnesses outside Christianity to the religious need of humanity. The Sufi is like the merchant in the Gospel who found the pearl of great price; he found one truth—the Reality of God and the worthlessness and emptiness of all apart from Him—and for that truth he sacrificed every other. But that truth is so great that it suffices to outweigh a vast amount of speculative error. The Sufi held fast to this, and consequently, in spite of his theoretic monism and pantheism, he preserves, unlike the Western philosophic monist, a genuine religious attitude. The Sufi may reason like a pantheist, but when he prays it is with the humility and adoration of a creature in the presence of his Creator.

Two

Christianity in the World

"Rome ploughed deep and far and the Christian Church cast the seed of the word in the furrows."
                                                    (Unpublished)

Introduction: Europe in Relation to World History

WORLD HISTORY, as it is understood today, is an entirely new subject. At the end of the past century, when Acton was planning the *Cambridge Modern History*, he saw it as a universal history which would not be a mere combined history of modern states, but a study of the development of universal historical forces. Yet at the same time he took for granted that this history would be a European one and that it was only, or primarily, in Europe and its colonies that the movement of world history was to be found. But the new conception of World History rejects this conception entirely and aspires to produce a work which will be ecumenical in treatment and scope, embracing the whole history of every people from China to Peru without preference or prejudice.

Throughout the past, down to a century or two ago, the historic world was not an intelligible unity. It was made up of a number of independent civilisations, which were in fact different worlds, each of them with its own historical tradition and its own view of world history. During the past thousand years these great world civilisations have been four in number—China, India, Islam, and Europe (or rather Christendom, for the divisions between Western Civilisation and its great Eastern neighbours was always religious rather than geographical).

It is true that the isolation of these four cultures was never complete. Europe was in contact with

Islam; Islam was in contact with India; and India was in contact with China. But these contacts did not go very deep. In particular they did not extend to a knowledge of one another's historical traditions, so that each civilisation tended to ignore one another's pasts. Moreover, these four civilisations were far from being worldwide. Altogether they represented only an island of higher civilisation in an ocean of darkness.

Now the unique significance of Europe for the development of world history is to be found in the part that it has played in breaking down the isolation of these ancient world civilisations and bringing the outer world into the light of civilisation and history.

The first step in this process—the breaking of the oceanic barriers of the Old World by the Portuguese and Spanish navigators—is no doubt familiar enough. The second stage of the European world movement —the penetration of the closed world of the other Old World civilisations—was a much more gradual process, since it began earlier in the thirteenth century with the first great travels of the Friars and of Marco Polo to Central Asia, India, and China and has continued throughout the centuries ever since. Here it was the Christian missionaries who played the leading part. The Jesuit mission to China in the seventeenth and early eighteenth centuries, above all, was unique for its double achievement in convincing Chinese scholars of the scientific values of European culture and in unveiling to Europe the whole extent of Chinese culture—its history, its literature, and its institutions.

The third phase of the process was introduced by three great changes that took place during the eighteenth century: first, the Europeanisation of Russia, the one province of Christendom that had remained isolated from the West since the Mongol conquest to the age of Alexis and Peter the Great; second, the establishment of an autonomous centre of Western culture outside Europe in North America; and third, the British conquest of India. Owing to these developments, the influence of European culture, which had hitherto been limited to the coast and the islands, penetrated to the heart of the Asian and American continents and gradually subjected the trade and the resources of the non-European world to the new Western economic and technical organisation.

During the great age of Western capitalism in the nineteenth century, the whole world lay open to the enterprise of the Western financier and merchant and to the skill of the Western technician and engineer. Nor was this expansion of Western culture purely material. It involved the advance of knowledge and the communication of ideas—and that in both directions. Towards the end of the eighteenth century, Western science took up the work of the Jesuit missionaries and began to reveal an unknown world of oriental religion and philosophy. The discovery of Sanskrit literature by Sir William Jones, Sir Charles Wilkins, and Henry Colebrooke was one of the most epoch-making events of modern times. In the West, it prepared the way for an oriental renaissance, which had a profound effect on European thought especially in Germany and France in the first decades of the nineteenth century. In the East, the influence of Western ideas combined with European interest in Sanskrit studies to produce important changes in Indian culture. The spread of education, the development of the vernacular literatures—above all, Bengali—and the influence of personalities like Ram Mohun Roy (1780–1833) and Rabindranath Tagore prepared the way for the revival of Hindu culture and the growth of a new educated class and a new national spirit. Thus it was the West that created Indian nationalism by giving India a new sense of its own cultural values and achievements.

This two-sided process of Western scientific study and Oriental cultural awakening went on all over the East during the nineteenth century and has extended in the present century to the more primitive peoples of Africa and the Pacific. Here Europe achieved something that had never been done before, since neither the Greeks nor the Arabs nor the Persians, in spite of their interest in the manners and customs of strange peoples, ever succeeded in getting inside the minds of the societies that they studied and comprehending their culture as a living whole. Today this has become the normal procedure of the modern social anthropologist, but its origins are much older than scientific anthropology and are to be found in the new oriental and historical studies, of which Lane's *Account of the Manners and Customs of the Modern Egyptians*, published in 1836, is a classical type, though by no means the earliest example.

But on the other hand, it may be argued that it was Kipling's "Sons of Martha," the engineers and civil servants and sanitary inspectors, who performed the essential task of breaking through the inherited tyranny of prejudice and custom and thrusting the new scientific and technical order on a hundred unwilling peoples. It may be objected that this function might have been performed by the oriental peoples themselves without Western control. But Japan is the only example of a people accepting a radical change in its way of life without being forced to do so by Western economic or political power. The natural reaction of oriental culture to Western contact was reactionary in both senses of the word. These reactionary nationalists or traditionalists who led the resistance to Western imperialism were by no means inferior in character to the leaders of the later nationalist movements—some of them like Abd el Khedir in Algeria, Shamyl in the Caucasus, the Khalifa Abdullah in the Egyptian Sudan, were heroic figures, but they were doomed to inevitable defeat because they did not possess the techniques and the scientific organisation of the civilisation that they resisted. All the triumphs of modern oriental nationalism have been the work of men of Western education, who were able to use the ideas and knowledge of the West in the service of their own peoples.

This new class was, however, literary rather than scientific in training. It was composed, especially in India and in the Near East, of lawyers and journalists and schoolmasters rather than engineers and doctors and economists. It remained for a long time suspended between two worlds—filled with enthusiasm for the material civilisation and democratic ideals of the West, but still profoundly attached to the memory of their ancient cultural tradition.

Hence the ambivalence of the modern nationalist movements. The Westernised intelligentsia acted as the spearhead of national mass movements which were animated by anti-Western xenophobia. But the moment that independence had been secured, they took over the role of the European administrators and proceeded to modernise oriental society far more drastically than the old colonialism had ever dared to do. And this tendency is most pronounced in communist states, where the traditional religious foundations of oriental culture are being destroyed just as ruthlessly as the much less deeply rooted alien power of Western capitalism. Thus the movement of world change that was inaugurated in Western Europe several centuries ago has now been so fully assimilated by the East that it is being carried forward by the very forces that are most overtly hostile to the West. And though this may well end the political predominance of Eu-

rope, it certainly cannot be used as an argument
against the significance of the Western achievement.
It is in fact a process which was foreseen and foretold
by some of the typical representatives of nineteenth-
century liberalism, for their idealism was cosmopolitan
rather than nationalist in its outlook.

This liberal idealism seems very remote from the
racial and cultural conflicts of the existing situation.
Nevertheless, we are witnessing far-reaching attempts
to establish relations between Eastern and Western
culture and to create an organised system of world
order, and both of these movements are the direct
products of nineteenth-century Western ideas. The
only real alternative to the tradition of Western liberalism is that of Eastern communism, and this is so
deeply committed to the principles of Western science and technology, and to one version of Western
social and political ideas, that it can hardly be regarded as representative of oriental culture.

The elements in Marxism which are derived from
the common tradition of Western socialism and democracy—the appeal to justice, humanity, and the
rights of man, even though they are not realised in the
totalitarian practice of the communist state—are still
absolutely essential to the success of communist propaganda in the East no less than in the West, and thus
communism remains committed to the Western side of
its inheritance.

So too with oriental nationalism. This also owes its
moral appeal and its positive qualities to the political
ideas it has acquired from the West. Modern nationalism is an exotic growth in Asia and Africa, and its
diffusion has followed closely in the spread of Western
education. If it loses this leaven of Western ideals and
becomes a negative xenophobic reaction against the
West, it also becomes a destructive force. We saw this
in India at the time of partition, when the old mass

loyalties asserted themselves in their naked elemental violence and the educated leaders of Indian nationalism recoiled in horror.

But perhaps the most striking example of the strength of Western influence on oriental nationalism is the case of modern Turkey, where the Kemalist revival, which arose in the hour of defeat to save the Turkish nation from external conquest, ended by transforming Turkey into a modern secular state planned on strictly Western lines.

Thus it seems impossible to avoid the conclusion that the new Asia and Africa which are emerging with such revolutionary suddenness do not represent simply the reaction of Asian or African culture against the influence of an alien civilisation, but rather the extension of Western civilisation and Western international society into the extra-European world.

And if we wish to understand the roots of the conflict and the source of the revolutionary movements of change that are transforming and possibly destroying the world, it is to Europe in the traditional sense that we must look. As the new science and technology are European in origin, so also is it with the political and ideological conflicts of the present age. These conflicts were in their origin European ones, going back to the age of the French revolution and to the party conflicts that divided Western socialists and liberal nationalists in the nineteenth century. But today these conflicts are being fought out by Asian mass societies which are neither bourgeois nor proletarian, and whose idea of nationality is founded on vast civilisations comparable to Europe or Christendom rather than to historical political unities like the Western European nations.

Nevertheless, the study of the European past is still relevant to modern world history, since Europe was the original source of the movement of change in which the whole world is now involved, and it is in European history that we find the key to the understanding of the ideologies which divide the modern world.

What we need is a new historical analysis of the whole process of world change, tracing the movement from West to East and taking account of the new factors which emerge at each stage in the process.

This process is so great that it transcends all the current ideological interpretations. It is not only an economic revolution in the Marxian sense, nor yet a process of colonial expansion on the part of the Western national states. It is the creation of a wider area of human communication, which is coming to embrace the whole world. In order to understand it, we shall need, on the one hand, the help of the Western historians who can trace its origins in the European past, and on the other, the work of the Orientalists who can appreciate the past of the non-European cultures and understand their reactions to the impact of modern civilisation.

Christianity and the Classical Tradition

IF EUROPE owes its political existence to the Roman
Empire and its spiritual unity to the Catholic Church,
it is indebted for its intellectual culture to a third
factor—the Classical Tradition—which is also one of
the fundamental elements that have gone to the making of the European unity.

It is indeed difficult for us to realise the extent of
our debt, for the classical tradition has become so
much a part of Western culture that we are no longer
fully conscious of its influence on our minds. Throughout European history this tradition has been the constant foundation of Western letters and Western
thought. It was first diffused through the West by the
cosmopolitan culture of the Roman Empire. It survived the fall of Rome and remained throughout the
Middle Ages as an integral part of the intellectual
heritage of the Christian Church, and in the age of
the Renaissance it arose with renewed strength to become the inspiration and model of the new European
literatures and the basis of all secular education.

Thus for nearly two thousand years Europe had
been taught in the same school and by the same masters, so that the schoolboy and undergraduate of the
nineteenth century were still reading the same books
and conforming their minds to the same standards as
their Roman predecessors eighteen hundred years
before.

It is almost impossible to overrate the cumulative

influence of so ancient and continuous a tradition. There is nothing to be compared with it in history except the Confucian tradition in China, and it is curious to reflect that both of them seem finally in danger of coming to an end at the same moment and under the influence of the same forces.

But the classical tradition of Europe differs from that of China in one important particular. It is not of indigenous origin, for though it is so closely linked with the Roman tradition, Rome was not its creator, but rather the agent by which it was transmitted to the West from its original home in the Hellenic world. The classical tradition is, in fact, nothing else than Hellenism, and perhaps the greatest of all the services that Rome rendered to civilisation is to be found in her masterly adaptation of the classical tradition of Hellenism to the needs of the Western mind and the forms of Western speech, so that the Latin language became not only a perfect vehicle for the expression of thought but also an ark which carried the seed of Hellenic culture through the deluge of barbarism. And thus the great classical writers of the first century B.C., above all, Cicero, Virgil, Livy, and Horace, have an importance in the history of Europe that far outweighs their intrinsic literary value, great as this is, for they are the fathers of the whole Western tradition of literature and the foundations of the edifice of European culture.

At the very moment when Rome had succeeded in extending her empire over the Hellenistic world, the empire of the Greek classical tradition over the Western mind was assured by the Latin literature of the Augustan age, and the influence of Hellenism continued to increase and spread throughout the first two centuries of the Roman Empire. Classical education was widely diffused throughout the Empire, and not only great cities like Rome and Antioch and Alexandria and Carthage, but provincial towns such as Madaura in Africa, Autun and Bordeaux in Gaul, Cordova in Spain, and Gaza and Berytus in Syria became the centres of an intense educational activity.

This culture was indeed purely literary. Science had little place in it, except at Alexandria. The rhetorical ideal of education was completely dominant, and the successful rhetorician was the idol of the educated public. But rhetoric had a much wider scope than anything which we understand by the name. It was the culmination of the whole cycle of liberal studies—arithmetic, geometry, astronomy, music, grammar, rhetoric, and dialectic—the forerunners of the mediaeval Quadrivium and Trivium. Even apart from this wide ideal of oratory, which was upheld by Cicero and Tacitus, the pure rhetorician, such as Quintilian or Aristides, was far from being a mere pedant. He aimed at something wider than technical scholarship—at a broad literary culture which is nothing less than humanism. In fact, the humanist ideal of culture, which has dominated modern education since the Renaissance, owes its existence to a deliberate revival of the old rhetorical training. But even in the Middle Ages, the latter survived to a far greater extent than is usually realised; indeed, there is no period of European history in which its influence is not perceptible. The very type of the publicist—the man of letters who addresses himself to the educated public in general—a type which is almost unknown in other cultures, is a product of this tradition: Alcuin, John of Salisbury, Petrarch, Erasmus, Bodin, Grotius, and Voltaire were all of them the successors and disciples of the ancient rhetoricians, and this is but one aspect of that classical tradition which has been one of the chief creative forces in European culture.

In the fourth century, however, the supremacy of the classical tradition seemed gravely threatened by

the victory of the new religion. Christianity was
founded on an oriental tradition which had nothing
in common with Hellenism, and its spirit and ideals
were sharply opposed to those of the pagan rhetorician and man of letters. The Christians acknowledged
no debt to the classical tradition. They had their own
classics—the Christian Scriptures—which were so fundamentally different in form and spirit from pagan literature that there was at first no room for mutual com-
prehension. "What has Athens to do with Jerusalem"?
writes Tertullian, "what concord is there between the
Academy and the Church"? St. Paul himself expressly
disavowed all claim to the graces of style and the wisdom of secular philosophy. "Where is the wise? Where
is the scribe? Where is the disputer of this world?
Hath not God made foolish the wisdom of this world?
For the Jews require signs, and the Greeks seek after
wisdom; but we preach Christ crucified, unto Jews a
stumbling-block and unto the Gentiles foolishness; but
with them that are called, both Jews and Greeks,
Christ the power of God and the wisdom of God."
(1 Cor. 1:20–27)

Thus Christianity made its appeal not to the so-
phisticated and sterile mind of cultivated society, but
to the fundamental needs of the human soul and to
the religious experience of the common man. In fact,
the early Christians were for the most part men of little education and culture. In the cities they belonged
mainly to the lower and the lower middle classes,
while in the country they were often drawn from a
peasantry which was almost unaffected by classical
culture and which preserved its native Syriac or Cop-
tic or Punic speech.

Nevertheless, though it was ignored by the leaders
of culture, there was going on all the time a process of
assimilation by which the Church was preparing for
the reception of the classical tradition and for the for-

mation of a new Christian culture. As early as the second century, educated converts such as Justin Martyr and Athenagoras were beginning to address the cultivated public in their own language, and attempting to show that the doctrines of Christianity were in harmony with the rational ideals of ancient philosophy.

The tendency which is already visible in the Apologists to assimilate Hellenic thought and culture reaches its highest development in the school of Alexandria in the third century. Origen and his predecessor Clement were the first to conceive the mediaeval ideal of a hierarchy of sciences culminating in Christian theology. As the Greeks had treated the arts and sciences as a propaedeutic to rhetoric and philosophy, so Origen proposed to make philosophy itself a propaedeutic to theology. He taught, writes his disciple, Gregory Thaumaturgus, "that we should philosophize and collate with all our powers every one of the writings of the ancients, whether philosophers or poets, excepting and rejecting nothing," save the writings of the atheists, "but giving a fair hearing to all." The result of this programme was a far-reaching synthesis of Christianity and Hellenic thought, which had a profound influence on the whole subsequent development of theology, but which from the first provoked considerable opposition on the ground that it was inconsistent with traditional orthodoxy, as indeed in some respects it certainly was. It is, however, important to note that this opposition to Origen did not necessarily imply any hostility to Hellenic culture, as distinct from Hellenic philosophy. There were Hellenists in both camps.

Thus, by the beginning of the fourth century, classical culture had gained a sure foothold within the Church, and the establishment of the Christian empire was actually followed by a considerable literary re-

vival. The Fathers of the fourth century, alike in the
East and the West, were essentially *Christian rhetoricians* who shared the culture and traditions of their
pagan rivals, but whose art was no longer an endless
elaboration of the worn-out themes of the lecture-
room, but had become the instrument of a new spiritual force. Once more the most profound issues were
debated with passionate earnestness before an audi-
ence drawn from every class, as when St. John Chry-
sostom delivered his great homilies to the people of
Antioch, while the fate of the city was hanging in the
balance. Even the most abstruse theological questions
were a matter of burning interest to the man in the
street, and the man who could speak or write of them
with eloquence and skill was assured of an almost
worldwide influence.

Moreover, the tendency of the Church to come to
terms with secular culture and to assimilate classical
literature and thought manifests itself in the West no
less than in the East. St. Ambrose adorns his sermons
with quotations from Virgil and Horace, and takes
Cicero as his model and guide in his most famous
work, *De Officiis Ministrorum*. The Ciceronian tradition forms an essential part of the new Christian culture and influences patristic literature from the time
of Lactantius to that of Augustine. St. Jerome, it is
true, speaks strongly of the dangers of pagan literature, and the famous vision in which he was condemned for being "a Ciceronian, not a Christian"
is often quoted as an example of the hostility of Christianity to classical culture. But the true significance of
the episode is that Jerome's devotion to classical literature was so intense that it had become a spiritual
temptation. Had he not reacted against it, he might
have become a rhetorician and nothing more. And in
that case, the Middle Ages would have lost the greatest of their spiritual classics: the Latin Vulgate. For in

his translation of the Bible, Jerome makes no attempt to adhere to Ciceronian standards, but allows the primitive grandeur of the Hebrew original to reflect itself in his style, so that he enriched the Latin language with a new range of expression.

The influence of Jerome was indeed second to none, not even to that of Augustine, but it was the influence of a scholar, not of a thinker or a theologian. In him the two great spiritual traditions of the classics and the Bible meet together, and from him they flow out again in a single stream to fertilise the culture of the Middle Ages.

The influence of the classical tradition is even more clearly discernible in the rise of a new Christian poetry, and the greatest of the Christian poets was the Spanish Prudentius, whom Bentley termed "the Christian Virgil and Horace." Of all the Christian writers, Prudentius shows the fullest appreciation of the classical tradition in both its literary and its social aspects. He yields to none of the pagan poets in his civic patriotism and his devotion to the great name of Rome. He does not look on Rome with the eyes of Tertullian and Augustine as a mere manifestation of human pride and ambition. Like Dante, he sees in the Empire a providential preparation for the unity of mankind in Christ.

To Prudentius, the old local patriotism of the city-state finds a new justification through the cult of the local saints. He shows us the cities of Spain presenting themselves before the judgment-seat of God, each bearing the relics of its native martyrs. The saint has become the representative and guardian of the city and imparts to it a share in his glory.

The reconciliation between Christianity and the classical tradition in the fourth and fifth centuries, which finds expression in the patristic culture and the new Christian poetry, had a profound influence on the for-

mation of the European mind. The modern is apt to
regard the whole rhetorical tradition as empty pedan-
try, and to dismiss Cicero himself as a pompous bore.
But it is to the rhetorician and his educational work
that we owe the survival of classical literature and the
whole tradition of humanism. Without them European culture would not only have been poorer, it
would have been fundamentally different. There
would have been no tradition of secular learning, no
secular literature, save that of the minstrel and the
saga-writer. The higher culture would have been entirely religious, as it has tended to be in the oriental
world outside China. The survival of classical literature and the rhetorical tradition not only made possible the rise of the modern European literatures, they
also formed the rational and critical attitude to life
and nature which is peculiar to Western civilisation.

It is true that this rhetorical and literary habit of
mind has its defects, and it is perhaps partially responsible for that artificiality which is one of the greatest weaknesses of our civilisation. Moreover, the coex-
istence of two intellectual traditions of disparate origin
has tended to produce a certain dualism and disharmony in European culture that is absent in civilisations of a simpler or more uniform type. Nor can it
be said that the rhetorical tradition was a complete
embodiment of the intellectual achievement of the
ancient world. It was a partial and one-sided development, which represents one aspect of the Hellenic
genius, but fails to do justice to its scientific and metaphysical achievements.

The scientific tradition still survived during the
later Empire, but it was confined to the East and flourished mainly in the schools of Alexandria and Athens,
and the Aristotelian revival, which had begun as early
as the third century, did not reach the Latin West, save

in a very rudimentary form through Boethius, until the twelfth and thirteenth centuries.

But although the later scientific development of Greek culture failed to affect the West, later Greek philosophy, as represented by Neoplatonism, had a direct influence on the new Latin Christian culture. Now at the very close of the imperial epoch the Latin world produced in St. Augustine a profoundly original genius, in whose thought the new Christian culture found its highest philosophic expression. But Augustine was not contented with the intellectualism of Greek philosophy. He demanded not a speculative theory of truth, but its experimental possession. This way he found only in Christianity—in the supernatural wisdom which not only shows man the truth, but gives him the means of attaining its fruition. His philosophy acquired its final character from the experience of his own conversion, the realisation of the intervention of a spiritual power which was strong enough to change his personality and to transform the notional order of intelligence into a vital order of charity.

Thus the philosophy of Augustine differs from that of Origen, the greatest Christian thinker of the Greek world, in its intensely personal character. It remains Hellenic in its insistence on the existence of a rational order pervading the world, and in its sense of the goodness and beauty of all created being. But it was both Western and Christian in its moral preoccupations and by reason of the central position which it accords to the will.

The philosophy of Augustine is essentially a philosophy of spiritual experience, and as such it is the source of Western mysticism and of Western ethics, as well as of the Western tradition of philosophic idealism.

In the fifth and sixth centuries, the influence of

Augustine became dominant throughout the Christian West. Orosius, Prosper of Aquitaine, Leo the Great, Fulgentius of Ruspe, were all of them Augustinians; and finally through St. Gregory the Great, the Augustinian tradition in a simplified form became the intellectual patrimony of the mediaeval Church. But this theological tradition was accompanied by a growing alienation from classical culture. The very profundity of Augustinian thought tended to narrow the range of intellectual activity and to concentrate all attention on the two poles of the spiritual life: God and the soul.

This view was destined to dominate the clerical and monastic culture of the Latin West for many centuries. Nevertheless, so long as the West preserved the Roman-Byzantine tradition of an educated bureaucracy trained in the schools of rhetoric, there was no risk of classical culture being undervalued. In Italy under the rule of Theodoric, the civil administration was still in the hands of highly cultivated officials like Boethius, Symmachus, and Cassiodorus, and they did all that was in their power to preserve the inheritance of classical learning. Boethius was not only the last of the classics, he was also the first of the Scholastics, a great educator, through whom the mediaeval West received its knowledge of Aristotelian logic and the rudiments of Greek mathematics. His tragic death put an end to the work of philosophical translation that he had planned, but in compensation it gave the world the *De Consolatione Philosophiae*—a masterpiece which, in spite of its deliberate reticence, is a perfect expression of the union of the Christian spirit with the classical tradition.

The same ideal inspired the work of Cassiodorus, who did even more than Boethius to build a bridge between the culture of the ancient world and that of the Middle Ages. In the first part of his life, as a minister of state in the service of the Gothic regime, he devoted himself to the promotion of religious unity and the reconciliation of the Germanic invaders to Roman culture, while his later life was dedicated to the service of the Church and to the reconciliation of classical culture with the needs of the new ecclesiastical society and the ideals of the monastic life.

Though he was forced to abandon public life and to take refuge in the cloister, Cassiodorus found an opportunity for the realisation of his ideal in the monastery that he founded in his great Calabrian estates at Vivarium. Here he collected a library and drew up his two programmes of monastic studies—the Institutes of Divine and Secular Letters—which are one of the fundamental documents for the history of mediaeval culture.

Thus Vivarium was the starting-point of the tradition of monastic learning that was afterwards to become the glory of the Benedictine Order. Western monasticism entered into the heritage of the classical culture and saved it from the ruin that overwhelmed the secular civilisation of the Latin West at the end of the sixth century. It is to the monastic libraries and scriptoria that we owe the preservation and translation of almost the entire body of Latin classical literature that we possess today. It is true that Italian monasticism was itself affected by this collapse, and Cassiodorus left no successors in his own land. His work was taken up and completed by the children of a new world—the Irish and Anglo-Saxon monks, who prepared the way for that revival of Christian classicism which finally emerged in the Carolingian period.

The Roman Empire and the Birth of the Christian Church

THE CONQUEST OF THE EAST by Alexander and the spread of Hellenistic civilisation over the greater part of the ancient world had first made possible a cosmopolitan society. The work of Alexander and his successors, however, remained incomplete until the age of Augustus and the coming of the Roman Empire. Thenceforward for five centuries the world state was a reality. Unlike the great oriental empires, this world state was a living organism to which every race and culture contributed their share. The form was created by Greek culture and Roman organisation, but under this form, the spirit of the oriental religions continued to live.

This was the environment in which the Catholic Church was born and in which it developed. This was the society it fought with and overcame, and the results of that intercourse are stamped deep on all subsequent history. The age that saw the birth of the Roman Empire was in truth altogether ripe for the appearance of a world religion. The whole current of the age was towards universalism—towards the union of the ancient world in one political organism and towards the combination of its cults and philosophies in a syncretist religious system.

Moreover, although the power of man had never been more triumphant, it was an age of demoralisation and disappointment—an age profoundly dissatisfied with its own powers and achievements. The conquest of the Mediterranean world by Rome was based on the ruin of the free landowner, on wholesale plantation slavery, and the new order had all the ugliness of a society based on unrestrained capitalist exploitation. The system had led directly to the horror of the civil wars, with their endless ruin and massacre.

Society seemed to have lost the power of self-control. The subject cities and peoples were powerless against Rome, and Rome herself was incapable of using the power she had acquired. The only hope was in some help coming from outside and from above, some authority that would take the reins out of the hands of the selfish soldiers and politicians who were wrecking the state.

This was the need that Augustus attempted to meet by the rallying of all the forces of order under the sanction of a revival of Roman traditions and religion. But in spite of the great minds that lent themselves to the task and in spite of the unique opportunity, the attempt to revive the Roman religion was artificial and sterile; however, the main work of Augustus was no failure. He created an authority with prestige great enough to bear the burden of the world power, and the new cult of Rome and of Augustus spread throughout the world state as an official religion that answered a real need and evoked real enthusiasm and loyalty.

The reason that the Augustan movement could do no more lay deep in the spiritual character of the age. No social reorganisation could satisfy an age that had come to despair of the body and the natural order and that demanded a transcendent satisfaction. The same disgust with life and the same longing for the infinite and absolute that had overcome Indian civilisation centuries before was now making itself felt in the Mediterranean world. Thus alongside of the political religion of the city-state, and the new cult of Rome and the Emperor, there began to spread everywhere the cults of the Eastern mystery religions, which offered initiation, immortality, and the knowledge of cosmic mysteries. These two religious currents, the political religion of the Empire and the syncretist mysticisms of the Eastern provinces, seemed to have the future in their hands.

The victory of Augustus involved a definite and conscious reaction against the rising tide of orientalism. In the West it produced a return to the national tradition and the restoration of the old Roman religion, while in the East it was followed by a revival of the prosperity of the Hellenistic cities and a renewed expansion of Greek culture. Even among the Jews, client princes like Herod the Great and Herod Agrippa did all in their power to introduce at least the external forms of Western civilisation, so that the leadership passed from oriental Jerusalem to Hellenistic Caesarea, and Jerusalem itself possessed a theatre and public games as in the days of Antiochus Epiphanes. The same policy was carried out with even more success in the lands to the east of Jordan and in the interior of Asia Minor, and the new provinces became covered with a network of Hellenistic cities, whose ruins even today are some of the most imposing memorials of the prosperity and culture of the Imperial Age.

However, this revival of Western civilisation was only partial. If on the one hand the Roman Empire inherited the tradition of the city-state and of Greek civilisation, it also inherited the tradition of the ancient oriental monarchy that had been handed down through the medium of the Egyptian and Syrian kingdoms. Looked at from the point of view of orthodox Roman constitutional theory, the empire was a federation of self-governing city-states under the hegemony of the city of Rome. In the eyes of the subject population, however, it was a world empire, ruled by an absolute deified monarch of the immemorial oriental type, and this conception was really more in accordance with the facts of the situation and the spirit of the age.

The hope in the appearance of a deliverer, who would put an end to oppression and war and bring in a reign of peace, already existed in the second century B.C., and by the middle of the following century it had reached a climax. Men believed that the end of a world cycle or aeon had arrived, and that the wars and revolutions of the period were the birth pangs of a new order. The most remarkable literary expression of this feeling is to be found in Vergil's fourth *Eclogue,* written in 40 B.C., in which he hails the birth of a child whose reign will bring back the wonders of the Golden Age. "Now comes the last Age of the prophecy of the Sibyl. The great order of the ages is born anew. Now too returns the Virgin, and the reign of Saturn. A new generation is sent down from heaven on high."

When such ideas filled mens' minds it was natural that the sorely tried provincials should see in Augustus, who put an end to the horrors of war and misgovernment, their longed-for deliverer and should pay him divine honours not merely out of oriental flattery, but in genuine gratitude and hope for the future. "The birthday of the God [Augustus] has brought good tidings to all the world," says an inscription discovered at Priene in Asia Minor. It is true that Augustus himself, and still more his successor Tiberius, did not aim at open self-deification, as Caesar and Antony had done. Their attitude is expressed rather in the noble utterance of Tiberius to the Senate, when he refused the divine honours offered him by the Spanish province. But Augustus could hardly prevent his deification in the eastern provinces, and the worship of Rome and Augustus became the established state cult of the empire outside Italy, and the religious bond of imperial unity. Even at Rome the Emperor was raised to the rank of the gods on his death by a formal apotheosis, and the degenerate successor of Tiberius—Caligula— insisted on the universal recognition of his divinity, and aped the manners of an Egyptian Pharaoh.

But the deification of a Caligula or a Nero reduced the imperial cult to a mockery. It contradicted the highest element in the Augustan programme, the ideal of moral purification and reform, which takes such a prominent place even in the poetry of Horace, and it offended all that was best in the mind of the age, whether Eastern or Western. In any case, the official religion of the empire could not satisfy the deeper needs of the time. The new religious spirit that manifested itself, alike in the neo-Pythagorean movement and in the oriental mystical cults, would not be contented with a merely material and earthly salvation. It looked for a supernatural deliverance from death and the bondage of material conditions.

Moreover, there still existed in the East an independent national and religious tradition, which was irreconcileable with the ideals of the Roman-Hellenistic culture. It condemned both the oppression and violence of Roman imperialism, and the materialism and luxury of the Hellenistic city. So at the same time that the Greeks and the Romans were looking for a deliverer who would restore the prosperity of Western civilisation, the Jews hoped for one who would destroy it all and set up a holy kingdom for the chosen people.

It was in this Jewish environment, with its strong national religious tradition and its apocalyptic hopes of a supernatural divine intervention that there arose the new movement that was to change the history of the world. It took the form not of a purely national and destructive reaction against the Roman power and Western civilisation, but of a moral and religious revolution that appealed no less to the supernatural hopes of the Hellenistic mystics than to the Jewish ideal of a world kingdom of righteousness.

Its most striking characteristic was its absolute novelty. The other mystery religions and oriental cults with which it is often compared, Mithraism—the Egyptian cults of Isis and of Serapis, the Syrian solar religion and the Babylonian astrological mysticism— were all representative of the survival, in however changed a form, of ancient oriental religious traditions. They were powerful agents in the orientalisation of the Roman Empire, but they were in no sense rivals or substitutes of the official state religion.

Christianity, on the other hand, was based on the life of a historical personality, no less real and actual than that of the founder of the empire itself. His teaching was profoundly original and individual—unlike the vague impersonal traditions of the oriental mystery cults, and the belief in the coming of His kingdom was as strong and vivid among his followers as was the belief in the present reality of the empire to the ordinary citizen. From the beginning the new religion appeared not as another addition to the multitude of strange sects that were adapting themselves without much difficulty to the cosmopolitan environment of the Roman state. It stood out in sharp contrast to them all, as an irreconcileable alternative to the whole dominant religio-political system.

Christianity appealed to all the elements that failed to find satisfaction in the material prosperity and civilisation of the Roman world: the poor and the oppressed; the subject oriental populations; those who were dissatisfied with the materialism and immorality of pagan society; above all, the growing class of men who had lost interest in the declining political life of the city-state and whose minds found compensation in the sphere of religion and mysticism. The work of St. Paul had removed the new religion from its Pales-

tinian environment and had assimilated it to the
minds of the Hellenistic world. Thenceforward it
spread with extraordinary rapidity not only in the
East, but throughout the empire, to Greece and Rome
and to southern Gaul.

But its exclusive character and irreconcileable hostility to the religious cults and ceremonies with which
the whole social life of the city-state and the empire
were inseparably connected at every turn, brought the
Christians into inevitable conflict with the government and with public opinion. To the man in the
street, the Christian was an anti-social atheist who
would take no part in the public feasts and the games,
which played such a large part in city life. To the authorities he was a passive rebel, who would neither
take his share of municipal offices nor pay loyal hom-
age to the Emperor. Hence the rise of persecution, and
the driving of the Christians into an underground existence, as a proscribed sect. The Church grew under the
shadow of the executioner's rods and axes, and every
Christian lived in peril of physical torture and death.
The thought of martyrdom coloured the whole outlook of early Christianity. But it was not only a fear, it
was also an ideal and a hope. For the martyr was the
complete Christian, he was the champion and hero of
the new society in its conflict with the old, and even
the Christians who had failed in the moment of trial
—the *lapsi*—looked on the martyrs as their saviours and
protectors.

In an age when the individual was becoming the
passive instrument of an omnipotent and universal
state, it is difficult to exaggerate the importance of
such an ideal, which was the ultimate stronghold of
spiritual freedom. More than any other factor, it secured the ultimate triumph of the Church, for it rendered plain to all the fact that Christianity was the one
remaining power in the world that could not be ab-

sorbed in the gigantic mechanism of the new servile state.

And while the Church was involved in this life-and-death struggle with the imperial state and its Hellenistic culture, it also had to carry on a difficult and obscure warfare with the growing forces of oriental religion. Under the veneer of cosmopolitan Hellenistic civilisation, the religious traditions of the ancient East were still alive and were gradually permeating the thought of the age. The mystery religions of Asia Minor spread westwards in the same way as Christianity itself, and the religion of Mithras accompanied the Roman armies to the Danube and the Rhine and the British frontier. The Egyptian worship of Isis and the Syrian cults of Adonis and Atargatis, Hadad of Baalbeck, and the sun-god of Emesa, followed the rising tide of Syrian trade and migration to the West, while in the oriental underworld new religions, like Manichaeanism, were coming into existence, and the immemorial traditions of Babylonian astral theology were appearing in new forms.

But the most characteristic product of this movement of oriental syncretism was the Gnostic theosophy, which was an ever-present danger to the Christian Church during the second and third centuries. It was based on the fundamental dualism of spirit and matter and the association of the material world with the evil principle, a dualism that derived more, perhaps, from Greek and Anatolian influences than from Persia, since we find it already fully developed in the Orphic mythology and in the philosophy of Empedocles. But this central idea was enveloped in a dense growth of magic and theosophical speculation that was undoubtedly derived from Babylonian and oriental sources.

This strange oriental mysticism possessed an extraordinary attraction for the mind of a society that was inspired with a profound sense of disillusionment and the thirst for deliverance. Consequently, it was not merely an exterior danger to Christianity; it also threatened to absorb it altogether, by transforming the historical figure of Jesus into a member of the hierarchy of divine Aeons, and by substituting the ideal of the deliverance of the soul from the contamination of the material world for the Christian ideals of the redemption of the body and the realisation of the kingdom of God as a social and historical reality.

If Christianity had been merely one among the oriental sects and mystery religions of the Roman Empire it must inevitably have been drawn into this oriental syncretism. It survived because it possessed a system of ecclesiastical organisation and a principle of social authority that distinguished it from all the other religious bodies of the age. From the first, the Church regarded itself as the New Israel, "an elect race, a royal priesthood, a holy nation, a people set apart." (1 P. 2:9) This holy society was a theocracy inspired and governed by the Holy Spirit, and its rulers, the apostles, were the representatives not of the community but of the Christ, who had chosen them and transmitted to them His divine authority. This conception of a divine apostolic authority remained as the foundation of ecclesiastical order in the post-apostolic period, and in this way the primitive Church survived both the perils of heresy and schism and the persecution of the imperial power and organised itself as a universal hierarchical society over against the pagan world-state.

Christianity in a Pagan World

THE WORLD into which the Church was born was an ancient and highly civilised world that was more of an international unity than any society that has existed down to our own days. It was a world of cities, each of which enjoyed some measure of self-government under the all-embracing sovereignty of Rome, a world in which all educated people talked a common language —Greek—and shared a common culture. At first sight it seemed a prosperous and peaceful world. The destructive wars, both wars of conquest and civil wars, that had brought so much misery to the world in the last two centuries of the pre-Christian era, had now come to an end, and the Roman peace that Augustus had inaugurated brought with it not only economic prosperity but also the ideal, if not the complete realisation, of the reign of law.

Yet on the other hand, things were not so good as they looked at first sight. For the whole social order rested on exploitation—the exploitation of the villages and the peasants by the cities, and finally on the existence of masses of people who were not merely underprivileged, but lacking the most elementary human rights—slaves who were treated not as human beings but as chattels to be bought and sold in the marketplace like cattle.

But in some respects this world was not unlike our own, especially in the great cities, like Rome, Alexandria, and Antioch which were its centres. These

were genuinely cosmopolitan cities, as New York is
today and as very few capitals in Europe have been.
These cities also had much higher standards of ameni-
ties and town planning than we are accustomed to in
Europe—a plentiful supply of public buildings. In fact,
there is some resemblance between the Hellenistic
and American way of life. This is seen most clearly in
the public baths, with their public libraries and gym-
nasiums—palatial luxury for the common man. These
great cities had a very high standard of personal comfort, like our cities—an excellent water supply brought
from a distance by great aqueducts, good drainage,
central heating, free amusements. All this was not the
creation of the Roman Empire. It had been the rule
in the Hellenistic cities, like Antioch and Alexandria,
for centuries, and had been made accessible to the
ordinary well-to-do middle-class citizen throughout
the Mediterranean world in Asia Minor and Africa
and Spain and in southern France. Of course, the
differences are still enormous. The ancient world knew
nothing of the wonders of modern science and the gigantic sources of power that we have tapped. Everything they had achieved was the work of direct human
labour with comparatively simple tools. Even so, it is
wonderful to see how much this could accomplish
when guided by the skill of the Roman engineer and
organised by the discipline of the Roman centurion.
And above all, this was due to the fact that all the resources of the civilised world were concentrated under
the control of a single government and a single man as
never before or since.

But there was one striking exception to the uniformity of this Roman-Hellenistic world. This was the Jewish people, who had stubbornly resisted the attempt of
the Greek kings of Syria to impose Hellenistic culture
upon them and had won their independence in a series of wars. Finally, however, in A.D. 6, Judaea was

incorporated in the Roman Empire as part of the province of Syria, and they were forced to submit to the control of a foreign pagan government that they bitterly resented on both national and religious grounds.

This was the world to which Christ came. He spent the greater part of his life in Galilee in northern Palestine, among a simple population of peasants and fishermen, a people of devout Jews whose hopes were centred in the coming of the kingdom and the supernatural deliverance of Israel from the Gentiles and who had hardly been touched by the influence of the dominant civilisation, although they were in close proximity to the Greek cities across the Lake of Gennesaret, which possessed a flourishing Hellenistic culture. It is curious to think that Meleager of Gadaris, who wrote so many charming love poems in the Greek *Anthology*, was a compatriot and contemporary of the Apostles.

The public ministry of Jesus culminated in the visit to Jerusalem, where his preaching aroused the opposition of both the priests and the Pharisees, so that he was handed over to the Roman procurator and put to death as an agitator who was a danger alike to the political authority of Rome and the religious authority of the Sanhedrin and the priesthood.

The Resurrection, the charge to the Apostles, and the descent of the Holy Spirit on the little group who were gathered in the Upper Chamber at Jerusalem were events that passed unnoticed by the great world. Yet they were the turning points that changed the whole course of human history. Gradually, almost imperceptibly, the Gospel and the Church were spread abroad, first to Samaria, then to Antioch, and by the mission of St. Paul to the Gentile world in Asia Minor and Greece, and finally to Rome itself. This apostolate was directed first to the Jews of the dispersion, Hellenistic Jews, like St. Paul himself, and then after great searching of heart to the Gentiles.

160 Christianity in the World

But meanwhile in Palestine, the Jewish people were being carried forward irresistibly to the great national catastrophe of the Jewish Revolt against Rome, which did not end with the destruction of Jerusalem and the Temple in A.D. 70, but was carried on through the two successive wars against Trajan and Hadrian until the Jews of Palestine had been almost exterminated, so that the religious and cultural centre of the Jewish world was eventually removed outside the Roman world to Babylonia, where Judaism was reshaped as a church rather than a nation by the influence of the Talmud.

The national catastrophe—above all, the fall of the Holy City—had been foretold by Jesus, as we read in the Gospels. But it did not stand alone, for the Christians were to some extent involved in the national disaster. After all, it was not very easy for Rome to distinguish between Jews and Christians. In any case, the Christians underwent terrible persecutions in the time of Nero and Domitian. It was a time of suffering and crisis, which lasted from the Neronic persecution, under which the leaders of the apostles, Saints Peter and Paul, were martyred, down to the end of the century.

To the Christians, as to the Jews, the destruction of Jerusalem was a sign of the end, and their hopes were fixed on the second coming of Jesus, when the triumph of the Church would be made manifest. Hence it was at this period that the tension and antagonism between the Church and the pagan world were most acute and find their most passionate expression in the pages of the Apocalypse, which were probably written in the latter part of the reign of Domitian. Here Rome is shown as Babylon the Great, the mother of harlots, drunken with the blood of saints and the blood of the martyrs of Jesus, while the Roman Empire is the Kingdom of the Beast, which seeks to destroy the Church but which is itself destined to destruction by the triumphant return of Jesus and the establishment of His kingdom.

This apocalyptic attitude finds its basis in the Gospels, for Jesus in his teaching frequently emphasised the catastrophic aspects of the coming of his kingdom, as an event of world-shaking character by which the old order of things is violently swept away, while at the same time his prophecy of the destruction of Jerusalem and the Temple is closely related to these themes.

Moreover, in the Gospels, the social dualism and opposition between the world and the kingdom is strongly marked, above all in the Fourth Gospel, for example, "Now is the judgment of the world. Now is the Prince of this world cast out," and in the numerous warnings to the disciples to avoid all contamination with the spirit of this world, which is the domain of Satan.

In spite of all this, there is nowhere in the Gospels or the Epistles any sign of direct hostility to the Roman Empire or the secular authorities. Nowhere is there a sign of sympathy or approval for the activist party, which was actually the strongest element among the Jews and which was so soon to inspire the desperate national resistance. Here the Christian attitude was markedly different, even from the sect of Wadi Qumran, which represented the most unworldly element in the contemporary Jewish world and whose moral attitude is in many respects so similar to that of the Christians. But this being so, it seems difficult to explain the continuous hostility of the government towards the Christians, which caused them to be treated with so much more intolerance than the Jews themselves, who had shown themselves to be a constant danger to the peace and security of the Roman world. One can only suppose that Rome regarded Christianity as an underground movement that undermined the foundation of society—a movement which was at once anti-social and anti-religious.

The Christians did all they could to exculpate themselves and to convince the authorities of their loyalty and good intentions. But it is doubtful if the works of the apologists were ever read by the people for whom they were intended, and especially the best writer among them, Tertullian, who was a born fighter who gloried in unpopularity and never attempted to conceal his opposition and contempt for the whole world of pagan culture.

In spite of these disadvantages and the continuous but very intermittent persecution, the Church continued to spread all over the civilised world, until by the middle of the third century it had become an organised world society such as the world had never seen before. It was already too great for any persecution to destroy it, even if the empire exerted its full power. But in fact the empire was no longer as strong as it was. The Goths and the Persians, civil war and pestilence had followed one another across the provinces that had once been so flourishing. Consequently, when a great Emperor arose at the end of the third century, it was no longer possible for him to restore the old empire and the prosperity of the Hellenistic cities or to maintain the privileges of the citizen class. He was forced to take revolutionary action and to create what was practically a new state—an absolute monarchy, based on compulsion, and a caste-like system of hereditary classes and professions and guilds. But though Diocletian with his colleagues made a last attempt to restore the old state religion and to destroy the Christian Church, he found himself unable to do so. And it was left to the successor of his Western colleagues, Constantine, to take the obvious step and to recognise Christianity as the new religion of the new empire and of the new capital at Byzantium.

To many Christians, like Eusebius of Caesarea, these events seemed to be the fulfilment of prophecy, and they accepted the ideals of the Christian empire as a final solution of the conflict and opposition between the Christian world and the pagan state. Henceforward, at least from the time of Theodosius I, loyalty to the Emperor and fidelity to the Christian faith went together; there were no longer two standards of life and two forms of culture. Nevertheless, much had been lost. The intense hope and expectation that had centred in the coming of Christ's kingdom and that had inspired the martyrs and the confessors with their heroic devotion gradually faded away, and the Church was faced with the problem of a new kind of secularism, since the "world" that the Christians renounced was also the Christian world that they accepted.

Now the instinctive reaction of the Church to this situation found expression in the new form of the religious life, which sprang up all over the Christian world in the fourth century. This was the monastic movement, which in its earliest form involved a flight from the cities to the desert and a total renunciation of all the pleasures and privileges of city life. It is impossible to exaggerate the impression that this movement made in the ancient world. It was not as it is today, when there are hundreds of different religious orders, all of which fulfil some special function. Then there was simply the sharp contrast between the life of the world and that of the desert ascetics, whose whole life was a visible contradiction of the way of the world. Thus the monks of the Byzantine Church were what the martyrs had been in earlier times, living witnesses to the inescapable demands of Christ's kingdom here on earth.

But the danger remained that the original tension between the Church and the world and the Christian and pagan ways of life should be changed into a division between the ordinary Christian who was content with the low standards of a nominally Christian world and the unattainable standards of the few who followed the life of perfection in the deserts and the mountains. But at this moment the greatest of the Western fathers, St. Augustine, reinterpreted the original Christian dualism between the Church and the world, between "the spirit" and "the flesh" by a new Christian philosophy of history, which was also a psychological philosophy. By this he showed that the old Christian tension between the two standards was a universal cosmic principle, running through the whole course of human history and human behaviour. Man is a dynamic being always driven by the attraction of his desires and the force of his affections. This is the Augustinian law of gravitation, which makes love or desire the spiritual principle of gravity. *Amor Pondus, pondus meum amor meus; eo feror quocumque feror.* (As a man's love moves him, so must he go and so must he become.) Now the natural man—what St. Paul calls the fleshly man—is impelled by the force of his natural appetite for temporal goods or pleasures, and the "world," the unregenerated world of which St. John and the Gospels speak, is the natural association of those who are drawn together by their appetites and desires. But such an association cannot produce real unity. "Associations of mortals," he writes, "scattered as they are throughout the world and confronted with the greatest possible diversity of local conditions, are nevertheless impelled by the bond of a common nature to pursue their respective advantages and interests. So long therefore as the object of appetation is insufficient for any or for all, since it does not possess this character, the association is normally divided against itself and the part that prevails oppresses the rest. The vanquished submits to the victor because he prefers peace and safety on any terms to mastery or even to freedom." (*The City of God,* XVIII 2.)

Since then the earthly city is founded on the principle of self-interest, it is essentially divided, a city of confusion and strife, and the world itself becomes the scene of a struggle for existence. "The world," says St. Augustine, "is a sea wherein men devour one another in turn like fish."

On the other hand, the Church and the kingdom of God are founded on a different principle—not merely on a true moral law, like the law of Moses, but on a new dynamic principle, which changes human nature by changing the direction of the force of spiritual gravity. This new force—charity—*amor Dei*—is a force of unity, whereas the old force of concupiscence or selfish appetite, *amor sui,* was the principle of confusion. Thus these two psychological principles are the animating principles of the two cities and the two social orders. The principle of charity, inspired by divine grace, is at work throughout the ages, building the new social order that is the city of God and the kingdom of Christ, whereas the principle of self-love is inevitably a divisive and destructive one, which creates the city of confusion—Babylon—which is the kingdom of the devil.

Now this vast generalisation, which comprehends the whole human race and the whole of human history, proved of inestimable value to the Church in its task of converting the world. For it was obvious that the conflict between the two loves and the two cities had not been brought to an end by the creation of the Christian empire. The forces of self-love, selfish ambition, lust and avarice, the unbridled desire for power, and the exploitation of man by man still continued— the battle between the two cities had to be fought out inch by inch within the Christian state, and similarly the monastic life, although it provided one pattern of

Christian perfection, could not be identified with the city of God, which it existed to serve.

The Augustinian principle provided a criterion by which both the world and the Church could be judged. The disappearance of paganism as the official religion of the state, which was the simple criterion by which the Christian had judged the secular world, presented the danger that now the Christian would accept the lower standards of secular culture, since they were veiled and dignified by Christian political forms. But St. Augustine restored the balance by showing the abiding truth and validity of the distinction between the two ways and describing how the essential principle of paganism—the exaltation of self-love and self-interest into the ruling principle in the social and moral order—still lived in every age and must continue to carry on their warfare against the city of God. In this way the thought of St. Augustine provided the necessary bridge between the two ages and inspired the leaders of the Western Church, above all St. Gregory the Great, with power to transform the half-Christian, half-pagan world of the barbarian kingdoms, which became the typical forms of Western society in the age that followed St. Augustine's death.

4

Byzantium and the Christian East

DURING THE LAST fifty years the interest in Byzantine culture and religion has been steadily growing until it has come to transform our conception of European history. A new appreciation of Byzantine art has probably contributed most to this change, but it also owes a great deal to religious causes. To earlier writers the Orthodox Church and Byzantine religious traditions were the true and almost the only representatives of oriental Christianity; they also represented the tradition of Eastern spirituality as against the materialism and rationalism of Western civilisation.

These views acquired immense popularity and prestige in modern times owing to the genius of Dostoyevsky and the influence of his disciples and admirers, first in Russia and later in the West. But they represent a specifically Russian movement of ideas, which owes comparatively little to the Byzantine tradition. Indeed, modern Byzantine studies are tending more and more to emphasise the nonoriental character of Byzantine culture. Thus to so distinguished a Byzantine scholar as Norman Baynes, "the elements that formed the complex civilisation of the Empire were the Roman tradition in law and government, the Hellenistic tradition in language, literature, and philosophy, and a Christian tradition which had already been refashioned on a Greek model."

If we accept this point of view we must abandon the traditional identification of the Orthodox Church with Eastern Christianity, since the Byzantine Empire must be regarded as an integral part of Western culture. But this is not to deny the existence of the problem of Eastern Christianity or the religious and cultural division between East and West. It only means that the crucial issue is not the conflict between Byzantine and Western culture but rather one between Byzantium and the East, which was fought out not only on the frontiers but within the empire in the relations of the Byzantine State and Church with the subject oriental population of Egypt and Syria and Armenia.

This conflict has a long history behind it, for Byzantium was not only the representative of the Roman Empire, it was also the heir of Alexander the Great and the Hellenistic monarchies. In fact, it represents the last phase of that great movement of conquest and colonisation which had carried Greek culture far into the heart of Asia and had founded cities and kingdoms on the Oxus and the Indus. The tide of this great expansion had begun to ebb long before the Byzantine Empire was founded, so that its whole history may be regarded as a long and stubbornly-fought rearguard action of Greek culture against the advancing forces of the resurgent East.

Throughout the whole of this period, however, the struggle between East and West acquired a new religious character owing to the conversion of the empire to Christianity and the Christianisation of Hellenic culture. The Orthodox Church became the bulwark of Hellenism, while the oriental powers which threatened the existence of the Empire—Sassanian Persia, the Islamic Khalifate, and the Turkish sultanates—were also the enemies of the Christian faith.

Nevertheless, this identification of Byzantium with Christendom was never so complete as it appeared in

the eyes of Byzantine patriotism and Hellenic orthodoxy, for between East and West there always existed
a wide transitional zone that was Christian in faith
but oriental in speech and culture. This zone extended
eastward far beyond the frontiers of the Empire,
while to the West it crossed the Byzantine frontier
and included a considerable part of the Eastern provinces of the Empire itself.

It is to this transitional zone that we must look if
we wish to study the problem of oriental Christianity
and the interaction and interpenetration of Byzantine
and Eastern culture. Unfortunately, there are few
fields of study that are so difficult and so unrewarding,
since it requires a knowledge of half a dozen oriental
languages and literatures and an intensive study of
the history and doctrines and mutual relations of half
a dozen independent churches.

If we study this field from outside, we shall inevitably tend to overestimate the importance of the dominant race and culture. Alike in the Hellenistic and the
Byzantine ages, the Greeks were characterised by a
boundless faith in the superiority of their culture. It is
true that they were comparatively free from racial intolerance. They freely admitted members of the subject races to citizenship and to social equality. But
they did so only so far as the subject peoples became
denationalised and adopted Greek language and culture.

The most remarkable example of this cultural imperialism is the case of Egypt, where the two peoples
and cultures lived side by side for nearly a thousand
years without ever blending with one another or creating a common civilisation. From first to last, Alexandria was one of the capitals of the Hellenistic world
and an active centre of Greek literature and learning.
But at its gates and below the surface of the ruling
society, the immemorial life of Egypt, which was old

when Hellas began, still maintained its separate existence. It is true that the native Egyptian population
possessed its own literary tradition, but it is the poorest and the least original of all the oriental literatures,
and the one which had the least influence on the dominant Byzantine culture. Nevertheless, this oppressed
and despised people was responsible for one great
creative achievement which did more to influence the
Byzantine Empire and indeed the whole Christian
world than any purely literary achievement could
have done, for it was in the Egyptian desert that monastic institutions and the ideals of Christian asceticism were originated and developed. However "Western" the Byzantine culture may have been, its greatest
cultural and spiritual organ was borrowed from the
East. St. Basil may have given the monastic ideal its
Hellenic form, just as St. Benedict translated it into
the tradition of Latin culture, but the lives of the
Desert Fathers and still more the Sayings of the Eld-
ers, *verba seniorum*, which represent the original au-
thentic tradition of oriental spirituality, continued to
exercise a vital influence on the monastic tradition
alike in the East and the West.

It was in Egypt that the dualism of Greek and oriental culture found its sharpest and most uncompromising expression. In Syria the relations between the
two cultures were far more complex, and the opportunities for mutual intercourse and understanding
were greater. Here the forces of Hellenism were not
concentrated in a single centre like Alexandria, but
were spread widely over the land in a hundred Greek
cities, which stood out like islands in an oriental
ocean. The policy of the Seleucid monarchy towards
the subject population had always been more liberal
than that of the Ptolemies in Egypt, and this difference of policy was maintained in Roman and Byzantine times. Consequently the culture of Syria was

largely a bilingual one, and the Greek-speaking Syrians played an important part in its diffusion. But this was always one-sided, as there were practically no Syriac-speaking Greeks. Here the importance of the oriental contribution is not to be measured by the existing remains of Syrian literature. Some of the greatest writers of the Byzantine age, such as Eusebius of Caesarea, Theodoret, and John of Damascus, were Syrians who wrote in Greek but whose mother tongue was Syriac, or in later centuries, Arabic.

Thus the Syriac world provided the main channel by which Greek culture penetrated into the oriental world and through which oriental influence permeated Byzantine culture. It embraced on the one side representatives of the most advanced type of Byzantine culture like Theodoret of Cyrrhus, and, on other, independent centres of oriental culture like the School of the Persians at Edessa and Nisibis, whence in turn the Syriac Christian culture was diffused through the Persian Empire and ultimately to Central and Eastern Asia.

It is easy to trace the eastern development, since it was a literary one due to the activity of the great Syriac writers and their schools. But the westward diffusion is much more difficult to follow, since it was mainly nonliterary and was due to the influence of Syrian monasticism and the cult of Syrian and Persian saints and martyrs, whose fame extended from one end of the Christian world to the other. Al Akhtal, the classical Arab poet, describes the Beni Taglib riding into battle under the banner of St. Sergius, and at the other end of the Christian world he was one of the great saints of Kievan Russia, and he possessed a cult at Rome as early as the seventh century. Here as in so many other cases the channels through which oriental Christianity reached the West were not literary but purely religious ones; they were the pilgrimage

routes, the famous sanctuaries and the oriental monastic colonies which were established at Constanti-
nople and elsewhere in the Byzantine world. Famous
monasteries like those of Egypt and Mt. Sinai and the
monastery of St. Symeon Stylites at Telnesin attracted
pilgrims from all over the Christian world, including
the Latin West, while in the opposite direction, the
famous community of the Acoemeti on the Bos-
phorus, which was of Syrian origin, was one of the
chief sources from which the cult and legends of the
Persian martyrs spread into the Byzantine world.

In these ways Syriac Christianity formed a kind of
subterranean channel between Eastern and Western
culture. Owing to unfavourable political conditions, it
was never able to create its own independent culture.
It remained submerged and divided between the dominant cultures of the Byzantine and Persian empires,
and later between Byzantium and Islam. In this respect it differs from the neighbouring Christian culture of Armenia, which was always characterised by
an intense consciousness of national individuality. Indeed, Armenia has some claim to be regarded as the
first example of cultural nationalism in the full sense
of the word. Armenian literature and cultural independence arose from the deliberate purpose of the
leaders of the Armenian people in the fifth century to
counteract the attempt of the Persian government to
incorporate Armenia in their empire. To this end they
despatched a mission to the centres of Syriac culture
at Edessa and Samosata. It was there that St. Mesrop,
with the help of Syriac and Syro-Hellenic scholars,
invented the Armenian script and alphabet and laid
the foundations of a national Christian literature.
Thenceforward the Armenian literature and script became the bulwarks of Armenian nationality and of
the national religion. Unfortunately, this identification
of the cause of Christianity with that of national sur-

vival was fatal to the cause of Catholic unity, for the adhesion of the Armenians to the Monophysite heresy was chiefly due to their desire to assert their national independence against the patriarchal see of Seleucia-Ctesiphon and the influence of the Syriac-Persian Church, which had now become Nestorian. It is probable that the Armenians had no idea of separating from the West by their action, since the Byzantine Empire itself was at this time heavily compromised with regard to Monophysitism. Later, however, when the orthodoxy of the Byzantine Church had been vindicated, the Armenians had come to look on the Byzantine Empire as an alien imperialism which threatened their national independence hardly less than Persia itself, so that their religious separation has remained to this day the symbol and pledge of their national existence.

But oriental nationalism did not always prove irreconcilable with Catholic unity. In fact, in the case of the Church of Georgia, it had just the opposite effect. Up to a point the development of Georgian Christianity and Georgian national culture followed exactly the same course as that of Armenia. The obscure origins of Christianity in Georgia were due to Syriac influences, and the first centres of literary culture arose on the Armenian frontier under Armenian inspiration. But the same causes which led the Armenians to separate themselves from the Nestorian Church of Persia and to become Monophysites caused the Georgians to assert their religious independence against Monophysite Armenia and to identify themselves with Byzantine orthodoxy. The little Christian kingdom in the Caucasus which was exposed to the continual danger of pagan and Moslem invasion secured the continuity of its cultural life by establishing Georgian monasteries in the centres of the Christian world—in

Palestine, in northern Syria, and in Greece and the Balkans.

The most important of these foundations was the famous monastery of Iviron on Mt. Athos, which became the greatest centre of Georgian learning and the source of the great revival of Georgian culture and literature in the eleventh and twelfth centuries. Here at last oriental Christianity achieved a satisfactory *modus vivendi* with Byzantine culture, which enriched the Georgian people with all the riches of Hellenic learning and Orthodox spirituality without threatening the independence of Georgian nationality and culture.

5

Christianity in a Barbarian World

St. Augustine has often been regarded as standing outside his own age—as the inaugurator of a new world and the first mediaeval man, while others, on the contrary, have seen in him rather the heir of the old classical culture and one of the last representatives of antiquity. There is an element of truth in both these views, but for all that, he belongs neither to the mediaeval nor to the classical world. He is essentially a man of his own age—that strange age of the Christian Empire which has been so despised by the historians, but which nevertheless marks one of the vital moments in the history of the world. It witnessed the fall of Rome, the passing of that great order which had controlled the fortunes of the world for five centuries and more, and the laying of the foundations of a new world. And Augustine was no mere passive spectator of the crisis. He was, to a far greater degree than any emperor or general or barbarian war-lord, a maker of history and a builder of the bridge which was to lead from the old world to the new.

Unfortunately, although there is no lack of historical evidence, the real importance of this period is seldom appreciated. Ever since the Renaissance, the teaching of ancient history has been treated as part of the study of the classics and consequently comes to an end with the age of the Antonines, while the teaching of modern history is equally bound up with the nationalist idea and begins with the rise of the existing European peoples. Consequently there is a gap of some five hundred years from the third to the seventh century in the knowledge of the ordinary educated person. It lasts from the collapse of the old Empire in the third century A.D. to the break-up of the reconstituted Eastern Empire in the seventh century under the stress of the Mohammedan invasions. This is the period of the Christian Empire, the Empire of Constantine and Justinian, the age of the Fathers and of the great councils. It deserves to be studied as a whole and for its own sake, instead of piecemeal and from conflicting points of view. Hitherto the secular historians have confined themselves to one side of the evidence and the ecclesiastical historians to the other, without paying much attention to each other's results. We have to go back to the days of Tillemont to find a historian who is equally competent in both fields. The modern historians of the period have shown themselves notably unsympathetic to its religious achievements. The greatest of them—Gibbon and Professor Bury—were freethinkers with a strong bias against Christianity, while the remainder from the days of Finlay and Burckhardt and Gregorovius to Seeck and Stein and Rostovtzeff in our time, all write from a secularist point of view. This is peculiarly unfortunate, not only because by far the larger part of the historical evidence has a religious character, but still more because the whole historical development becomes inexplicable when viewed from a purely secular standpoint. To neglect or despise the religious achievement of the age is as fatal to any true understanding of it as a complete disregard of the economic factor would be in the case of nineteenth-century Europe. For the real interest and importance of that age are essentially religious. It marks the failure of the greatest experiment in secular civilisation that the world had ever seen, and the return of society to spiritual principles. It was at once an age of material loss and of spiritual recovery, when amidst the ruins of a bankrupt order men strove slowly and painfully to rebuild the house of life on eternal foundations.

After much persecution, much apostolic work, and much deep theological study, the Church succeeded in overcoming the pagan world and creating the world of the Christian Empire and the Byzantine culture in the age of the Fathers.

But before this work had been accomplished in Western Europe, it was all swept away by the barbarian conquests, and the Church had to face quite a different situation—that of a world given over to barbarism.

In the first age of the Church, it was a question of the Christians who were largely underprivileged and uneducated people facing the resistance of a highly educated rich and powerful civilisation, which despised them for their lack of culture.

Now the situation was completely reversed. It was the Christians who were the civilised people, and they were confronted with the challenge of brute force and barbarism by people who were prepared to destroy everything that they valued—cities, churches, schools, literature, law and order, justice and humanity: by people who were not conscious of the value of what they were destroying, who were satisfied with a far lower standard of life, so long as they had power and freedom to live their own lives.

It was hard for a civilised Roman Christian to face this predicament. We say today, "Better dead than Red," and in those days there were many people who said, "Better dead than slaves to the barbarians." That was the normal human reaction to paganism. When the Macedonians captured Stagyrus or one of the Greek coastal cities, the citizens held a great banquet the night before, which ended in their passing round a cup of poison, and this was the normal practice of many peoples—as we see in the fine reliefs on Trajan's Column, which show the Dacian chiefs passing round the poison bowl after their defeat.

But this attitude never received the approval of the Church, which regarded Cato's refusal to accept the verdict of history as an act of pride—an example of St. Augustine's saying that "the virtues of the pagans are splendid vices." Christians had to submit to the verdict of history, which in this case was the defeat of a Christian civilisation by pagan barbarians, and study how best they should carry their cross.

The problem was a double one, as the greatest living Catholic of that age, St. Augustine, soon found out. First of all, Christians had to face a severe barrage of criticism from highly cultured and influential pagans, the representatives of the old Roman tradition, who attributed all the disasters that were falling on the civilised world to the abandonment of the good old Roman traditions and the introduction of this new-fangled religion, which to them seemed both irrational and anti-social. It was to answer these critics that St. Augustine wrote his great work, *The City of God*, which some have thought to be his greatest work, which it is not, but which nevertheless was the book which gave Western Christendom an intelligible theory of universal history on which it was to base its view of the world for twelve centuries and more.

But the second problem was a much more pressing one: the practical duty of Christians in this crisis that threatened everything—their lives, their property, their religion, their hopes for the future of their children. This problem St. Augustine also had to face in its most acute form in the last year of his life when he was, by the standards of the time, a very old man (aged about seventy-six). This is how his disciple and friend Possidius, who was with him to the end, described the catastrophe:

It was not long after this, however, that, by God's will and providence, there poured into Africa from across the sea in ships from Spain a huge host of savage enemies armed with every kind of weapon and trained to war. There were Vandals and Alans, mixed with one of the Gothic peoples, and individuals of various nations. They overran the country, spreading all over Mauretania and passing on to our other Provinces and territories. There was no limit to their savage atrocities and cruelties. Everything they could reach they laid waste, with their looting, murders, tortures of all kinds, burnings, and countless other unspeakable crimes. They spared neither age nor sex, not the very priests and ministers of God, not the ornaments and vessels of the churches, nor the buildings.

Our man of God did not view all this running riot and devastation by a ferocious enemy in the same light as other men. He brought to its origin and progress loftier and profounder considerations. He saw in it chiefly the danger and the death it brought to souls and, more than ever, "tears became his bread by day and night" ("more than ever" because "he who adds to knowledge adds to trouble" and "a heart that understands is like a worm in the bones").

These days, therefore, that he lived through, or endured, almost at the very end of his life, were the bitterest and most mournful of all his old age. A man such as he had to see cities overthrown and destroyed and, with them, their citizens and inhabitants and the buildings on their estates wiped out by a murderous enemy, and others put to flight and scattered. He saw churches denuded of priests and ministers; holy virgins and others vowed to chastity dispersed, some among them succumbing to tortures, others perishing by the sword, others taken captive and losing innocence of soul and body, and faith itself, in evil and cruel slavery to their foes.

He saw the hymns and divine praises ceasing in the churches, the buildings themselves in many places burnt

down, the solemn sacrifice owed to God no longer offered
in the appointed places, the holy sacraments no longer
wanted, and, if they were wanted, ministers of them hard
to find. He saw men taking refuge in forests, on the mountains, in caves, in the rocks, in dens, or in any strong
places; others forced out of them and their escape cut off;
others, again, stripped and deprived of all means of subsistence and slowly perishing of hunger; the very bishops
and clergy of the churches (if, by God's favour, they did
not encounter the enemy or escaped from encounter)
robbed and denuded of everything and begging in the ut-
most need, when there was no possibility of supplying
them with all that was necessary for their support.

Of the countless churches, he saw only three survive,
those of Carthage, Hippo, and Cirta, which by God's favour were not uprooted; and there cities still stand, but-
tressed by human and divine support. (After his death the
city of Hippo was burnt to the ground by the enemy after
being abandoned by its inhabitants.) And amidst these
calamities he used to console himself with the maxim of a
certain wise man who said, "No great man will think it a
great matter when sticks and stones fall and mortals die."

Over all these events, then, in his own wise way, he
daily and deeply mourned. Then, to his other griefs and
sorrows, there was added the arrival of this same enemy
to besiege Hippo-Regius itself, which had so far been left
alone. Their reason was that a certain Count Boniface
with an army of allied Goths had taken up his position to
defend it. For nearly fourteen months their investment of
the city was complete, for their lines even deprived it of
its sea-coast.

I myself, and other bishops from neighbouring regions,
had taken refuge there and were in the city during the
whole of the siege. We had many talks together, saying,
as we pondered the dread judgments of God that were
being executed before our eyes: "Just are Thou, O Lord,
and righteous are Thy judgments." And as we sorrowed,
sighed, and wept together, we implored "the Father of
mercies and the God from whom all consolation comes"

that He would see fit to support us in our present tribulation.

In this situation the clergy had to decide whether they should stay at their post with the prospect of almost certain death or whether it was permissible for them to escape while they could. One of St. Augustine's bishops, Honoratus of Thisbe, stated the case of the escapists very clearly in the letter he wrote asking for directions. He says, "If we are to stay with our congregations, I cannot see what good we should be doing either to ourselves or to the people. All that will happen will be that the slaughter of men, the outraging of women, and the burning of churches will take place under our eyes and we ourselves will die under torture when they are trying to get from us something that we have not got." To this Augustine replies at length most unequivocally that there are no circumstances that can justify the clergy leaving their flock. If the laity have to die, the clergy can help them to die properly or at least die with them; if some of the laity survive, they will still need clergy, and it is quite possible that some of the clergy may be spared too. If all the laity die, then there is no object in the clergy surviving. While if there is a division, and some Christians take flight and others remain, then let the clergy do the same, and draw lots which of them are to go and which to remain, so that there should be no ground for future controversies and recriminations.

It was in this age of ruin and distress that St. Augustine lived and worked. To the materialist, nothing could be more futile than the spectacle of Augustine busying himself with the reunion of the African Church and the refutation of the Pelagians, while civilisation was falling to pieces about his ears. It would seem like the activity of an ant that works on while its nest is being destroyed. But St. Augustine saw things otherwise. To him the ruin of civilisation and the destruction of the empire were not very important things. He looked beyond the aimless and bloody chaos of history to the world of eternal realities from which the world of sense derives all the significance it possesses. His thoughts were fixed, not on the fate of the city of Rome or the city of Hippo, nor on the struggle of Roman and barbarian, but on those other cities that have their foundations in heaven and in hell, and on the warfare between "the world rulers of the dark aeon" and the princes of light. And, in fact, though the age of St. Augustine ended in ruin and though the Church of Africa, in the service of which he spent his life, was destined to be blotted out as completely as if it had never been, he was justified in his faith. The spirit of Augustine continued to live and bear fruit long after Christian Africa had ceased to exist. It entered into the tradition of the Western Church and moulded the thought of Western Christendom so that our very civilisation bears the imprint of his genius. However far we have travelled since the fifth century and however much we have learnt from other teachers, the work of St. Augustine still remains an inalienable part of our spiritual heritage.

We have a remarkable case of this same spirit in another part of the Empire. St. Severinus, a monk of Pannonia, came to Noricium higher up the Danube, where the Christian Roman population had been left to itself at the mercy of the barbarians. He spent the rest of his life there—nearly thirty years—acting as the guide and protector of those forlorn remains of Christian civilisation, proving again and again that the barbarians themselves could be overcome by a man of strong moral character who was absolutely fearless. We see the same thing in Gaul in the fifth and sixth centuries, where the barbarian conquerors increasingly underwent the influence of the Catholic bishops and monks so that the Church gradually became the strongest power in the country.

Nevertheless, the trial was a long and severe one, for the level of civilisation was continually declining, so that the situation became more unbearable to each successive generation.

We see this very clearly in the writings of St. Gregory the Great. There has never been a stronger character or a man of more courageous temperament than Gregory. Yet he shows a most profound pessimism in what he wrote. He even sees the great pestilence that was then devastating Italy as a welcome relief from the suffering his people had to endure at the hands of the Lombards.

"When we consider the way that other men have died, we find a solace in thinking of the form of death that threatens us. What mutilations, what cruelties have we seen inflicted upon men, for which death is the only cure and in the midst of which life was a torment." (*Epistolae* X 20.)

Yet it was just in this age, in the midst of the Lombard invasions, that the foundations of a new civilisation were being laid by St. Benedict in Italy and by the Irish monks in the West. The Benedictine rule was the Church's answer to the problem of how to preserve the elements of Christian culture in a barbarous world. The Benedictine monastery was a real society, with its own constitution, its own economic foundation, its own rule of life, and its own spiritual ideal. As a self-sufficient rural community, it resembled the Latin Roman villa, containing workshops and kitchens and refectories, an oratory, a library, a guest house, a novitiate, and an infirmary, and if possible a well, a mill, and a garden, all within a walled enclosure. Where it differed from the ordinary villa was that it was based on a threefold renunciation, which denied the three natural instincts on which the ordinary society is founded—the sexual instinct, the economic motive, and the desire for individual power, so that it was in St. Benedict's words "a school for the service of the Lord," in which it would be possible to live a completely Christian life without any surrender to the forces of disorder that ruled the barbaric society that surrounded it. The extraordinary thing was that it worked. It was a successful experiment in communal living that spread far and wide through barbarian Europe. Barbarian kings and princesses became monks and nuns, the barbarian warrior and the Roman peasant lived and worked side by side in the same community, which was dedicated to the law of charity and embraced the threefold obligation of prayer, study, and manual work. And it thus became the seed or germ cell of a new culture. All that barbarian Europe possessed of culture and letters and education came to it from the monasteries, which like an ark carried the tradition of the old Christian culture over the floods of barbarism to a new age that was yet unborn.

But perhaps the most remarkable achievement of the Church among the barbarians was its conversion or reconversion of the British Isles. This was almost entirely the work of the monks, though to a great extent it belongs to the pre-Benedictine period.

Of course, we know very little of what was happening to the Roman Christians in Britain in the last age of the empire. We know that the famous Pelagius, the great opponent of St. Augustine, was a Briton and a man of high culture. And so was St. Faustus, who was an abbot of Lerins (the great monastery off the Riviera) for a quarter of a century and afterwards bishop of Riez for another thirty years, until he was finally sent into exile by the Arian king of the Visigoths.

But in the British Isles themselves the great figure was St. Patrick, one of the most remarkable men produced by that time of stress. He was a Roman Briton, son of a Roman official who was also a deacon, and he was carried off as a captive to Ireland in one of the barbarian raids early in the fifth century. After six years he escaped and eventually returned to his family. Here he had a dream or vision in which he heard the voice of the Irish who dwelt by the wood of Foclut, which is by the western sea, imploring him to come over and help them, and he then determined to devote his life to their conversion.

But first he had to go to Gaul, probably for many years to Lerins and St. Germanus at Auxerre, to study and be ordained as bishop, returning to Ireland probably in 432.

Although he had to undergo much opposition from the Druids and the chieftains and from the rebarbarised Celts from Britain who joined with the heathen Picts to raid his new convents, his mission was extraordinarily successful, so that a century later Ireland had become a Christian country: the only land of the Western barbarians to become Christian by its own efforts—like Armenia and Georgia in the East—and to produce a Christian culture that was all its own.

This Christian culture was almost entirely a monastic one, and it was the monks from Ireland, like St. Columba and St. Columbanus, who co-operated with the Benedictine monks from Italy in restoring the Christian culture of Europe after the age of barbarian invasions. And the two movements came together in England in the seventh century, when they produced between them the great age of Northumbrian culture of the age of Bede. Thanks to Bede we actually know more about the history of Christianity in England than we do about Ireland, which is regrettable, since it was Ireland that offers the best example of an intact barbarian culture accepting Christianity without any loss of its own cultural traditions.

Of course, Irish culture remained barbarous in the

technical Graeco-Roman sense. It had no cities and consequently no diocesan episcopate like the rest of the Western Church, and it also maintained many pagan customs and usages. But it was no longer barbarian in the destructive sense. There were no more Irish raids carried out against Christian peoples. If the example of St. Patrick had been more widely followed, it is conceivable that Holland and Saxony and Scandinavia might have been converted peacefully without any interference with their native cultures and traditions, so that Europe might have been spared the second wave of barbarian invasions of the Viking period, which practically destroyed the peaceful monastic culture of Ireland and Northumbria. But this is a doubtful speculation.

Christian Europe actually had to undergo all the evils of barbarian invasion for a second time in the ninth and tenth centuries, when they had fewer spiritual and cultural resources to fall back upon than the Church of the later Roman Empire possessed. Even so, Christianity withstood the test as it had before, with the result that almost the whole of Europe, including Russia and Poland and Hungary, had become Christian by the eleventh century.

Now we are in somewhat the same situation today as was the Christian Empire in the fourth and fifth centuries. If we were prepared, like St. Augustine and St. Patrick, St. Benedict and St. Gregory, to accept the solution of the cross, I believe there is no doubt that Christian civilisation would ultimately triumph. But there is a much greater temptation today to rely on our superiority in material power and resources and to put our trust too much in "the arm of the flesh," as St. Gregory would have said.

6

The Church in a Christian World

AT THE BEGINNING of the eleventh century the long
process of the conversion of the barbarians by the
Church was completed, with the conversion of Russia
in the East, Scandinavia and Iceland in the North, and
Hungary and Poland in central Europe. Henceforward
the whole of Europe was to be a Christian continent,
excepting a few peripheral regions such as the Baltic
and Finnish people southeast of the Baltic; the remaining footholds of Islam in Spain and Sicily, which were
soon to become Christian; and finally the south Russian steppes, which were to remain an open door to
the nomad peoples of central Asia, such as the Turks
and the Tartars. Apart from these outlying regions,
Europe became more and more identified with Christendom, especially since in the course of the eleventh
century the remaining territories of the Byzantine Empire in Asia Minor were overrun by the Turks and
were permanently lost to Christendom.

This change was the more important because from
the eleventh century onwards, Western Europe witnessed a great explosion of cultural and religious energy, which was most evident in France, West Germany, and North Italy. The most active elements in this
movement were the monks and bishops who had inherited the Carolingian tradition of Christian culture
and who were the only part of the society who possessed some degree of higher education. These men
became the leaders of a movement of religious reform

which, beginning with the monasteries, like Cluny and Fleury in the tenth century, gradually extended to the papacy and the whole Western Church. They aimed both at moral reform and at the restoration of canonical discipline, which had become entirely neglected in the age of civil war and barbarian invasions, which had followed the decline of the Carolingian Empire. And this inevitably led to a conflict with the secular powers in order to vindicate the freedom and independence of the Church.

The victory of the papacy over the empire in the long conflict that followed had a far-reaching effect on Western culture. It meant that Western Christendom was not regarded as a single state after the fashion of the Byzantine Empire, but rather as a wide collection of kingdoms, principalities, and cities united by their common faith under the leadership of the papacy. Thus Christendom was a Church rather than a state, and while the Western states were ununified and unorganised, the Church during the twelfth and thirteenth centuries developed an elaborate centralised system of international government and control, extending from the Pope and the Roman curia down to the diocese and the bishop's court and below that to the rural parish.

That this system was an effective one which gave a real sense of unity and a principle of leadership to the Christian people was shown by the success of the crusading movement from the end of the eleventh century to the middle of the thirteenth.

The very idea of a religious war is apt to shock the modern mind, but we cannot understand mediaeval religion, at least in its more popular aspects, unless we realise the strength of the religious emotion which drove so many myriads of Christians to take the cross and to leave their bones on the long road through Asia Minor, or to rot in the prisons of Egypt and Syria. The significant thing about the crusading movement is that it was an attempt to Christianise mediaeval society in its most vital but least Christian aspect, and thus it denotes a real fusion between the native tradition of the warrior peoples of Western Europe and the ideals of the Church and the Christian tradition. We see in early mediaeval literature—for example, in the *Chansons de Geste*—how wide was the gulf between these two traditions and how much of the leaven of pagan barbarism still remained in the feudal society of the twelfth century. Yet in the following century the crusading ideal finds expression in the life of St. Louis, which is one of the noblest examples of mediaeval religion. Here the leaven of paganism is entirely purged away, while the characteristic heroic idealism of the northern warrior tradition remains. This demonstrated how the papacy was able to mobilise the forces of Western Europe for a common object independently of the larger states which, in the beginning at least, made a comparatively small contribution to the common effort.

In the First Crusade, especially, the participation of so many different elements in a common effort and the fact that it ultimately succeeded in achieving a concrete political objective, that is, the foundation of the kingdom of Jerusalem, were very important factors in making the Western people conscious of the existence of a great supernatural society which claimed their allegiance.

But from the Church's point of view the crusading movement was of secondary importance. The essential task was rather the internal one, the reform of the Church herself; first by the reassertion of her authority as an autonomous universal spiritual society, which was achieved by the succession of provincial and general councils, which culminated in the Fourth Lateran Council of 1215; and second, the work of the spiritual reform which was carried forward by the great monastic reformers, notably by St. Bernard and the Cistercians in the twelfth century, and in the thirteenth century by the work of St. Francis and St. Dominic and the orders of the Friars Minor and the Friars Preachers.

These new orders were essentially international institutions, which were emancipated from the ties of property and from the influence of feudalism and territorialism, which had affected the older monastic orders. They were classless societies which were able to preach the Christian way of life to the democratic society of the new urban communes as well as the peasants and the poor in the villages.

No less important than these movements of ecclesiastical and spiritual reform was the intellectual revival that accompanied them. Beginning in the eleventh century, it spread from the monastic and episcopal schools, like Chartres and Laon and Liège, until it became a universal movement that affected every side of mediaeval thought and culture.

The renewed contact with Greek and oriental science and culture which was established by the translation of Arabic works by the Jewish and Christian scholars who were active in Spain and elsewhere during the twelfth century, especially at the episcopal school of Toledo, had a very stimulating effect on the Western mind. Now it was at this moment that the first universities were being founded, and they soon became the points at which the new intellectual influences were concentrated. The mediaeval university was essentially a corporation of students and teachers, like the craft guilds which were so numerous and flourishing at this time. Like these, it was a free self-governing professional union, which conferred the right of teaching on its graduates, whether masters or doctors, and the greatest of these universities, like Paris and Oxford and the great law school of Bologna in Italy, developed during the later twelfth and early thirteenth centuries into centres of study for the whole of Western Christendom, and Paris, above all, acquired papal recognition as the authorised centre of higher theological studies. At the same time, the new orders of the Dominicans and the Franciscans established themselves there and rapidly assumed a position of intellectual leadership.

It was under these conditions that the great synthesis of mediaeval Christian thought was worked out by a series of great systematic thinkers, such as the Franciscan, St. Bonaventure, the Dominicans, St. Albert the Great and St. Thomas Aquinas, and the Augustinian, Aegidius Colonna. I say synthesis rather than syntheses, because though the philosophies differed, they all comprehended the same elements, Christian theology, Greek or Graeco-Arabic metaphysics, physics and mathematics, and politics. In other words, they were all different versions of a total synthesis of all that was known or could be known by the mediaeval mind.

It was this creation of a universal synthesis of knowledge which was the greatest achievement of the thirteenth century, and it left its mark on the whole culture of the age, which possessed an extraordinary unity that is to be seen in its art and architecture and social institutions, no less than in its theology and philosophy. The measure of its success in these latter fields is to be seen in the way that the work of the greatest of the thirteenth-century systemizers, St. Thomas Aquinas, had remained down to our own age as the classical and official exponent of the Catholic conception of reality.

In spite of this, it is difficult for us at the present day to understand the mediaeval view of reality and the nature of the mediaeval cosmos, without the help of some work of creative imagination like Dante's great

poem, by which we can see the mediaeval world
through mediaeval eyes.

Seen in this way, we can understand how the relation of man to the universe was essentially different
from what it is today. The mediaeval universe was
essentially theocentric. It sought the explanation of all
things in God, and related every facet of experience
and every form of art and science to their divine soul
and centre; for the universe is nothing but a reflection
or image of the glory of God. From the sphere of pure
light and fire that lies beyond the stars down through
the nine heavens to the earth and the depths below,
the whole creation glows and burns with the light of
divine wisdom and the strength of divine power, as St.
Bonaventure expressed it.

Man stands on the lowest steps of this divine ladder,
poised dizzily between heaven and the abyss, and yet
he possesses a unique function which even the pure
intelligence which rules the heavens cannot share. He
is the mediator between the two worlds of spirit and
matter, the high priest of the sublunary world whose
mission it is to bring spiritual life and light into the
sensible world. This hieratic function can only be fulfilled through the ecclesiastical hierarchy, which is the
earthly counterpart of the angelic hierarchy of the
heavens and which builds and organises mankind into
a spiritual society, which is the living temple of God
on earth. Thus the human existence is dependent at
any stage on the spiritual order which surrounds and
transcends it. The visible world is a shadow, and the
importance of man is not to be found in this shadow
existence, but in the place that he occupies on the ladder of being, which rises from nothingness to God and
to his actual and potential participation in the spiritual
world on the frontier of which he is placed.

Thus the mediaeval view was essentially unitary
and dynamic. It is true that the dynamic concep-

tion takes a somewhat different form in the Augustinian Neoplatonic synthesis from that which is seen in the Aristotelian-Thomist one, since the former emphasises the will of the soul to the Supreme Good, and the latter, the satisfaction of the intellect in the Beatific Vision. But the difference is not very important, since in this matter a Thomist like Dante found no difficulty in reconciling the Neoplatonism of Dionysius the Areopagite with Christian Aristotelianism in St. Thomas. A spiritual dynamism was common to both systems, and its influence is to be seen in almost every aspect of mediaeval thought and culture. It is particularly evident in the mediaeval art which came to its flowering in the same age as mediaeval philosophy and expresses the same dynamism and the same domination of matter by form.

Aesthetic appreciation of this spiritual unity of mediaeval culture was very characteristic of nineteenth-century mediaevalism: We find it first in the German romantics, like Novalis and Schlegel, then in the writers of the French Catholic revival, like Lacordaire and Montalembert, and most of all perhaps in the English and American mediaevalists, from the time of Pugin and Kenelm Digby through Ruskin to William Morris and finally in W. R. Lethaby and R. A. Cram.

It is only natural that in the present century there has been a strong reaction against these views, so that perhaps at the present time there is a tendency to depreciate the mediaeval achievement and to reject any attempt to identify mediaeval culture with the Catholic tradition. Among the factors in this reaction there is, on the one hand, the strong liberal prejudice against mediaeval intolerance as seen in the Crusades and still more in the Inquisition, and on the other, the equally strong Protestant prejudice against the practical abuses of mediaeval society and the moral standards of the

mediaeval clergy, an attitude that found its typical expression in the writings of G. G. Coulton.

Nor is this view without some justification, inasmuch
as our knowledge of mediaeval culture is inevitably
biased by the fact that the clergy was the only element
in medieval society that was fully literate and articu-
late, so that all the historians, philosophers, and legists
were drawn from the same class and represent the
same point of view. And, above all, there was the
Inquisition.

The revival of Western culture had been accompanied from the eleventh century onwards by a new
heretical movement which, in the twelfth and thirteenth centuries, became a serious danger to Catholicism. This was the Catharist movement. It should perhaps be regarded not so much as a heresy as a rival
religion, since it was rooted in the non-Christian and
perhaps pre-Christian dualism of the ancient East,
which was transmitted to the West, through the Bal-
kan peninsula, by the Paulicians and the Bogomils. In
any case, it is of the greatest importance for the history
of medieval religion, and we cannot understand the
latter unless we realise that Catholicism's most dangerous foe was not some form of simplified or rationalised Christianity, but a religion that regarded the
body and the whole material world as the creation of
Satan, and condemned marriage and child-bearing
as essentially sinful. It was forbidden for the Catharist
not only to marry, but to kill any living thing, or to eat
anything that was the fruit of sexual generation. But
this life of strict asceticism belonged only to the "perfect," who had received the *consalementum*, "the baptism with the spirit and with fire," which was the
sacrament of the Catharist religion. The ordinary
Catharist was merely a "believer" who shared neither
the privileges nor the privations of the "perfect,"
through whom alone he could hope to attain contact

with the spiritual world. Thus Catharism combined extreme asceticism with considerable laxity, and even antinomianism, in practice.

It is not surprising that a heresy of so fundamental a nature, which regarded the God of the Catholics as an evil power and the Church itself as the creation of Satan, should have been met with remorseless repression. Indeed, the rise of Catharism in Western Europe seems to have been largely responsible for the new attitude to heresy and persecution that marked the later medieval Church. Hitherto, it is true, the Church had regarded the suppression of heresy as part of the duty of the state, but it had shown itself averse from extreme measures, and the sentence *"Ecclesia abhorret a sanguine"*—"The Church abominates bloodshed"—had been accepted as an established maxim. But the Catharists were in an entirely different category to other heretics. Manichees, and such the Catharists substantially were, were regarded alike by pagans and Christians as enemies of the human race. Even before the advent of Christianity, Manicheanism had been treated as a capital offence by Roman law, and the Byzantine Empire had attempted to exterminate the Paulicians by fire and sword. Though isolated rulers or bishops from the eleventh century onwards had executed heretics, the Church had given no official sanction to their capital punishment, and the leaders of orthodox opinion, such as St. Bernard and Gerhoh of Reichersberg, continued to condemn it. When, however, the Church had taken the lead in preaching the Crusade against the infidel abroad, it seemed inconsistent to condemn the use of the sword against the heretic at home, above all in face of a heresy so radically subversive as Catharism. Accordingly, in the second half of the twelfth century we find a growing movement in favour of a Crusade against the Albigenses, and the Crusade was in fact declared in 1208.

Nevertheless, though Innocent III, under the influence of Roman law, assimilated heresy to the crime of high treason (*laesae majestatis*), for which the penalty was death, he still stopped short of the death penalty, and decreed only exile and confiscation in the anti-heretical legislation of the Fourth Lateran Council.

The final step seems to have been taken in consequence of the action of that brilliant and sinister figure, Frederick II, who covered his own doubtful orthodoxy by the zeal with which he persecuted heretics and the ruthlessness of his anti-heretical legislation. In 1224 he made heresy punishable by burning. It is probable that his action was due to a desire to assert his authority in religious matters at the expense of the ecclesiastical authority. In any case, the Pope (Gregory IX) was unwilling to leave the "inquisition" of heretics to the civil power, and he accordingly appointed special commissioners for the purpose in 1231, which may be regarded as the date of the official foundation of the Inquisition.

The very name Inquisition has become so highly charged with emotion that we are disposed to see in its operation nothing but cruelty and injustice. The excesses of two of the earliest inquisitors, the Dominican Robert le Bougre and his contemporary, the Premonstratensian Conrad of Marburg, are indeed deserving of such condemnation. Even so, the former was removed from his office by Pope Gregory IX and condemned to lifelong imprisonment; and the latter combined with his fanatical intolerance, zeal for social justice in defense of the poor against noble or princely oppressors.

Far more representative was the fourteenth-century inquisitor Bernard Gui, whose manual of procedure (*Practica*) is a serious attempt, however defective by our judicial standards, to secure justice. Out of 930 sentences passed by Gui, only 42 delivered the accused to the secular arm for capital punishment. At Pamiers and Toulouse at about the same period the proportion was respectively 1 in 15 and 1 in 22. Lea, the Protestant historian of the Inquisition, concludes: "The stake consumed few victims."

Both the legislation of Frederick and that of the Popes were affected by the influence of the revived Roman law as, for example, in the use of judicial torture, introduced into the Inquisition in 1251 and one of its worst features. This was a serious breach with the older mediaeval tradition, for the Church had opposed the use of torture not only in patristic times, but also in the darkest period of the Dark Ages, when Pope Nicholas I had insisted on its essential folly and injustice in his letter to the converted Bulgarians. Here the attitude of the Dark Ages seems more enlightened than that of the later mediaeval and Renaissance periods. The same is true of the belief in witchcraft: Belief in its reality was opposed as a relic of pagan superstition by Nicholas I and Agobard, and the ecclesiastical advisers of Charlemagne. Witch-burning, however, spread like a contagion through Europe at the close of the Middle Ages and reached its height in the post-Reformation period.

It is easy to exaggerate these negative aspects of mediaeval culture. The life of the mediaeval Church with its feasts and fasts, its pilgrimages and its devotion to the saints in whom every locality and every occupation had its appropriate patron, was the common possession of the whole Christian people, and it was in his membership in the Church rather than the state that mediaeval man found his true citizenship. No man was ever too poor or too wretched to be included in this community—even the beggars and the lepers possessed their own spiritual dignity, which was solemnly recognised by the powers of the world when the King washed the feet of the poor on Maundy Thursday and fed them at his own table.

This ideal of Christian democracy or fraternity found its highest expression in the Franciscan movement, with its cult of poverty and its apostolate of the poor. The influence of the Friars was all-pervading in the thirteenth century: It affected every level of society and culture, and was especially strong in the case of St. Louis IX, who took the Friars as his advisers and ministers as well as his friends. It is, however, in St. Francis himself that mediaeval religion finds its most sublime expression, and one that makes a unique appeal not only to the mediaeval mind but also to that of modern times. And the secret of this appeal is to be found precisely in the Christocentric character of the life and doctrine of St. Francis. What impressed his contemporaries and still impresses us to-day is the "conformity" of St. Francis to the pattern of the divine humanity, so that, in the words of a mediaeval writer,* "St. Francis became as it were the *picture of Christ,* and was transformed at all points into Jesus, the Lord Himself completing and finishing this work by the impression of the stigmata."

But St. Francis was not only a master of the spiritual life, he was also among the greatest of the leaders of the reforming movement, and his order, together with that of St. Dominic, were the most efficient and devoted agents of the papacy in its universal mission.

Unfortunately, the left wing of the Franciscan order, the so-called "Spirituals," developed revolutionary tendencies, which brought them into conflict with orthodox Catholic tradition and with the authority of the Holy See. This weakened both the reforming movement as a whole, and especially that alliance of the

---

* The author of the *Meditationes vitae Christi,* which were falsely attributed to St. Bonaventure (John de Caulibus?).

spiritual reformers and the papacy that had been the basis of the whole religious movement from the eleventh to the thirteenth centuries. At the same time, the growth of nationalism destroyed the international unity of mediaeval culture and prepared the way for that great schism between northern and southern Europe that came to a head at the Reformation. The last two centuries of the Middle Ages saw the gradual disintegration of the unity that had been built up in the previous age. The spiritual vitality of mediaeval religion was still strong, but it had lost its centre of unity and its constructive power. The last great attempt to reform the Church and to restore the unity of Christendom—the conciliar movement—was a failure because it based its action on a kind of ecclesiastical constitutionalism that was inconsistent with the divine authority of the Holy See. Thus the papacy, deserted by the reformers and opposed by a strong Gallicanising movement, was forced to make its own terms with the new secular powers, and became itself increasingly absorbed in the secular politics and humanist culture of Renaissance Italy.

It was indeed at Rome that the Middle Ages first came to an end. Already in the first half of the fifteenth century, the age of St. Joan, the Curia was thronged with bright young men who regarded the whole mediaeval development as an unfortunate episode that was best forgotten, and who looked back to pagan antiquity with romantic enthusiasm. More than a century was to pass before the old alliance of the papacy and the spiritual reformers was renewed by St. Ignatius and the heroes of the Counter-Reformation. But in the meantime, the great revolt had taken place, and northern Europe had ceased to be Catholic.

What gave mediaeval culture its Christian character was not that the Church enforced a universal Christian standard on everybody to the exclusion of

all scandal and evil, but that it turned men's eyes to a
vision of spiritual perfection that could be attained by
all sorts of people in all sorts of ways; a man might be
a contemplative monk, like St. Bernard, or a tough
fighting man, like a Knight Templar; he might be a
philosopher, like St. Bonaventure and St. Thomas, or a
politician, like Simon de Montfort the Younger. He
might be a beggar, like St. Francis, or a king, like St.
Louis; a poet, like Wolfram von Eschenbach, or a scientist, like Roger Bacon. All shared a common faith
and a common purpose, and each had his own personal goal of spiritual perfection, which had its allotted place in the completed order of the city of God.

Needless to say, this domination of Western culture
by the Church and of the Church by the ideal of reform was always incomplete, and endured only from
the Lateran Council of 1059 to the Council of Lyons in
1274, just over two centuries. After the death of
Gregory X in 1276 the union between the papacy and
the reformers that had created the dynamic unity of
mediaeval religion and culture was lost, and the crusading ideal was lost with it. The sense of Christendom
as a living social reality was gradually replaced by the
rivalry of conflicting states and nationalities, which left
no room for the supernatural institutions and ideals
of the earlier period.

The men of that generation were not altogether conscious of what was happening. We see this not only
in the complaints of the spiritual reformers on the dangers that threatened the Church, but also among the
laity, with the poets who expressed the general feeling
of Christendom on the failure of the Crusades. I quote
the moving line that Ruteboeuf devoted to Geoffrey of
Sergines, the knight whom St. Louis left in charge of
the defence of the Holy Land and who was the last
representative of the old ideals:

"Master Geoffrey de Sergines, I no longer see any

sign that they will send you succour. Let the men of Aire make a great cemetery: That is what they will need. The path is overgrown with weeds, which men once trod gladly to offer their 'souls as though they were burning tapers.'"

For two hundred years the armies of Christendom had thronged that path that was at once a way of pilgrimage and a way of the cross. The blood and wealth of Europe had flowed out through it like an open vein. No one can measure the good and the evil, the heroism and the destruction of that long-drawn-out *via dolorosa*. Now the path was closed and the account was ended. Nothing remained but the ruins of the great crusading castles that still remain stranded on the slopes of Lebanon or the shores of the Mediterranean as impressive witnesses to the power of the crusading ideal. It is very appropriate that the order of the Templars that represented this idea and the last Pope who embodied the universal claims of the mediaeval papacy should both of them have been destroyed only a few years later by the first great representative of the new power of the national state and the new monarchy that was to dominate the following age.

7

Renaissance and Reformation

THOSE TWO GREAT INTERNATIONAL MOVEMENTS—the Renaissance and the Reformation—had a profound effect on European culture which cannot be explained in political or national terms. Neither can they be explained in terms of one another. In spite of the intimate and complex relations between them, both alike are aspects of the great cultural revolution which was due to the dissolution of the mediaeval unity of Western Christendom and to the reorganization of the different elements of Western culture according to new patterns.

The European situation was ripe for an explosion. Martin Luther was simply the revolutionary leader whose passionate genius fired the train. He was the living embodiment of all the elements in Northern Europe which were most alien from Rome and from the new Mediterranean culture. He appealed from Hellenism to Hebraism, from Italian humanism to Northern religious emotion, from the authority of the Roman Papacy to the Christian Nobility of the German Nation. There was, however, one respect in which he agreed with the humanists: he shared their distaste for asceticism. The circumstances of his conversion caused him to react with extraordinary violence against the monastic life and the ascetic ideal on which it was founded, above all the ideal of virginity. And this was one of the most revolutionary aspects of his work, for the monks had been the makers of Western Christendom. They had dominated mediaeval culture from its beginnings down to the thirteenth century, when their influence had been replaced by that of the friars, who represented the same ascetic ideal in a more popular and personal form.

Moreover, monasticism was not peculiar to Western Christendom. It was common to the whole Christian world from Russia to Abyssinia, and to the whole Christian past since the fourth century, so that its destruction changed not only the social and institutional pattern of mediaeval culture but also the moral and spiritual ideals of the Christian life. Religion was secularised in the sense that it was reorientated from the cloister to the world and found its centre in the family and in the active fulfilment of man's earthly calling. No doubt all this was secondary in Luther's eyes to the fundamental evangelical doctrine of salvation by faith alone. But the destructive element of the Protestant revolution was more far-reaching than the positive, and was to some extent independent of it, as we see in the early history of the English Reformation.

For Henry VIII had no sympathy or understanding for Luther's religious ideas. The tradition to which he appealed was that of Philip le Bel and Louis of Bavaria, as we see from his publication of works like Marsilius' *Defensor Pacis* and the *dialogus inter Militem et Clericum*, of which English translations were produced in 1533 and 1535. And so long as his schism followed these conservative lines it met with little resistance from clergy or people. But when from political and economic motives he followed the Protestant example and attacked the monasteries, the revolutionary character of his work became clear, and it aroused a wave of popular Catholic feeling which under more vigorous leadership might have changed the course of history.

The Reformation was a revolutionary movement not

merely on account of the excesses of fanatical minorities, like the Zwickau prophets or the Anabaptists of Münster, but because it changed both the spiritual and social order of the mediaeval world. Nothing is more remarkable than the rapidity with which the movement spread across the whole of Northern Europe in the course of a few years, from Switzerland to the Rhine to Scandinavia and the remote territories of Livonia and Courland. In these years the resistance of the Catholics was insignificant. The religious orders, notably the Augustinian Friars, were themselves the leaders of the revolt, and before the Catholic forces had had time to rally, Germany had become three quarters Protestant and Scandinavia and the Baltic almost completely so. Only Iceland stood out for a little. When the first Icelandic monastery was destroyed by the Danes in 1539, the perpetrators were outlawed by the Althing and the governor was deposed. It was not until 1550 that the last Catholic bishop, Jan Arason, the poet, was executed at Skalholt with his two sons.

But while it is impossible to exaggerate the importance of Luther as the source of the revolutionary movement which destroyed the unity of Christendom and split Europe asunder, his achievements as a constructor and organiser were relatively small, and it is very doubtful whether Lutheranism would have withstood the Catholic reaction that followed if it had been left to its own resources. The wider development of Protestantism as a European movement which met the Catholic Counter-Reformation on its own ground was mainly due to a genius of a very different type.

John Calvin was a French bourgeois, the son of a lawyer at Noyon, who brought to the service of the Protestant cause the logic and discipline and legal acuteness of the Latin mind. Unlike Luther, he was essentially an intellectual who had the gift of ruling men, and from his study he was able at once to govern a state and to direct a world-wide movement of religious propaganda and ecclesiastical organisation. In place of the somewhat shapeless and incoherent mass of doctrines and tendencies represented by Luther and the German reformers, he fashioned a coherent logical body of doctrine and an iron system of discipline, and in place of the state-controlled Lutheran territorial Churches, he created an autonomous Church which claimed theocratic authority. In this respect Calvinism inherited the tradition of the Catholic reforming movement of the Middle Ages, since it maintained the supremacy of the spiritual power as uncompromisingly as St. Gregory VII had done, and was equally ready to resist any attempt on the part of the state to interfere in the government of the Church.

Thus in spite of the theological principles that were common to Lutheranism and Calvinism, their social appeal and their political effects were entirely different. Lutheranism had appealed to the princes and had transferred to the state the prerogatives and power and property which had belonged to the Church. Calvinism, on the other hand, appealed to the people, and especially to the newly educated middle classes, to which Calvin himself belonged. In the same way, while in Germany Protestantism soon lost the support of the humanists, so that Luther found his most formidable opponent in Erasmus, the leader of the intelligentsia, in France it was in humanist circles that the success of Calvinism was most pronounced, so that the leaders of Cisalpine humanism in the later sixteenth century, like J. J. Scaliger and Isaac Casaubon, were found among the Calvinists. In this way the Reformation in its second phase did a great deal to promote the cause of learning. The Calvinists, no less than their enemies, the Jesuits, fully realised the importance of education, and wherever they went, even as

far as Massachusetts Bay, they brought not only the
Bible but also the *Latin Grammar*.

Nevertheless, this humanism was of a strictly utilitarian kind. Its adherents were the friends of education, but they were the enemies of culture and did
their best to destroy and dissipate the wealth of religious art and imagery that had been accumulated by
centuries of Christian culture. It was this fierce spirit
of iconoclasm and the harsh intolerance that the Calvinists showed towards all the manifestations of Catholic piety which made any reconciliation between
Protestantism and the movement of Catholic reform
impossible and doomed Europe to more than a century of religious war and sectarian controversy.

The reaction to the tremendous changes brought
about by Luther and Calvin also spread to the Mediterranean world. When Luther launched his revolt, the
culture of humanist Italy had reached its maturity,
and Leo X, the son of Lorenzo de Medici, had made
Rome the centre of a brilliant literary and artistic culture. Centuries later, men looked back on the Rome of
Leo X as a golden age. Voltaire writes of it as one of
those rare moments in the history of the world that
vindicate the greatness of the human mind and com-
pensate the historian for the barren prospect of a thousand years of stupidity and barbarism. To Luther, on
the other hand, the Rome of Leo X was a sink of iniquity, its culture was pure materialism, and its religion was gross superstition.

Neither of these extremes is justified. Leo X's generous patronage of culture cannot redeem his failures
in his spiritual and international leadership. And the
worldliness and moral laxity of Italian society do not
prove that Italian religion was moribund. On the contrary, its vitality is shown by the unbroken series of
saints and mystics and reformers who flourished
throughout the Renaissance period and who are to be

found not only among the representatives of the mediaeval tradition like Savonarola but also among the leaders of humanist culture. At Rome itself in the age of Leo X, the Oratory of Divine Love, out of which the Theatine Order arose a few years later, formed a centre of spiritual renewal which united leaders of the Catholic reform like St. Cajetan and Cardinal Carafa (afterwards Paul IV) with humanists and members of the papal court, like Sadolet and Manetti, and later Reginald Pole, Alexander, and Contarini.

The spirit of this Italian reforming movement was at once more mediaeval and more modern than that of the German Reformation. It aimed at applying the interior spirituality of the Italian mystical tradition—the spirit of St. Catherine of Genoa—to the task of ecclesiastical reform, and instead of revolting against the monastic and the ascetic traditions like Luther, it sought to adapt them to the needs of the age by providing a corporate quasi-monastic way of life in which the clergy could carry on their pastoral work while living by rule in community. This innovation proved extraordinarily popular and successful. It exerted its influence not only by training priests and bishops but even more by providing an example which was to be followed by a series of similar institutions, the Barnabites of St. Antonio Maria Zaccaria, the Somaschi of St. Jerome Emiliani, and above all the Roman Oratory of St. Philip Neri. It was this movement, even more than the Spanish Counter-Reformation, that was the real source of the Catholic revival and of the new forms and ideals of modern Catholicism.

Nevertheless, it did not possess the dynamic quality that was necessary to meet the challenge of the Reformation. The Christian humanists might have reason and authority and tradition on their side, but they were too civilised to cope with the titanic forces that had been released by Martin Luther.

But the Mediterranean world also possessed a new source of spiritual energy, which was still intact. The rising force of nationalism was making itself felt in the Iberian Peninsula no less than in Germany, but in Spain, unlike Germany, it was directed and unified by a strong central power. After centuries of division and strife, the Spanish kingdoms had been united in 1474 by the Catholic kings, who set themselves to organise and reform the whole national order, alike in Church and state. In this task they were able to appeal to the age-long tradition of the crusade against the infidel, which had always been the dynamic force in Spanish history, so that they could unite their peoples externally by the reconquest of the remaining Moslem territories in Southern Spain and internally by the liquidation of the non-Christian minorities through the tribunal of the Inquisition, which was the organ of national unity as well as of Catholic orthodoxy and helped to identify the spirit of Spanish patriotism with Spanish religious ideals.

It was this Spanish crusading spirit which was to become the motive force of the Counter-Reformation. By degrees it communicated itself to Charles V and his advisers, so that eventually, and still more under his successor, the whole resources of the Spanish Empire were mobilised in a new holy war against European Protestantism.

Nevertheless, this militant aggressiveness was only one aspect of Spanish Catholicism. Still more important was its internal spiritual mission for the reform of the Church and the restoration of Catholic culture, which found its expression in the work of St. Ignatius Loyola and the Society of Jesus. The beginnings of Ignatius were those of a spiritual Quixote, a knight errant in search of a crusade. But his retreat at Manresa, which coincided with that of Luther at the Wartburg, transformed his character and his aims and revealed to him his true mission, which was both internal and universal. The society which he created united the spirit of the Spanish Counter-Reformation with that of the Italian movement of spiritual reform which was represented by the Theatines and later by the Oratory. Unlike the former, it was essentially international in character, and was directly dependent on the Papacy, but it also embodied the Spanish crusading ideal in a sublimated form, as we see above all in the heroic achievements of St. Francis Xavier, the apostle of the Indies.

No less important, however, in the long run, was the activity of the Society of Jesus in education and culture. From the sixteenth century onwards, the Jesuits set themselves to adapt the new methods of humanist education to Christian ideals, and their colleges, which were established all over the Catholic world from Peru to Russia, were the organs of a common type of humanist Catholic culture. Their work did more than anything else to restore the prestige of Catholic education, which had been so much damaged by the assaults of the humanists against the old Scholastic tradition. And at the same time the work of the Jesuits as directors of conscience and spiritual advisers brought the influence of the Catholic revival to bear on the courts and cabinets, which were the key points of social influence and had hitherto been the centres of the disintegrating movements that had underminded the unity of Christendom.

But great as the contribution of the Society to the Catholic revival was, it was only a part of a much wider development. For example, the revival of the contemplative life and the new flowering of Christian mysticism, which was the spiritual climax of the whole movement, owed less to the Jesuits than to the Carmelite Reform, which arose slightly later and did not attain its full influence on the Catholic world until the

early years of the seventeenth century. St. Teresa and
St. John of the Cross, no less than St. Ignatius and St.
Francis Xavier, are a proof of the extraordinary dynamism of the Spanish religious genius, and their
achievement is even more representative of the Spanish religious tradition than that of the great Jesuits,
since it is the culmination of a mystical tradition that
was already flourishing, especially among the Spanish Franciscans, like Francisco of Ossuna, Bernardino
of Laredo, and St. Peter of Alcantara. Nevertheless, it
would be a mistake to ascribe the mystical revival of
the sixteenth century entirely to Spanish sources. It
had its independent roots in Italy, where one of the
greatest of Catholic mystics, St. Catherine of Genoa
(1447–97), had had a profound influence on the spiritual life of Renaissance Italy through Christian humanists like Ettore Vernazza.

It is difficult to overestimate the share of the mystics
in the Catholic revival and their influence on the new
Catholic culture. The Protestant criticisms of Catholicism as a religion of external practice lost all their
force when they were confronted with this new out-
pouring of divine grace and with the ideal of spiritual
perfection manifested in the lives of the saints. At the
same time, mysticism provided the antidote against
the rationalist and materialist tendencies in Western
society and enlarged the range of humanist culture by
a deeper and more sublime vision of spiritual reality,
which inspired poets and artists as well as theologians
and philosophers.

This too is an important factor in the Catholic revival, for the centres of the Catholic renaissance were
also the centres of artistic production, so that Catholic
art became one of the great channels for the diffusion
of Catholic culture. Thus it was that the new Baroque
art gave its name to the new culture, which became
the last great corporate expression of Western reli-

gious ideals. For the expansion of the Baroque culture was not merely an ideological movement, like the Enlightenment in the eighteenth century or the diffusion of nineteenth-century liberalism. It appealed to the heart as well as the head, and satisfied the emotional as well as the intellectual needs of human nature. And thus it was never merely the culture of an educated minority, since its religious ideals embodied in painting and architecture and music were the common heritage of the people as a whole and not the exclusive possession of a privileged class.

Owing to this character, the Baroque culture possessed exceptional powers of diffusion, even among peoples of alien traditions. On the whole, the modern expansion of European culture has been external and material. It has forced non-European peoples to recognise the superiority of Western techniques and Western scientific knowledge, but it has failed to bridge the spiritual gap between East and West. But within the sphere of the Baroque culture this was not so. Mexico and Peru and the Portuguese settlements in Asia assimilated the Baroque culture and produced their own local styles of Baroque art.

Thus by the seventeenth century, Europe and the New World were sharply divided between two apparently exclusive and antagonistic forms of culture. The Inquisition and the ecclesiastical control of books and ideas, on the one hand, and the penal laws against Catholicism, on the other, seemed to create an impassable barrier which divided Catholic and Protestant Europe and America into two closed worlds. How was it, under these circumstances, that the unity of Western culture survived? Why did not the Baroque culture of Catholic Europe and the Protestant culture of the North go their own ways and gradually become as mutually incomprehensible and as spiritually remote as Christendom and Islam?

The reason for this is to be found not so much in their common Christianity but in their common humanism. Both Catholic and Protestant Europe shared the same humanist education and the same classical literature, so that in spite of their spiritual separation they still maintained a certain community of intellectual life, which prevented the divergence between Catholics and Protestants from completely destroying the unity of Western culture.

8

Christianity in a Rationalist World

WHEN ONE CONSIDERS the progress of the Catholic revival in the sixteenth and seventeenth centuries and the apparent strength of religious faith and practice both in Catholic and Protestant Europe at that time, it is difficult to understand how European culture ever became secularised. In the middle of the seventeenth century, Europe, and America also, were divided between opposing forms of religion and culture—the Baroque culture of the South and the Protestant culture of the North—but both of them were intensely religious and sincerely Christian. Yet in a century and a half all this was changed, and Europe had become the Europe that we know. Religion had become a matter of private opinion, and the public life of the state and the intellectual community of culture had become almost entirely secularised.

This change was even more revolutionary than that of the sixteenth century, although it was less spectacular. For it was not the result of the French Revolution. The spiritual revolution had been already accomplished before there was any question of a political one.

How then are we to explain so vast a change? It was not, as is sometimes supposed, the direct consequence of the Reformation, nor was it due to the political or cultural victory of the Protestant North over the Catholic South. Yet on the other hand, it had no roots within the Baroque culture itself, for the latter had attained a state of social and political equilibrium which might have endured for centuries if it had not been disturbed from without. Spain and Italy were as impervious to Protestantism as Scotland and Scandinavia were impervious to Catholicism. And so too in America, there was no possibility of mutual influence or understanding between the Protestants of New England and the Catholics of New France or New Spain.

But to this rule there was one great exception. Throughout the decisive period in which the new Catholic and Protestant cultures were becoming stabilised, the largest national state in Western Europe remained divided between the two religions. The French religious wars of the sixteenth century had ended in a kind of stalemate by which the leader of the Protestants became the representative of French national unity by himself becoming a Catholic, while at the same time guaranteeing the rights and privileges of the Protestant minority. The Edict of Nantes not only secured freedom of conscience for the Protestants; it recognised their corporate existence as an organised society—a state within a state—with their own religious and political assemblies, their own fortresses and practically their own army.

Nevertheless, these very generous terms did not represent a Protestant triumph, but rather a victory for the party of conciliation, the so-called *Politiques*, who were prepared to sacrifice the principle of religious unity to the cause of national unity and who found their leader and representative in Henry IV himself, who repeatedly changed his religion according to political circumstances; once insincerely in order to save his life after the massacre of St. Bartholomew, and once with apparent sincerity at the moment when his conversion gave him the crown and defeated the European hegemony of Spanish Catholicism.

The work of Henry IV was carried on by Cardinal Richelieu, the classical representative of *raison d'état*, who did more than Gustavus Adolphus or Cromwell to defeat the international policy of the Counter-Reformation and to destroy the political unity of Catholic Europe. And this ruthless system of power-politics, which established the greatness of France on the ruin of central Europe, went hand in hand with an equally ruthless system of internal centralisation, which prepared the way for the absolute national monarchy of Louis XIV.

The effects of this revolution were not only political, they were also religious and cultural. The Gallican Church became more and more an autonomous ecclesiastical organism, and French culture became progressively detached from the Baroque culture of Catholic Europe. This new national culture still shared the ideals of the humanist culture, but instead of applying them, as the Baroque society had done, to the service of an international religion, it used culture, in the Augustan manner, as an instrument of government and empire. This ideal found its most complete expression in the palace of Versailles and the elaborate ritual of the court of Louis XIV.

The watch-words of the new culture were order and regularity, good taste and good sense, reason and clear ideas. Its spirit was essentially classical, but it was also rationalist, and this rationalist element gradually permeated the whole culture until it underminded and ultimately destroyed the authoritarian orthodoxy of the Gallican Church and the authoritarian absolutism of the French monarchy.

The source of this rationalist tradition was, however, quite distinct from that of the academic classical culture. For at the same time that Richelieu was reorganising the political and social order according to the principle of *raison d'état*, another great man, Descartes, was reorganising the world of thought according to abstract mathematical principles. He was essentially a revolutionary genius who made a clean sweep of authority and tradition and created a new intellectual world by the unaided powers of individual reason. And yet there was a profound affinity—and even a spiritual identity—between the rationalism of this most independent of thinkers who lived in voluntary exile in Holland and the spirit of the new classical culture. So that in spite of the opposition of all the vested interests in the Church and the universities, the Cartesian movement won the support not only of the scientific world but of all the leaders of French culture and French religion, with the partial exception of Pascal—whether they were Gallicans like Bossuet, Jansenists like Arnauld and Nicole, or mystics like Malebranche.

Nor was this development confined to Catholic Europe, for a parallel movement was taking place in England, which destroyed the religious unity of Protestant culture and prepared the way for its secularisation. In England as in France, the nation had gone through a period of civil and religious strife which had made men look for some principle of unity that stood outside the field of theological controversy. As the religious wars in France had discredited both the Huguenots and the Catholic League, so the English Civil War had discredited the intransigence both of the Puritans and of their Episcopalian opponents. But in England, unlike France, the monarchy itself had been defeated. Strafford, who might have been the English Richelieu, had lost his head. So too had Charles I, and though the act of regicide had shocked the popular conscience, it dealt a blow to the doctrine of divine right from which the English monarchy never entirely recovered. Henceforth the English people sought a middle way, which it found, after a very unrevolutionary Revolution, in a regime of limited monarchy and limited religious toleration combined with unlimited individualism and freedom of thought.

This English solution was exactly the opposite to that of the French, and the two nations were involved for twenty-seven years in almost continuous war. Yet in spite of their national and political differences, both English and French culture show a similar reaction against mysticism and religious "enthusiasm" and a similar trend towards science and rationalism.

It is true that there is a sharp contrast between the geometrical reason of Descartes and the empirical common sense of Locke, which reflects the difference in spirit of the two cultures. Nevertheless, these two schools of thought met and mingled with one another in the culture of the Enlightenment. The philosophy of Voltaire and the Encyclopaedists was that of Locke rather than of Descartes. Yet the driving force behind it is still the Cartesian rationalism, with its sublime confidence in the infallibility of reason, its dissolvent criticism of received beliefs and traditions, and its determination "never to accept anything for true which I did not clearly know to be such."

Thus the spiritual barriers which divided the two post-Reformation cultures of Catholic and Protestant Europe were broken down, not by the victory of one over the other but by the weakening of religious convictions before the self-confident, superficial rationalism of the new lay intelligentsia.

9

The Age of Revolution

THE ORIGINS OF MODERN DEMOCRACY are so closely
bound up with the history of liberalism that it is a
matter of considerable difficulty to disentangle them
and to distinguish their distinctive contributions to the
common political tradition of modern Western culture. For this question also involves that of the relation between the three revolutions, the English, the
American, and the French, which transformed the
Europe of the *ancien régime,* with its absolute monarchies and state churches, into the modern world.
Now all these three revolutions were liberal revolutions, and all of them were political expressions of the
movement of the European enlightenment in its successive phases. But this movement was not originally
a democratic one, and it was only in the second half
of the eighteenth century that the democratic ideal
was clearly formulated. On the continent of Europe
the revolution of ideas preceded the political and economic revolutions by half a century, and the revolution of ideas was not in any sense of the word a
democratic movement; it was the work of a small minority of men of letters who looked to the nobles and
the princes of Europe rather than to the common people, and whose ideal of government was a benevolent
and enlightened absolutism, like that of Frederick the
Great or the Empress Catherine of Russia. There was
an immense gulf between the ideas of Voltaire and
Turgot, of Diderot and D'Alembert, and the opinions

of the average man. The liberalism of the philosophers was a hothouse growth which could not be easily acclimatised to the open air of the fields and the marketplace.

Even in France, which was the most unified continental state, the influence of the feudal past still made itself felt in the diversity of provincial institutions, each of which had its own economic life only remotely affected by the fashions and opinions of the great world. The Church still maintained its power over men's minds, and its festivals and pilgrimages played a great part in the life of the people. There was a deep undercurrent of religious life in the Age of Enlightenment, which is nonetheless important for being ignored by the philosophers and men of letters. The age of Voltaire and Bolingbroke and Frederick the Great was also the age of Wesley and Tersteegen and St. Paul of the Cross. It is true that this movement is most evident in the Protestant world, with the Moravians and Pietists in Germany, the Methodists in England, and the Great Awakening in America, but it was by no means lacking in Catholic Europe during the eighteenth century, as we see from the foundation of the new missionary orders in Italy, the building of great baroque monasteries and pilgrimage churches such as Wies, Vierzehnheiligen, Melk, and Neresheim in Germany and Austria, and the vitality of popular religious life. Nothing shows the divorce between the bourgeois rationalism of the Enlightenment and the religious traditions of popular culture better than the figure of the beggar saint Benedict Joseph Labre (1748–83), who lived the life of a mediaeval ascetic and miracle worker in the age of Gibbon and Adam Smith.

But in spite of its internal resources, the Church, because of its close alliance with the state, was rendered exceptionally vulnerable to any attack from

above. Consequently, the substitution of the enlightened despotism of Joseph II and Choiseul and Charles
III of Spain for the Catholic absolutism of the Baroque
period deprived the Church of its traditional method
of social action, and neutralised its activities for two
generations. The situation was ripe for the rise of a
new spiritual force which would fill the void created
by the temporary breakdown of Catholic action and
give an outlet to the religious instincts that found no
satisfaction in the rational culture of the Enlightenment, for the Enlightenment had swept and gar-
nished the Western mind without bringing anything
to take the place of the religion that it had destroyed.
The typical man of the age, like Voltaire or Frederick the Great or Horace Walpole, was the final
product of an aristocratic humanist culture. He had
all the gifts that a purely intellectual culture could
bestow, but the hard-polished surface of his mind reflected light without warmth. If the liberal ideas of
the Enlightenment were to penetrate beyond the
limited world of the privileged classes and change the
thought and the life of the people, they had to make
an appeal to psychological forces that lay beneath
the surface of rational consciousness. They had to be
transformed from a philosophy into a religion, to cease
to be mere ideas and to become articles of faith.

This reinterpretation of liberalism in religious terms
was the work of Jean-Jacques Rousseau, who thus became the founder and prophet of a new faith—the
religion of democracy. In 1749, as he walked to Vin-
cennes on a hot summer afternoon to visit Diderot,
he experienced a sudden flash of inspiration which
revealed to him his true mission and converted him
from an unsuccessful man of letters into the prophet
of a new gospel. He saw that all the ills of man and
all the evils of society were due not to man's own sin
or ignorance but to social injustice and the corruptions

of an artifical civilisation. If man could return to nature and follow the divinely inspired instincts of his own heart, all would be well. The savage child of nature was happier than the spoiled child of civilisation, and the simple faith of the peasant wiser than all the science of the philosophers. He pleads the cause of the individual against society, the poor against the rich, and the people against the privileged classes, the cause of love against convention and of intuition and religious sentiment against the philosophers and the libertines.

It is impossible to exaggerate the effect of Rousseau's teaching on his generation. It came into the brilliant artificial world of the Enlightenment like a warm west wind from the fields into a lighted salon, extinguishing the tapers and filling the air with the scent of damp earth and rain-soaked vegetation. No wonder that the aged Voltaire gnashed his teeth in rage at the daring of this madman and charlatan, who was a traitor to the philosophic cause and who divided the forces of progress. For it was no longer to Voltaire but to Rousseau that the new generation turned for guidance and inspiration. He was the spiritual father of the makers of the new age, and the source of that spirit of revolutionary idealism which finds expression not only in liberalism but in socialism and anarchism as well. It was he who first fired men's minds with the ideal of democracy not as a mere system of government but as a new way of life, a vision of social justice and fraternity which is nothing else than the kingdom of God on earth. It is true that Rousseau himself was not a revolutionary in the ordinary sense. The revolution that he preached was not a political or an economic one but a spiritual one, and he fully realised the practical danger of any sudden disturbance of the existing order. But these cautious reservations did little to lessen the effect of his tremendous denunciation of the inequality and injustice of the existing social order. Although he was no socialist, he had no sympathy with the ideals of the capitalist economy; and though he admired the freedom and republican simplicity of Swiss Protestant society, he denounced its spirit of bourgeois individualism.

Rousseau himself had no wish to apply his principles to a large, highly centralised state like eighteenth-century France. He believed that political equality was unattainable unless economic conditions were favourable to social equality, and that democratic institutions were only suitable to small states whose citizens could participate directly in public life and government, such as the Swiss peasant cantons or the city-states of antiquity.

But while his eyes were turned to the past, towards an idealised picture of Sparta and Rome, a democratic state was actually coming into existence in the New World across the Atlantic, and there is a curious analogy between the philosophical abstractions of Rousseau's theory of democracy and the historical realities of American democracy. A century and a half before the *Social Contract* was written, the little band of Puritan exiles who landed on the virgin soil of New England signed a real Social Compact by which they constituted themselves a "civil body politic" and promised their individual obedience to the general will. Moreover, under the surface the Puritan tradition still retained its power and vitality, as we see from the Great Awakening of 1740 and the development of sectarian activity that followed it. It was in the eighteenth century that American Puritanism produced its greatest religious teacher, Jonathan Edwards; and about the same time the diary and writings of the Quaker John Woolman (1720–72) show that the religion of the people sometimes possessed a strain of social idealism no less high and even more profound than that of the liberal Enlightenment. Woolman denounces social injustice and corruption no less strongly than Rousseau, but instead of confining himself to generalities, he spent his life working against the iniquities of slavery and the acquisitive spirit that was characteristic of the new bourgeois society.

It is true that as the movement of revolt became politically self-conscious, the leadership was inevitably taken by the non-democratic elements, lawyers, politicians, and men of wealth and position like Washington and the Lees. But the driving force behind the movement was a democratic one, and even among the leaders there were representatives of the Enlightenment, like Franklin in Pennsylvania and Jefferson in Virginia, through whom the democratic principles implicit in the American Revolution finally received their classical formulation in the Declaration of Independence. For the progress of the controversy itself had forced the lawyers and politicians to abandon the narrow ground of constitutional precedent and to fall back on the fundamental dogmas of the new religion. Owing to the influence of Paine, Jefferson, and Franklin, the American cause became identified in the eyes of the world with this revolutionary idealism, and the conflict was transformed from a local quarrel concerning taxation and colonial rights into a crusade for the rights of man and the cause of humanity.

Nowhere did it find more wholehearted acceptance than in France, where the ground had been prepared by the work of Rousseau and the Enlightenment and where the cause of American independence had the supreme good fortune to have a representative of the genius of Benjamin Franklin, who possessed just that combination of cosmopolitan culture with personal originality and the exotic flavour of American democracy which appealed to the romantic liberalism of the age of Louis XVI, and his relations with philosophers and physiocrats and freemasons admitted him to the inner circle of French aristocratic society. He concealed the astuteness and finesse of a born diplomat under the legendary figure of patriarchal virtue and democratic simplicity, so that he was able to direct the vague idealism of philosophic liberalism towards concrete political ends. In this way the French intelligentsia came to see in America the realisation of Rouseau's ideal of a state and a social order based on natural principles and inspired by a spirit of fraternity and equality. They forgot the mob law, the tarrings and featherings, and the ruthless proscription of minorities by which New England democracy had vindicated the rights of man. They forgot that the liberal culture and the spacious life of Monticello and Mount Vernon were only rendered possible by the existence of negro slavery. They saw only the generous idealism of a Jefferson, the republican virtue of a Washington, and the mellow wisdom of Franklin.

Thus the myth of the American Revolution acquired definite shape in France long before the United States themselves had acquired political form, and exerted a far stronger influence than the latter on public opinion and the development of democratic ideals in France. In the eyes of Turgot and Mably and Reynal, of Brissot and Condorcet and Lafayette, the United States owed their importance not to what they actually were but to what they might become, and still more to what humanity might become by following their example.

In the victory of the American Revolution, European liberals saw the justification of their ideals and the realisation of their hopes. It turned the current of the Enlightenment in a political direction and infused a revolutionary purpose into the democratic idealism of Rousseau. The young nobles, like Lafayette, who returned from America with the prestige of heroes and apostles; the young bourgeois, like Brissot de Warville, who looked to America as the promised land of liberty and democratic virtue, became the centre of a new patriotic movement which demanded the reform of the French government based on the democratic principle of the rights of men and equal citizenship.

At the same time that the revolutionary criticism of the Enlightenment had undermined the religious foundations of the traditional order, the functional basis was being destroyed by economic change. The new financial system and the new capitalist economy were irreconcilable with the hierarchic and authoritative principles of the *ancien régime*. The nobility had ceased to be the natural leaders of the nation, whose privileges were the reward of their service to the state, as was still the case with the Prussian officer caste. It had preserved its caste spirit and its feudal privileges, while it had lost that control over local administration and agriculture which gave the English aristocracy its power and social prestige. It had become merely a rich leisure class, whose chief social function was to provide a brilliant and expressive setting for the royal court. But since the heavy Baroque group of Versailles was no longer in fashion, even this function had become a sinecure, and in the eyes of public opinion, the nobles were regarded as social parasites who sucked the life blood of the peasantry and battened on the resources of a discredited and bankrupt state. Above all, they had lost faith in themselves. With the exception of a few eccentrics like the Marquis de Mirabeau and the old guard of zealous Catholics, which had lost its leaders with the dissolution of the Jesuits and the death of Louis XV's eldest son and his pious wife, the nobles were in the forefront of the movement of Enlightenment. They ridiculed the Gothic barbarism of the old order. They applauded the anti-clerical

propaganda of the philosophers, the democratic senti-
ments of Rousseau and Beaumarchais, and the biting
satire of Chamfort. As Ségur wrote in an often quoted
passage, "They trod lightly on a carpet of flowers towards the abyss." And when the crash came, some of
the ablest and the most exalted of them—Talley-
rand, the Bishop of Autun; Hérault de Séchelles, the
Comte de St. Simon; even Philip of Orleans, the first of
the princes of the blood—were on the side of the Revolution and assisted in the work of destruction. It was
only in the more remote provinces, where the nobility
had preserved its traditional relations with the land
and the peasants and where the influence of the Enlightenment was non-existent, that they put up a formidable resistance to the progress of revolution. Elsewhere, the proudest and most ancient aristocracy in
Europe, which had its roots deep in history, fell like a
rotten apple at the first blast of the storm, and
resigned its rights and privileges almost without a
struggle.

Behind the liberal aristocrats and lawyers who
formed the majority of the States General, there lay
the vast anonymous power that had made the monarchy and had been in turn shaped by it, and now it
was to make the Revolution. To the liberal idealists—
to men like Lafayette and Clermont Tonnerre, to the
Abbé Fauchet and the orators of the Gironde—the
Revolution meant the realisation of the ideals of the
Enlightenment, liberty and toleration, the rights of
men, and the religion of humanity. They did not see
that they were on the edge of a precipice and that the
world they knew was about to be swallowed up in a
tempest of change which would destroy both them
and their ideals. "Woe unto you who desire the day of
the Lord. It is darkness and not light. As if a man did
flee from a lion and a bear met him, or went into the
house and leaned his hand upon the well and a ser-

pent bit him"; they were a doomed generation, fated to perish at first by ones and twos, and then by scores and hundreds and thousands, on the scaffold, in the streets, and on the battlefield. For as the Revolution advanced, it gradually revealed the naked reality that had been veiled by the antiquated trappings of royalty and tradition—the General Will—and it was not the benevolent abstraction which the disciples of Rousseau had worshipped but a fierce will to power which destroyed every man and institution that stood in its way. As de Maistre wrote, the will of the people was a battering ram, with twenty million men behind it.

Nevertheless, it would be a great mistake to ignore or minimise the importance of the intellectual factor in the Revolution, as many modern historians have done, in reaction to the idealist conceptions of Louis Blanc and Lamartine and Michelet. If we are to deny the influence of liberalism on the French Revolution, we should have to deny the influence of communism on the Revolution in Russia. In fact, the movement of ideas was wider and deeper in France than in Russia and had a far greater influence on the course of events. At every stage of the Revolution, from the Assembly of the Notables in 1787 down to the fall of Robespierre in 1794, the battle of ideas decided the fall of parties and statesmen, and it was carried on not only in the National Assembly and in the meetings of the Clubs and Districts, but in the press, the streets, and the cafés.

So the French Revolution falls into place as part of a world revolution which would restore to mankind the original rights of which it had been robbed at the very dawn of history by the tyranny of kings and priests. "Political popery, like the ecclesiastical popery of old, has had its day and is hastening to its exit. The ragged relic and the antiquated precedent, the monk and the monarch, will moulder together." (*Rights of Man,* Part IV.)

This is the same faith which inspired the speculative Freemasonry of the eighteenth century and that expresses itself in a mystical form in the early prophecies of William Blake. The Declaration of the Rights of Man made it the official creed of the French Revolution and gave the political and economic discontent of the French people a philosophical or rather theological basis on which a new social order could be based.

It is this ideological background which gave the French Revolution its spiritual force and its international significance. Without it, the Revolution might have been nothing more than a new Fronde. With it, it changed the world.

The men who did so much to bring the new gospel out of the *coulisses* of the salons and the masonic lodges onto the stage of history had no idea where their ideals would lead. Their generous illusions blinded them to the dangers in their path, and they thought that the Revolution was accomplished when it had hardly begun. But nonetheless, they played an essential part in the revolutionary drama. Lafayette, "the hero of two worlds," on his white horse posing as a French Washington, seems an absurd or pathetic figure (Cromwell-Grandison, as Mirabeau said) in comparison with the men who were to make history, such as Mirabeau, Danton, and Bonaparte. Yet had it not been for Lafayette, these might never have had the chance to play their part. To the French bourgeoisie in the opening years of the Revolution, Mirabeau and Danton seemed sinister figures who were ready to play the part of a Cataline or a Clodius. And as Mirabeau was not trusted by the bourgeoisie, so neither did he trust the people. He realised the meaning of revolution and the meaning of authority, but he cared nothing for the metaphysical abstractions of the Declaration of

Rights or the moral principles which inspired the liberal idealism of the moderate reformers no less than the Puritan fanaticism of Robespierre and Saint-Just. Lafayette, on the other hand, was a thoroughly respectable person, a man of high character and high principles, a good liberal and a good deist but no enemy of property and religion. And so the bourgeoisie were ready to fall in and march behind his famous white horse in defence of the cause of liberalism against both the forces of disorder and the forces of reaction.

But if it was a time of freedom and hope, it was also a time of illusion. The Constituent Assembly went to work in a mood of boundless optimism without any regard for the facts of history or the limitations of time and place, in the spirit of their arch-theorist Sieyès, who said that the so-called truths of history were as unreal as the so-called truths of religion. When their work was finished, Cerutti declared that they had destroyed fourteen centuries of abuses in three years, that the Constitution they had made would endure for centuries, and that their names would be blessed by future generations. Yet before many months had elapsed, their work was undone and their leaders were executed, imprisoned, or in exile. They had destroyed what they could not replace and called up forces that they could neither understand nor control. For the liberal aristocracy and bourgeoisie were not the people, and in some respects they were further from the people than the nobles and clergy who remained faithful to the old order. On the one hand, there were the vast inarticulate masses of the peasantry who were ready to burn the castles of the nobles but who were often equally ready to fight with desperate resolution for their religion. On the other hand, there was the people of the communes, above all the Commune of Paris. For Paris was still

at heart the old city of the League, and it needed no
teaching from America or England to learn the lesson
of Revolution. It remembered the night of St. Bartholomew and the killing of Henry III, and its crowds ral-
lied as readily to the preaching of the new Cordeliers
and the new Jacobins as to that of their Catholic predecessors who led the mob against the Huguenots and
held the city for five days against Henry of Navarre.
Already in the days of July the people of Paris had asserted their power in unequivocal fashion and had
regained their liberty by force of arms. Henceforward
the people of Paris were an independent power,
and a power which possessed far more political self-
consciousness and revolutionary will than the people
whose representatives sat in the National Assembly. It
is true that in the first years of the Revolution the mu-
nicipality was still in the hands of the bourgeoisie,
but this was not the case with the assemblies of the districts and sections, which were the real centres of political action. Here was democracy in action; not the
representative democracy of the liberal constitutionalism, but the direct democracy of the mediaeval communes and the Greek city-states—the democracy of
which Rousseau and Mably had dreamed. It was this
new and terrible power which was to undo the work
of the aristocratic liberals and remake the Revolution,
and already in the days of the Constituent Assembly it
had found its leader in Danton and its philosopher and
teacher in Marat. For the venomous and diseased little
Swiss doctor, who was regarded as either a criminal
or a lunatic by the respectable politicians of the Assembly, saw more clearly than they the fundamental
issues of the Revolution and the bloody road that it
was to travel. From the first he denounced the new
constitution as the work of a privileged class, and he
marvelled at the way in which the workers had risked
their lives to destroy the Bastille, which was not their

prison but that of their oppressors. He even warned the Assembly that if the bourgeoisie rejected the political rights of the workers on the ground of their poverty, they would find a remedy in the assertion of their economic rights to share in the possessions of the rich. "Where is the country of the poor?" he writes in November 1789, in reference to the question of conscription. "Everywhere condemned to serve, if they are not under the yoke of a master, they are under that of their fellow-citizens, and whatever revolution may come, their eternal lot is servitude, poverty, and oppression. What can they owe to a state which has done nothing, nothing but secure their misery and tighten their chains? They owe it nothing but hatred and malediction."

This is very different from the optimistic liberal idealism which was the prevailing spirit in 1789-90. In fact, Marat was anything but a liberal. From the first he had preached the gospel of terror, and his political ideal was a popular dictatorship rather than any kind of liberal constitutionalism. But he understood the mind of the people better than Lafayette and the makers of the Constitution of 1791, and it was not liberalism but his creed of revolutionary democracy which became the creed of the Commune, the Jacobins, and the Republic in the decisive years that followed.

10

Christianity and the Modern World:
The Ideal of Democracy

OF ALL THE ELEMENTS of the European tradition, transformed so profoundly in the past hundred years, democracy is the one that is most difficult to appreciate in an objective and impartial spirit. It has been surrounded by an atmosphere of loose thinking, which has obscured its true nature and has degraded it until it has become an empty catchword that covers every kind of political sentimentality and falsehood.

And yet it stands, nonetheless, for an element in European life that is of permanent value and importance. It is the most characteristic expression of European political ideals, and if we attempt to separate it from its historical roots in European culture and to identify it with an abstract ideal that had its first conception in the mind of Rousseau, we shall inevitably misunderstand both democracy and Europe. There are two mistaken views of democracy, both of which have caused infinite misunderstandings in the past and which even today are not altogether extinct. One of these regards democracy as a crude destructive force that cares nothing for the finer values of civilised life, that is indifferent to culture and scientific knowledge, and seeks only to satisfy the vanity and greed of the masses. This is the fallacy of the reactionaries. And, on the other hand, there is the ideal of democracy that is founded on false belief in the perfectibility of human nature. It regards all the evils of society as due to the misdeeds of kings and governments and believes that if once the power is put into the hands of the common people, everything will go well, everyone will be happy, and the world will be transformed into a Utopia.

In reality, democracy is neither the enemy of culture nor a cure for all the ills of humanity. It is simply the culmination of the old European tradition of social and political freedom that has always been one of the essential elements in Western culture.

The basis of democracy is the idea of public law and civic rights which Europe inherited from Greece and Rome and which is almost absent in oriental societies, however advanced they may be in civilisation. Consequently, the fundamental opposition is not that between democracy and aristocracy, but that between citizenship and despotism. In the East the individual is nothing and the state is everything. It is a divine power —the Shadow of God on Earth, as the Sultan of Turkey used to call himself—and any claim to independent rights against that power on the part of the individual is inconceivable.

But in the West a man has his rights, even against the state. The whole history of Europe is the story of the vindication of these rights and the affirmation of human freedom, whether by classes or communities or individuals, from the English barons at Runnymede, the free cities of the Middle Ages, the Swiss peasants, and the English House of Commons, down to the final affirmation of the Rights of Man by the fathers of the United States and the founders of the French Republic. It was inevitable that these rights should begin as the rights of a privileged class and gradually be extended to the rest of the community, for unfortunately, they are not the natural birthright of the human race, as the early Liberals used to believe. They are the culmination of a long process of social development—the flower of an advanced civilisation.

The free man who was the ideal of the eighteenth-century democrats was not a mere nobody, he was an ideal type—no less ideal than the mediaeval knight or the Renaissance gentleman, and in the same line of descent. In fact, the ideal was first launched by aristocrats of the type of Alfieri and Mirabeau, and the English Whigs and the Virginian planters. The famous lines of Burns, "The rank is but the guinea stamp, a man's a man for a' that," do not mean that *quality* doesn't matter; on the contrary, they mean that quality is so important that it far outweighs the conventional labels that society has substituted for it.

Thus, paradoxical as it may appear, the democratic ideal has its origin in the aristocratic principle. In fact, Western democracy is essentially *aristocracy for all*. It was just the same with the Greeks. Greek democracy was not a proletariat; it had its origin in the extension to the majority of the civic rights that had originally been the jealously guarded privilege of a small body of patricians. Athens, the greatest of Greek democracies, was in reality one of the most aristocratic communities that has ever existed.

And this ideal, whether ancient Greek or modern European, has nothing in common with the Oriental ideal of the absolute state. The free man has no place in the latter; it is the impersonal power of the community, whether embodied in an absolute monarch or a priesthood or a democracy, that is all in all. Of course, this ideal is also capable of acquiring a popular form. The absolute state may represent the interests of the whole people rather than of a privileged class; it may even, as in Communist Russia, become the instrument of a dictatorship of the proletariat. But this does not make it democratic in the Western sense. Bolshevism is a popular version of Tsarism, just as democracy is aristocracy for all. The essential note of democracy is the recognition of the dignity and the rights of the individual citizen. And thus it is very closely associated with the traditions of humanism and of humanitarianism. In fact, apart from humanitarianism, democracy becomes an empty and meaningless form. The political rights of democracy presuppose the moral rights of humanity, and if the humanitarian movement had not inspired Western society with an enthusiasm for social justice and for the cause of the weak and oppressed, modern democracy would never have come into existence.

But in spite of the superiority of the democratic ideal—at least to the Western mind—we must admit that it is much harder to realise than the ideal of the absolute state. The despotic regime is the one that has succeeded, at least in the past. And even today, the vast and rapid advance of democracy should not blind us to the fact that the opposite ideal is still vigorous and that in some respects it is once more gaining ground at the expense of democracy.

The chief cause of this is not political but economic: the problem of economic equality is the real crux of democracy. You can give nominal political rights to every citizen without much difficulty, but when you attempt to put into practice the full programme of real democracy—that is to say, to give every citizen equal opportunities of happiness and an equal share in the good things of life—you are faced with a serious dilemma. Complete economic equality seems attainable only by state socialism, and any thorough-going system of socialism seems to involve, as in Russia, the omnipotence of the state and all the dangers of a return to despotism and the negation of individual rights which that implies. The democratic ideal in its economic aspect is neither that of pure individualism nor that of pure state socialism; it is the ideal of a free co-operative economy in which every man has control over his own life and possesses an economic foundation for his social liberty. In other words, economic democracy means capitalism for all: it means an extension of the rights of property to every citizen rather than the abolition of private property in the interests of the state. It is inconsistent with the individualistic society in which a small number of very rich men control the lives of the great masses of their fellow citizens; but it is also inconsistent with the communist society in which the economic life of the individual is even more completely controlled by the machinery of an all-powerful state.

We must, in fact, recognise (and it is very seldom recognised) that the idea of equality is not necessarily or exclusively democratic. Pure democracy leads to equality, but so does pure despotism. And as a matter of fact, it is easier to attain the negative ideal of a dead level of equality in equal servitude than to achieve the positive ideal of equality in freedom and fulness of life.

But, as I have said, democracy is aristocracy for all; it is levelling up, not levelling down. The true democrat does not wish to attain equality by lowering the cultural standard of society and by reducing everyone to a drab uniformity of existence. He desires the richest and fullest life that is possible. In the communist Utopia, there is no room for a Wordsworth or a Beethoven. The artist, no less than the engineer or the bureaucrat, is the servant of the economic machine, and his highest aim is to be a kind of publicity-agent for the communist state. But in the democratic Utopia, the state would be the servant and not the absolute master of the human personality, and the development of individual genius would be encouraged as much as possible, for one Mozart adds more to the real wealth of society than a hundred millionaires or political organisers.

All that the democrat demands in the name of equality is that no man shall be debarred by economic or social privileges from developing his own genius or from enjoying the results of the genius of others.

Every society must have its élite; the only question is what kind of an élite it desires to have. In a despotic society the élite are the picked servants of the state, like the Communist Party in Russia, the later Roman bureaucracy, or the priests and officials of the old Oriental despotism. We find the extreme development of this ideal in those oriental states, like mediaeval Egypt or Turkey under the Ottoman Sultans, in which the country was governed by picked slaves and members of the subject races who owed everything to the sovereign power and had no rights of their own. But in the civic type of society, whether it is a democracy or an aristocracy, the élite are not bound to the service of the state. They are free men with the right to live their own life and develop their own personalities under the most advantageous conditions.

The only difference between the aristocracy and the democracy is that in the one case the élite forms a hereditary class which tends to monopolise political power and social privilege, while in the other they are the leaders of their fellow citizens, who set the standard of culture for the rest of the community and use their opportunities for the enrichment of the common social life.

This was the secret of the achievements of Greek democracy. The élite at Athens had no monopoly of political power, but they possessed a cultural leadership. Their aristocrats, like Pericles, were great democratic leaders, and their rich men were expected to use their wealth to provide for the public amusements of the citizens. And thus the brilliant achievements of Greek art and literature were not the selfish monopoly of the few, but the common posses-

sion of the whole body of citizens; as we see, above
all, in the case of the Greek drama, perhaps the greatest civic art that has ever existed.

It may be objected that this is not real democracy,
and that the Athenians would have done better to
abolish their élite and to use their wealth for the increase of the ordinary citizen's income. But though it
is true that you cannot enjoy the higher goods of culture if you have not enough to eat, it is also true that
you cannot get twice as much culture by doubling the
amount you eat. The truly rich society is not the one
that goes on piling up economic wealth as an end in
itself, but the one that uses its wealth as the foundation on which to build a rich and many-sided culture. From this point of view, a country like ancient
Greece, in which hardly anybody could afford more
than one good meal a day, was richer than the United
States at the height of its prosperity.

The great fault of modern democracy—a fault that
is common to the capitalist and the socialist—is that
it accepts economic wealth as the end of society and
the standard of personal happiness. We have made
the increase of wealth the one criterion of social improvement, and consequently our aristocracy is an
aristocracy of money-makers, and our democratic
ideal is mainly an ideal of more money for everyone.
But the standard of life is really not an economic but
a vital thing; it is a question of how you live rather
than how much you live on. Just as a man who buys
one's house does not buy one's family and friends and
interests—all the things that made up the life that was
lived in that house—so two men may possess the same
money income and yet have totally different standards of life.

Even if we could guarantee every unemployed
person a reasonable income, we should not have
solved the vital problem of unemployment, which is

the problem of social maladjustment. St. Francis of Assisi possessed no income at all, and his material standard of life was below that of a modern tramp. But for all that, he was infinitely better off than the modern unemployed, because he had achieved a complete measure of social adjustment. To take a less extreme instance, during the happiest and most productive part of his life, Wordsworth had, I believe, an income of about £70 a year, and he would have been no better off with a million, because he had found the way of life that suited him.

The great curse of our modern society is not so much lack of money as the fact that the lack of money condemns a man to a squalid and incomplete existence. But even if he has money, and a great deal of it, he is still in danger of leading an incomplete and cramped life, because our whole social order is directed to economic instead of spiritual ends. The economic view of life regards money as equivalent to satisfaction. Get money, and if you get enough of it you will get everything else that is worth having. The Christian view of life, on the other hand, puts economic things in the second place. First seek the kingdom of God, and everything else will be added to you. And this is not so absurd as it sounds, for we have only to think for a moment to realise that the ills of modern society do not spring from poverty; in fact, society today is probably richer in material wealth than any society that has ever existed. What we are suffering from is lack of social adjustment and the failure to subordinate material and economic goods to human and spiritual ones.

11

Christianity and Communism

THE CONFLICT between Christianity and Marxism—between the Catholic Church and the Communist party—is the vital issue of our time. It is not a conflict of rival economic systems, like the conflict between Socialism and Capitalism, or of rival political ideals —as with parliamentarism and Fascism. It is a conflict of rival philosophies and of rival doctrines regarding the very nature of man and society.

The importance of this conflict was by no means clearly realised by the founders of Communism themselves. Catholicism was something quite outside the orbit of Marx's thought. He seems to have regarded it, not as a dangerous rival, but as a dying force which belonged essentially to the past. In his historical theory, Catholicism is bound up with feudalism: it is the ideological reflection of feudal society, and consequently it had little significance for the modern world, save in a few backward regions where the social structure was that of a past age. The real enemy in Marx's eyes was not Catholicism or Christianity, but the power that had, so Marx believed, already dethroned God and set up a purely secular culture and new secular standards of value—the power of Capitalism.

In Marx's view, the whole structure of society is determined by economic production, and consequently it is justifiable to define a state of society by its economic character. But it may also be defined sociologically by its characteristic social type, and this is what Marx does when he speaks of bourgeois society and bourgeois civilisation, as indeed is his usual practice.

Finally, it is possible to define a state of society ideologically by its characteristic ideas and system of thought. For example, Capitalist and bourgeois society is characterised by the doctrines of free trade and economic individualism, and by the ideals of progress, freedom of thought, and democratic institutions—in a word, by Liberalism.

Now, Marx himself did not regard ideologies as of prime importance, since they were to him merely the theoretical reflection of social realities which are primarily economic and material. But he fully realises —no thinker more so—that ideology and sociology are indissolubly linked, that is, that capitalism, bourgeois society, and Liberalism are *three aspects of the same social reality*. If, however, we interpret history in a more spiritual fashion than that of Marx, we shall tend to emphasise the importance of this ideological, or we may rather say, spiritual, factor. And I should myself be inclined to regard liberalism, for example, as one of the creative forces in the formation of the new order, and not merely as a reflection of that order in men's minds.

In any case, it is important to remember the existence of this element in connection with capitalism. For not only socialists, but social reformers of all kinds, including Catholics, are only too apt to treat capitalism as a kind of abstract bogy which is responsible for all our ills, and not to remember that Capitalism is nothing else but *economic Liberalism*, and that it has a very close relationship not only with political Liberalism, but also with liberal philosophy and liberal idealism. Very few English Socialists seem to realise this, but Marx and Engels and Lenin say it

clearly enough, and that is why they devoted so much
of their time to philosophical controversy and why
they regarded Socialist idealists as a greater danger to
the true Communist faith than any number of open reactionaries and even Christians.

Thus the issue raised by Communism is a three-
sided one that involves politics no less than economics, and philosophy and religion even more than
politics. And the conflict is also a three-cornered one.
It is not a straight fight between Communism and
Catholicism or between Communism and Capitalism.
It is a fight of each against all.

First, Liberalism, following in the steps of Protestantism, revolted against Catholicism, and its victory
brought in the secularised culture of bourgeois Capitalism. And now Communism has risen against this
culture and seeks to destroy it, while at the same time
retaining all and more than all of its secular spirit and
its hostility to the Catholic tradition. But though Communism is the enemy of both Catholicism and Capitalism, it stands far nearer to Capitalism than to
Catholicism.

For Marx had a genuine admiration for the achievements of bourgeois and capitalist civilisation. He
admired its material achievement and power, its conquest of the world by machinery and economic organisation. He appreciated still more its revolutionary
achievement: its breaking down of the old social
forms and institutions, its revolt against religious tradition, and its thoroughgoing secularisation of life. In
all these respects Marx regarded Communism as
destined to carry on the capitalist or bourgeois tradition, and Capitalism as a first step towards the new
system of economic world organisation. But on the
other hand, Marx was bitterly hostile to the ideological
side of the bourgeois culture—that is to say, to the
liberal ideals which the bourgeois themselves re-

garded as the real justification of their material achievement. All these ideals of Freedom, parliamentary democracy, humanitarianism, and the rest, Marx regarded as nothing but shams, plastered onto the front of society in order to hide the naked reality of exploitation and class interest.

Of course, Marx did not consciously blame the bourgeois for being governed by class interest, for class interest is, according to the Marxian theory, the supreme dynamic force in social life. The bourgeois can no more help exploiting the proletariat than the wolf can help eating the lamb, the only difference being that the proletarian lamb is being transformed by the dialectic of history into a Communist wolf that will in turn devour the bourgeois lamb. What aroused Marx's indignation was the hypocrisy of the bourgeois culture, which refused to recognise these facts and put up a smoke screen of liberal idealism to hide them.

We, however, as Christians, may well take a diametrically opposite view of all this development. We may condemn the ruthless subordination of human life to economic ends and the wholesale secularisation of culture as evil; and we may look on the faith of the nineteenth century in liberal ideals, in freedom and justice and humanity and progress as a redeeming trait in the harsh and unlovely features of bourgeois civilisation. This faith was no sign of conscious hypocrisy—indeed, men like Adam Smith and John Stuart Mill were just as sincere as any idealists who have ever lived.

On the other hand, we may well agree with Marx in his belief that it is the material element in bourgeois culture that is the permanent one and that the idealist liberal element is incapable of maintaining itself by its own inherent resources. For European liberalism is a temporary phenomenon which belongs to the phase of transition between a Christian culture and one that is completely secularised. European culture had already ceased to be Christian in the eighteenth century, but it still retained the inherited moral standards and values of a Christian civilisation. And so it attempted to erect these standards into an independent system by providing a rational philosophical justification for them. This was the Liberal idealism that was the faith of the nineteenth century—not a religious faith, but a quasi-religious substitute for one.

But as Liberalism did not create these moral ideals, so, too, it cannot preserve them. It lives on the spiritual capital that it has inherited from Christian civilisation, and as this is exhausted, something else must come to take its place. Once society is launched on the path of secularisation, it cannot stop in the halfway house of Liberalism; it must go on to the bitter end, whether that end be Communism or some alternative type of "totalitarian" secularism.

Here Marx and Engels were right, but our agreement with their judgment of facts only emphasises our opposition to them on the vital question of values. Marxism condemns in Liberalism just the element that we can approve, namely, its partial acceptance of Christian moral standards: and it approves just what we condemn, that is to say, the secularisation of life and the entire subordination of man to economic ends. This is the vital issue of Marxism, which has come more and more to the front as time goes on and which will, in the future, I believe, quite dwarf the original conflict between capital and labour. We are at the present time witnessing a profound revolution in European culture. All those Liberal achievements which seemed so secure half a century ago are to-day either lost or in peril. Here the responsibility of Communism is a very heavy one, for it has originated that cult of violence and that contempt for the value of human life which have spread like an epidemic from Eastern to Central Europe and may spread yet farther.

In Russia, there is no contradiction between the State and the Communist party. The State has become nothing more than the instrument of the party, and the power of the party is shown by the Assyrian ruthlessness with which it has in the last few years destroyed the independent life of the Russian peasantry at the cost of an incalculable amount of human suffering. And these events show more clearly than any abstract argument the real issue of Communism. It is not an issue between the capitalists and the proletariat, for it is obvious that the real proletarians are the starving peasants of the Ukraine and not the well-fed bureaucrats of Moscow. The vital issue is the subordination of man, body and soul, to the economic machine of the secular State. And the greatest obstacle to the fulfilment of this end is not Capitalism, nor the bourgeois culture, but the Christian faith.

It is becoming increasingly clear that the opposition between Capitalism as a working system and Communism as an economic ideal is not an absolute one. If only Communism could show itself to be efficient, if only its five-year plans could attain an outstanding success, then the leaders of Capitalism, the professional economists, and the whole tribe of economic planners and organisers would have no difficulty in rallying to the Communist cause. And in the same way the leading representatives of bourgeois culture are also coming to terms with Communist ideals. It is precisely these people—left-wing peers and bourgeois intellectuals—who are the leading admirers and apologists of the Soviet regime in this country. They have lost their faith in the traditional creed of Liberalism, and they rally to Communism, because in spite of its cruelties and intolerances, it seems modern and progres-

sive and anti-religious. As Mr. Malcolm Muggeridge
has pointed out with such biting emphasis in his
Winter in Moscow, all these Platonic admirers of
Communism from the West find in Russia something
that they can understand—a State run on advanced
lines by advanced people; whereas the victims of the
Soviet system, the wretched peasants and unprivi-
leged workers and priests, are people of the underworld with whom they have nothing in common and
whose sufferings seem distant and unreal.

Of course, the orthodox Communist will deny that
this total subordination and sacrifice of humanity to
the State machine is of the essence of Communism, for
did not Marx and Lenin expressly teach that the dictatorship of the proletariat is only a temporary phase,
and the State itself will eventually wither away and
give place to a classless and Stateless society? But how
will this end be attained? Only when the individual
is so completely socialised that he will instinctively
devote all his energies to working for society and will
be unable even to conceive of any end other than that
of the economic organism of which he forms part. In
such an order there would be no need for a State any
more than it is necessary for ants or bees to have a
State. But is it a human order, and is it possible for
humanity to rise or sink to such a level?

At first sight it may appear strange that a system
which sets as its goal the bleak and inhuman ideals
of economic totalitarianism can possess any attractions
for idealists and social reformers. Yet nothing can
be more clear than that in Western Europe at least it
is the idealists, the humanitarians, and the intellectuals who are most sensitive to the appeal of Communism. Nothing could be more unlike the men of blood
and iron who founded the Soviet State than the
amiable idealists who are the leaders of advanced
thought and advanced politics in this country. But

while the former never disguised their contempt for the idealists, the latter have preserved a romantic admiration for Communism which manifests itself in countless speeches and articles, and pilgrimages to Moscow. Sentimental as much of this propaganda is, it is perfectly sincere and it bears witness to a certain fundamental weakness in Western society. The fact is that the bourgeois culture of the modern Capitalist state fails to satisfy the deepest need of the human spirit, so that the hungry and the dissatisfied turn for relief even to the dry husks of Communism. And what, in fact, drives men to Communism is not mere economic discontent, nor even dissatisfaction with the existing social order. It is something deeper than these —a discontent with human life itself: a divine discontent that can only find full satisfaction in the sphere of religion.

This strange paradox of a godless religion and a materialist spirituality has its basis in the internal contradictions of the revolutionary tradition of which Communism is the final product. For that tradition unconsciously drew its dynamic force from religious sources, though it denied and rejected them in its rationalised consciousness. In the same way the Marxian theory of history, for all its materialism, is dependent to a degree that Marx himself never suspected on the antecedent religious view of history which had been formed by the Jewish and Christian traditions. Consequently, in order to understand both the religious appeal of Communism and its points of contact and conflict with Christianity, it is necessary to go beyond politics and economics and to study the relations between Communism and Christianity at the point where their contact is closest and their conflict most acute—that is to say, in their philosophy of history.

12

The Problem of European Unity

ALL THE LIVING FORCES that are moving the world to-day, whether scientific, economic, or political, have their roots in European culture and would wither if that culture were to break down. Even the United States, which alone stands on an equality with Western Europe in material and technical organisation, is not in a position to take the place of Europe and carry on the work of world organisation. For it is not merely that the world is indebted to Europe for the scientific inventions and the economic technique that have changed the external conditions of human life; it also owes to her the ideals of political liberty and social justice that have brought a ferment of change into the stationary societies of Russia and the East. Even the bitterest enemies of Europe borrow from Europe the weapons and the ideas that they turn against her.

But if Europe is, after all, a benefactor to humanity, why is not humanity more grateful? The answer is obvious enough. Western civilisation is morally discredited, and even the Western peoples themselves no longer possess any faith in its spiritual value. National particularism has deprived Western culture of its moral unity and its common spiritual ideals and has left it naked before the world as a purely material effort of economic exploitation and predatory imperialism. It has to meet the revolt of the subject peoples and the internal danger of social unrest and revolution with no spiritual resources and no higher appeal than self-interest and practical expediency.

The ancient world passed through a similar crisis in the age of the civil wars that marked the decline of the Roman Republic. Then also the power of the West was threatened alike by the revolt of the oriental world and by its own disunity and social discontent. Rome, like modern Europe, had conquered and organised the world and lost its own soul in the process. The ancient Roman, no less than the Victorian Englishman, had been a man of strict, though narrow, moral ideas, who had inherited from his peasant ancestors an ideal of duty and devotion to public interests under the sanction of traditional religion. He was firmly convinced of his moral superiority to the clever and immoral Greeks and the idle and superstitious Orientals, whom it was his business to conquer. A type like the elder Cato with his forbidding appearance—"all teeth and red hair," as a contemporary observed—his moral censoriousness, his sense of duty, and his devotion to money-making, has much more in common with the makers of the Industrial Revolution than with a modern Italian or an ancient Greek. But it was the fate of this society, like our own, to destroy the foundations on which its strength rested. The old Roman virtues withered away when the peasant republic became a capitalist oligarchy, based on a mercenary army and a horde of tax-collectors and money-lenders. The successors of the Catonian tradition were millionaires who accumulated vast fortunes by the exploitation of the subject peoples—like that model republican, Brutus, who forced the cities of Cyprus to borrow money from him at a rate of 48 per cent in order to pay the war indemnities that had been levied on them. Even Cicero, who represented all that was best in the liberal republican tradition, was not ashamed to defend the cause of "those most worthy and distinguished people, the financiers" and to advocate a war "in defence of national glory, public revenue, and private investments," with a naïve effrontery that even a modern politician might envy.

This orgy of exploitation called forth an equally violent explosion of revolutionary feeling. It expressed itself in the revolt of the subject oriental peoples and the Italian allies, in the risings of the slaves, and above all in the movement of social revolution, which attempted to destroy the rule of the oligarchy by the confiscation of the great estates and the proscription and massacre of the capitalists themselves. Thus in the first century B.C. Roman society was faced by a revolutionary crisis, complicated by the rebellion of the subject nationalities and the horrors of class war. It seemed as though society would tear itself to pieces, and that the complete collapse of ancient civilisation was at hand. If the Roman Empire had fallen in the first century B.C. instead of five hundred years later, the history of the world would have been changed, and European civilisation, as we know it, would never have come into existence. But she succeeded in surmounting her difficulties at the cost of immense effort and suffering, and thanks to the Augustan achievement, the Roman organisation of the world became the basis of a new order on which the whole later development of Western civilisation has been based.

Modern Europe stands today very much in the same position as that of the Roman Empire in the first century B.C. Like Rome, it has conquered and organised the world. By destroying the old tribal separatism and breaking down the barriers between East and West, it has laid the foundations of an incipient world order. But its work, like that of Rome, has been vitiated by its lack of spiritual purpose and by selfishness and economic exploitation. Our civilisation stands in no less need of moral and social reconstruction than that of the ancient world in the time of

Augustus, though the task of restoration is infinitely more difficult than it was then.

The task of European restoration is at once more difficult and more hopeful. Rome at least possessed the materials of a political unity and the unified military control with which to realise it. But we have no political European unity and no hope of creating it by the direct means of a centralisation of military power. If Europe ever achieves political unity it will be as an international federation, not as a centralised empire; and this can only come about by the slow and difficult process of social and economic co-operation.

But on the other hand, Europe possesses an infinitely richer spiritual heritage than that of ancient Rome. The Roman world empire was an artificial unity, with no common spiritual tradition behind it, whereas modern Europe rests on the foundation of an age-long community of religion and of intellectual culture. If we could recover that tradition and become as conscious of our European community as we now are of our national particularism, international co-operation would cease to appear as an insoluble problem and would become natural and almost inevitable. The problem of Europe is fundamentally a spiritual one, and the true foundation of European unity is to be found not in political or economic agreements but in the restoration of the spiritual tradition on which that unity was originally based.

The crisis of Europe is the crisis of the world. As Maritain has written, "A new world is emerging from the obscure chrysalis of history." But it is only in and through Europe that this new world can realise itself. Europe has been led, as it were in spite of itself, to break down the barriers that divided peoples and cultures and to sow broadcast through the world the seeds of a new order. It is true that without spiritual leadership this movement may cause the enslavement of mankind to economic machinery and thus produce an inhuman and anti-spiritual order which is nothing but a kingdom of Antichrist. But it is equally capable of serving a higher end. The material organisation of the world by European ideas and Western science is a necessary preparation for that spiritual unification of humanity that it is the mission of Christianity to accomplish.

More than a century ago Joseph de Maistre, the last representative of the old pre-nationalist Europe, an exile in the city of Peter the Great and Lenin, discerned with almost prophetic insight the meaning of the revolutions that had destroyed his own happiness and broken down the traditional order of European life that he valued so highly. France and England, he writes, in spite of their mutual hostility, have been led to co-operate in the same work. While the French Revolution sowed the seeds of French culture throughout Europe, England has carried European culture into Asia and has caused the works of Newton to be read in the language of Mahomet.

"Man in his ignorance often deceives himself as to ends and means, as to forces and resistance, as to instruments and obstacles. Sometimes he tries to cut down an oak with a pocket-knife and sometimes he throws a bomb to break a reed. But Providence never wavers, and it is not in vain that it shakes the world. Everything proclaims that we are moving towards a great unity which, to use a religious expression, we must hail from afar. We have been grievously and justly broken, but if such eyes as mine are worthy to foresee the divine purpose, we have been broken only to be made one."*

* De Maistre, *Soirées de Saint Petersbourg*, 2eme Entretien, ad fin.

Three

The Nature and Destiny of Man

"There is a point at which the world of spirit comes into conscious contact with the world of matter. That point is man. It is surely rational to suppose that the world of thought and of spiritual values, on the threshold of which man has the consciousness of standing, is a real world, an order no less great than the material order, and that it is in this alone that we shall find a solution to the otherwise hopeless conflict of man's spiritual aspirations and the limitations of his material existence."

The Nature and Destiny of Man (1920)

Introduction: The Crisis of Civilisation

TODAY CHRISTIANITY seems to many a thing of the past, part of the vanishing order of the old Europe, and the new powers that are shaping the world are non-Christian or even anti-Christian.

It is no wonder that the conscience of Christians is uneasy. On the one hand, there are those who still retain an internal bond with the Christian culture of the past, and a deep love and reverence for it; and in that case they must feel that something in the nature of a national apostasy has occurred and that they bear some share of the guilt. And on the other hand, there are those who have lost contact with that social tradition and who know only the new secularised world. These are likely to feel that the Christian culture of the past failed because it was not really Christian and that it is for us or our successors to discover or create for the first time a new way of life that will be truly Christian.

I believe both these points of view are fundamentally true. They represent the two aspects of Christian culture in our time, and they are wrong only insofar as they are one-sided. I do not think it is possible to deny the fact of Christian culture as an objective social reality. It is hardly too much to say that it is Christian culture that has created Western man and the Western way of life. But at the same time, we must admit that Western man has not been faithful to this Christian tradition. He has abandoned it not once, but again and again. For since Christianity depends on a living faith and not merely on social tradition, Christendom must be renewed in every generation, and every generation is faced by the responsibility of making decisions, each of which may be an act of Christian faith or an act of apostasy.

No doubt it is very seldom that a society is clearly conscious of what is at stake. The issues are complicated by all kinds of social, economic, and political influences, so that the actual decision usually takes the form of a compromise.

Now the creative activity which is the essence of the Christian life takes place far below the visible surface of culture; and the same thing is true of the spiritual failures and apostasies which are the other side of the picture. But this does not mean that religion and culture are two separate worlds with no relation to each other. The assumption of such a separation has been the great error of the Western mind during the last two centuries. First we have divided human life into two parts—the life of the individual and the life of the state—and have confined religion entirely to the former. This error was typical of bourgeois liberalism, and nowhere has it been more prevalent than in the English-speaking countries. But now men have gone further and reunited the divided world under the reign of impersonal material forces, so that the individual counts for nothing, and religion is viewed as an illusion of the individual consciousness or a perversion of the individual craving for satisfaction.

This is the typical error of Marx and Engels and of the totalitarian mass state in all its forms.

But to the Christian, the hidden principle of the life of culture and the fate of nations and civilisations must always be found in the heart of man and in the hand of God. There is no limit to the efficacy of faith and to the influence of these acts of spiritual decision, which are ultimately the response of particular men to God's call, as revealed in particular historical and personal circumstances. Burke wrote very truly and finely that the so-called laws of history which attempt to subordinate the future to some kind of historical determinism are but the artificial combinations of the human mind. There always remains an irreducible element of mystery. "A common soldier, a child, a girl at the door of an inn have changed the face of the future and almost of Nature."

But to Christians the mystery of history is not completely dark, since it is a veil which only partially conceals the creative activity of spiritual forces and the operation of spiritual laws. It is a commonplace to say that the blood of the martyrs is the seed of the Church, yet what we are asserting is simply that individual acts of spiritual decision ultimately bear spiritual fruit. We admit this in the case of the Church, and we have admitted it so long that it has become a platitude. But we do not for the most part realise that it is equally true in the case of culture and history.

For the great cultural changes and the historic revolutions that decide the fate of nations or the character of an age are the cumulative results of a number of spiritual decisions—the faith and insight, or the refusal and blindness, of individuals. No one can put his finger on the ultimate spiritual act which tilts the balance and makes the external order of society assume a new form. In this sense we may adapt Burke's saying and assert that the prayer of some unknown Christian or some unrecognised and unadmitted act of spiritual surrender may change the face of the world.

The process of secularisation arises not from the loss of faith but from the loss of social interest in the world of faith. It begins the moment men feel that religion is irrelevant to the common way of life and that society as such has nothing to do with the truths of faith. It is important to distinguish this secular separation between religion and society from the traditional opposition between the Church and the World—or between the present world and the world to come—which has always been so deeply rooted in the Christian tradition. It is often difficult thus to differentiate, since what is described as the "other-worldly" type of religion is in some cases directly connected with the divorce between religion and culture of which I have spoken. In other cases the opposition springs from the Christian dualism which finds expression not only in St. Augustine, or in the later mystics, but in all ages of the life of the Church from the New Testament to the twentieth century. Indeed, it is this vital tension between two worlds and two planes of reality which makes the Christian way of life so difficult but which is also the source of its strength. To live for eternal truths, to possess the first fruits of eternal life, while facing every practical responsibility and meeting the demands of the present moment and place on their own ground—that is the spirit by which a Christian culture lives and is known. For Christian culture involves a ceaseless effort to widen the frontiers of the Kingdom of God—not only horizontally, by increasing the number of Christians, but vertically, by penetrating deeper into human life and bringing every human activity into closer relations with its spiritual centre.

The return from a secular civilisation to a Christian way of life no doubt involves a reversal of many historical forces that transcend the limits not only of our personal experience but even of our particular society. But in spite of the modern totalitarian tendency to control the development of culture by the external methods of legislation and international organisation and the control of parties and political police, it is still the individual mind that is the creative force which determines the ultimate fate of cultures. And the first step in the transformation of culture is a change in the pattern of culture within the mind, for this is the seed out of which there spring new forms of life which ultimately change the social way of life and thus create a new culture. I do not, of course, mean to assert that new ideas are more important than new moral action and new spiritual initiative. Knowledge and will and action are inseparable in life, and the soul is the principle of all life. But I do believe that it has been on the plane of ideas that the process of the secularisation of culture began, and that it is only by a change of ideas that this process can be reversed. It has always been the weakness of the Anglo-Saxon tradition to underestimate the influence of ideas on life and of contemplation on action, and the result of this error has been that many Christians in England and America never realised the existence of culture until the culture of the age had ceased to be Christian.

In the last century they were complacent and uncritical in their attitude to their own bourgeois culture: so long as men went to church and read the Bible and abstained from gambling and drunkenness and open immorality, it did not matter that they were at the same time helping to turn England into a hideous and disorderly conglomeration of factories and slums in which the chapel and the gin palace provided the only satisfaction for man's spiritual and emotional needs.

The reaction against this degradation of Christian culture has carried us very far in the opposite direction. And the improvement of social conditions—one might almost say the civilising of our industrial society—has coincided with the secularisation of English culture.

This secularisation has been the great scandal of modern Christendom. For the Christian cannot deny the crying evils of that nineteenth-century industrial society from which the ordinary man has been delivered by the social reforms of the last fifty or one hundred years, while at the same time he is forced to reject the purely secular idealism which has inspired the new culture. Nevertheless, this has been a salutary experience for Christians. It has made us examine our conscience to see how great has been our responsibility for this decline of Christian culture and for the conversion of our society to a new kind of paganism.

But we ought not to concentrate our attention on the failures of nineteenth-century Christianity. Today we are faced with a new situation and an entirely different range of problems. The modern world is in a state of violent confusion and change, and it is not the traditional Christian culture of the past but the secularised culture of the present which is being tried and found wanting. The material security and the confidence in the future which have long been characteristic of Western civilisation have suddenly disappeared. Nobody knows where the world is going. The course of history has suddenly been changed from a broad, placid river into a destructive cataract.

Christianity is not left unaffected by this change, for it threatens all the values and traditions which the liberal secularism of the last age still respected and preserved. Yet this catastrophic element in life, which had been temporarily exiled from the nineteenth-century world, is one that is very familiar to Christians. Indeed, in the past it formed an integral part of the original Christian experience, and the changes of the last forty years have confronted us with a situation which is not essentially different from that which the primitive Church faced under the Roman

Empire. The eschatological aspect of Christian doctrine, which was so alien to the Edwardian age, has once more become relevant and significant. For even though we may not believe in the imminent end of the world, it is hardly possible to doubt that *a* world is ending. We are once more in the presence of cosmic forces that are destroying or transforming human life, and therefore we have a new opportunity to see life in religious terms and not merely in terms of humanism and social welfare and political reform. Arnold's ideal of culture as a "general harmonious expansion of those gifts of thought and feeling which make the peculiar dignity, wealth, and happiness of human nature" obviously belonged to an age and a class which could reckon on social security. For that age the four last things—Death and Judgment and Heaven and Hell—had become remote and unreal. But today they are real enough even for the unbeliever who knows nothing of the Christian hope of eternal life. The Christian way of life has indeed become the only way that is capable of surmounting the tremendous dangers and evils that have become a part of the common experience of modern man. No doubt, as the Gospel says, men will go on eating and drinking and buying and selling and planting and building, until the heaven rains fire and brimstone and destroys them all. But they do this with only one part of their minds; there is another part of their minds which remains uneasily conscious of the threat that hangs over them; and in proportion as they realise this, they feel that something should be done, and they seek a way of salvation, however vaguely and uncertainly.

In a sense this has always been so, and men have always been partially conscious of their spiritual need. But there has been during the last generation a fundamental change in the nature of their anxiety. During the last few centuries the appeal of Christianity has been largely personal. It has been an appeal to the individual conscience and especially to the isolated and introverted types. It is the experience which finds a classical expression in Bunyan's *Pilgrim's Progress,* which is all the more classical because it was also popular. But today the appeal is greatest to those who have the strongest sense of social responsibility, and it is no longer merely a question of individual salvation but of the salvation of the world—the deliverance of man in his whole social nature from the evils that express themselves in political and social forms, in anonymous mass crimes and criminal instincts which nevertheless are not less opposed to the Christian spirit than are the sins of the individual. This is the reason why the chief rivals to Christianity at the present time are not different religions but political ideologies like Communism, which offers man a social way of salvation by external revolution, by faith in a social creed, and by communion with a party which is a kind of secular church.

Nor is it surprising that these secular counter-religions should tend to produce the very evils from which men are seeking to be delivered. For this is just what the early Church experienced with the pagan counter-religions which tried to satisfy the spiritual needs of the ancient world in opposition to the Christian way of salvation.

And the anti-Christian character of the forces which are making an attempt to conquer the world is also another sign of the relevance of Christianity to the problems of the present age. Religion is ceasing to be a side issue—it is no longer regarded as belonging to a private world remote from the real world of business and politics and science. It is once more felt to be a vital issue even by its enemies who are determined to destroy it.

Consequently, in spite of the increasing secularisation of culture both in the West and in the world at large, I feel that the outlook for Christian culture is brighter than it has been for a considerable time—perhaps even 250 years. For if what I have been saying about spiritual changes and their cultural fruits is true and if the changes of the last 40 years have the effect of weakening the barrier between religion and social life which was so strong a century ago, then the new situation opens the way for a new Christian movement of advance.

This is no excuse for facile optimism. For even if the change has begun, it must go a long way before it can affect the structure of social life and bear fruit in a living Christian culture; and meanwhile things must grow worse as secular civilisation undergoes the inevitable process of corruption to which it is exposed by its nature. From all that we can see, and from the experience of the past, it is practically certain that the period of transition will be a time of suffering and trial for the Church. Above all, we have little or no knowledge of how Christians are to meet the new organised forces with which they are confronted. However much these forces may have misused the new techniques that science has put into their hands, these techniques cannot be ignored, and they are bound to become an integral part of the civilisation of the future, whether it is Christian or anti-Christian. So long as it is only a question of material techniques —of the machine order and all that it implies—Christians are ready enough to accept the situation, perhaps almost too ready. But what of the social and psychological techniques on which the totalitarian state relies and which may almost be said to have created it? All these methods of mass conditioning, social control by centralised planning, the control of opinion by propaganda and official ideologies, the control of behaviour by methods of social repression are not restricted to defending society from the evil-doer but are directed against any type of minority opinion or activity. Most of these things have been condemned and rejected by Western opinion, whether Christian or secular, yet many of them are already invading and transforming Western society, and they are likely to become more and more a part of the modern world. Seen from this point of view, the Nazis and the Communists are not the only totalitarians, they are only parties which have attempted to exploit the totalitarian elements in modern civilisation in a simplified and drastic way in order to obtain quick results.

The whole tendency of modern life is towards scientific planning and organisation, central control, standardisation, and specialisation. If this tendency was left to work itself out to its extreme conclusion, one might expect to see the state transformed into an immense social machine, all the individual components of which are strictly limited to the performance of a definite and specialised function, where there could be no freedom because the machine could only work smoothly as long as every wheel and cog performed its task with unvarying regularity. Now the nearer modern society comes to the state of total organisation, the more difficult it is to find any place for spiritual freedom and personal responsibility. Education itself becomes an essential part of the machine, for the mind has to be as completely measured and controlled by the techniques of the scientific expert as the task which it is being trained to perform.

Therefore the whole society has to move together as a single unit. Either it may be a Christian unit which is governed by spiritual standards and directed towards spiritual ends, or it is wholly secular—a power machine, or a machine for the production of wealth or population.

As I have said, this is an extreme conclusion, and at the present time even the most totalitarian forms of society are not and cannot be as totalitarian as this. Nevertheless, the modern world is moving steadily in this direction, and the margin between the old forms of liberal or social democracy and this new Leviathan is growing narrower every year. Hence we can hardly doubt that when ultimately a conflict takes place between the new state and the Christian Church, it will be far more severe in character than anything that has been known before.

Here again the trend of events is following the same pattern as in the early days of Christianity. Nothing was clearer to the Christians of that age than the imminence of a tremendous trial, in which the mystery of iniquity that was already at work in the world would come out into the open and claim to stand in the place of God Himself. It was with the constant awareness of this coming catastrophe that the new Christian way of life took form, and it was this that made the Christian belief in a new life and in the coming of a new world, not an expression of other-worldly pietism, but an active preparation for vast and immediate historical changes. There is no need to idealise this behaviour. At times the actual outburst of persecution was followed by wholesale apostasies, as in the time of Decius in the year 250. Yet in spite of such failures, throughout the long periods of persecution and semi-persecution a gradual change was taking place beneath the surface until finally, after the last and fiercest persecution of all, the world suddenly awoke to find that the Empire itself had become Christian.

We today are living in a world that is far less stable

than that of the early Roman Empire. There is no doubt that the world is on the move again and that the pace is faster and more furious than anything that man has known before. But there is nothing in this situation which should cause Christians to despair. On the contrary, it is the kind of situation for which their faith has always prepared them and which provides the opportunity for the fulfilment of their mission.

It is true that we do not know where the world is going. We cannot say it must go towards a Christian culture any more than towards destruction by atomic warfare. All we know is that the world is being changed from top to bottom and that the Christian faith remains the way of salvation, that is to say, a way to the renewal of human life by the spirit of God, which has no limits and which cannot be prevented by human power or material catastrophe. Christianity proved victorious over the pagan world in the past because Christians were always looking forward, while the secular world was looking back. This note of hope and expectation is one of the characteristic notes of Christianity; it runs through the New Testament from beginning to end. One of the most striking expressions of this is to be seen in St. Paul's last letter to his first European converts—the Philippians—written during his captivity and trial, yet making even his trial a ground of encouragement, since it was providing a means to spread the knowledge of the faith in the Roman praetorium and the palace of Caesar. And after describing all his gains and all his losses, he concludes:

"Not that I have already reached fulfilment. I do not claim to have attained. But this one thing I do. Forgetting all that is completed and reaching out to the things that lie before, I press on to the goal for the prize of the high calling of God in Christ Jesus." (Philippians 3:12–14.)

This attitude to detachment and confidence in the future which St. Paul expresses in such an intensely personal, vivid way is also the social attitude of the Church as a whole, and it is this which gives Christianity such a great power of spiritual renewal.

Nevertheless, though Christianity is prepared to accept every external change, though it is not bound to the past in the same way as a particular form of society tends to be, it has its own internal tradition, which it maintains with the most scrupulous fidelity and which it can never surrender. Looked at from the secular standpoint, the primitive Church might have seemed to lack everything that the educated Roman regarded as culture. Yet in reality it was the representative of a cultural tradition older than that of Greece and Rome. To the Christian, the people of God was a real historical society, with its own history and literature and its perennial philosophy of divine wisdom. And when eventually the world became Christian, this specifically religious culture-tradition came to the surface and was accepted by the new world as the source of the new Christian art and literature and liturgy.

The same tradition exists today, for though the Church no longer inspires and dominates the external culture of the modern world, it still remains the guardian of all the riches of its own inner life and is the bearer of a sacred tradition. If society were once again to become Christian, after a generation or two or after ten or twenty generations, this sacred tradition would once more flow out into the world and fertilise the culture of societies yet unborn. Thus the movement toward Christian culture is at one and the same time a voyage into the unknown, in the course of which new worlds of human experience will be discovered, and a return to our own fatherland—to the sacred tradition of the Christian past which flows underneath the streets and skyscrapers of the new Babylon as the tradition of the patriarchs and prophets flowed beneath the palaces and amphitheatres of Imperial Rome.

The Meaning of History

THERE IS NO GETTING AWAY from history. Man carries it with him wherever he goes and whether he knows it or not. His thoughts and his actions are alike influenced by this invisible burden, which is not a dead weight but an active force that impels him forward along the path he has to travel. Men may make a new start, like the Pilgrim Fathers when they landed at Plymouth Rock, but at the same time they were "making history" and realised very strongly that they were doing so.

Long ago, not only in English but in all the Western languages, the word "history" has been extended from its original sense of the written or oral records of the past to cover the process with which such records deal, that is to say, the whole movement of change and persistence in time through which mankind has passed down to the present moment. Only a divine or angelic intelligence could comprehend the whole of this process in its almost infinite complexity. Yet even the savage and the completely uneducated man is not totally ignorant of it, for he is aware of the existence of the past and preserves a certain traditional knowledge of it. Between these two extremes lies the field of historical study, which is always extending its frontiers and striving towards a universality and omniscience which can never be completely realised.

In modern times the extension of this field of knowledge has been one of the most remarkable features of Western civilisation. We usually think of the modern age as an age of physical science and technology, but it has also become the great age of historical research. Never since the world began has the barrier of time been pushed back so far and so fast as during the last century or 150 years. It is not merely that our knowledge of our past has been extended and deepened; what is still more remarkable is that we have reconquered great tracts of history that had been lost for thousands of years, the history of the great civilisations of the ancient world—Egypt, Sumer, and Babylon; the history of civilisations previously unknown, like that of the Hittite Empire; the history of the living civilisations of the Far East, that were barely glimpsed by us in the past; and finally the history of the peoples who left no written records, but whose past has been unveiled by the patient labour of the archaeologists. Although the time has not yet come, we can look forward with some confidence to the advent of a real world history which will integrate all the different forms and stages of human culture into an intelligible unity.

All this knowledge is not just an accumulation of useless archaeological lumber. It has a meaning and a value for human life today. For paradoxical though it may appear, there can be no doubt that the people who are most ignorant of history are those who are most dependent on the past, and the most enslaved to the bondage of tradition and custom; while the more we know of the past, the more free we become to choose the way we will go.

Moreover, without history we cannot understand even the world we live in. Each society and culture becomes imprisoned in the narrow confines of its present experience. The attitude of the natural non-historical man to other cultures finds a classical ex-

pression in the famous conversation between Jim and
Huckleberry Finn. "Is a Frenchman a man? Well den,
why doan he *talk* like a man? Yu answer me dat!"
So in the past it was only natural for uncivilised peoples to call themselves some name signifying "man"
like Eskimo, Innuit, and countless other examples,
with the assumption that other peoples were some-
how not altogether human. And it is not only the uncivilised peoples who have made this mistake. The
Greeks themselves dismissed all the non-Greek-
speaking peoples as "barbarians"; and we ourselves
almost down to the present day used to describe peoples whose history we knew nothing of as "savages,"
implying thereby that they had a sort of halfway position between us and the animals. If only our predecessors two centuries or even a century ago had known
what we know today about the history and culture of
the native peoples of America and Africa, how much
unnecessary waste and suffering might have been
avoided! And even today with our vastly increased
resources of knowledge and understanding, we still
find it difficult to apply our knowledge in the right
place and at the right time. For it is usually only in
time of war that serious attempts are made to mobilise
our resources of knowledge, and then only for purposes of psychological warfare and the like.

Perhaps in some degree the historians and the social
anthropologists are themselves not without blame for
this failure. For the knowledge of history, however
exhaustive, is not a panacea that will solve all our
political problems and cure all our social ills. That is
the fallacy of *historicism*, of which we have heard so
much in recent years. For during the nineteenth century the intoxication of the new knowledge and the
influence of evolutionary theories led men to believe
that history was a kind of progressive revelation
which would gradually lead us to a wider knowledge,

to larger moral values, and ultimately to universal truth. This view was propagated, on the one hand, by the French and English and of course American, liberal philosophers who believed in the theory of social progress, and on the other by the German philosophers who constructed their vast systems of speculative idealism and their philosophies of history.

Now it is true enough that history leads us to wider knowledge, but only to a knowledge of historical phenomena. It does not create truth or moral values. The historical world left to its own resources is a world of pure relativism, and the more completely we immerse ourselves in it, the more difficult it is to see beyond it or to grasp any ultimate truth to which we can hold fast. The only lesson we can learn from it is that which the Greeks had learnt—the lesson of humility—that man is a drop in an endless stream, but he cannot see where the stream is going. The philosophers of history have judged differently because they had their philosophy already and applied it to history, like Hegel, who saw history as the progressive revelation of the Absolute Spirit, because he had a metaphysical conviction that whatever is real is rational, and whatever is rational is real. Therefore the historical process must represent a kind of dialectic by which the universal mind develops its thought. And so one does not feel that Hegel actually learnt much from history; he discovered his principle of historical dialectic by a process of philosophical speculation, and he then applied the principle (not always very happily) to the facts of history as he saw them.

This kind of philosophy of history is out of fashion today, and there are very few Hegelians to be met with, but there are plenty of Marxians, and Marxism makes use of just the same principle of historical interpretation, although its dialectic is a materialistic instead of a spiritual one. And still more numerous than the Marxists are the historians and writers who possess a kind of subconscious or unacknowledged philosophy of history. Indeed, the belief in progress has been preached so long and so widely in the modern world that it has become accepted by most people as a necessary part of the democratic outlook and way of life.

Nowhere is this point of view more widespread than in America, where a belief in the historic destiny of the American people as the leaders of the nations of the world towards a golden age of freedom and plenty dates back to the very origins of the republic. No doubt there have always been discordant voices—indeed, the pessimism of the thoroughgoing American pessimist like Robinson Jeffers surpasses anything that the Old World can show. But it is just because the American pessimist is so exceptional that he is so extreme. He has to speak violently to make his voice heard. But the great mass of Americans have always had a much stronger faith in the future than any other people, and they owe this faith not to any philosophical theory or ideology like that of Marxism, but to a spiritual tradition or climate of opinion into which they have been born and with which the nation has grown up from the beginning.

In this respect it is very instructive to compare the case of America with that of Germany. The Germans are perhaps the most historically minded of all the Western peoples. No people has produced greater historians or more philosophers of history. But their concern with history is bound up with a continual anxiety about history, and their philosophies of history often seem like attempts to reassure themselves against underlying doubt. Thus in the later nineteenth century, during the Bismarckian period, when the historical optimism of the nationalist historians and of the Hegelian philosophers seemed to have been justified by events, the critical attitude towards history found classical expression in the writings of Burckhardt and Nietzsche. Both of them regarded the philosophy of history as a delusion which led either to a vulgar cult of success, as with the nationalist historians, or to the secularisation and nationalisation of Christianity, as with the liberal Protestant theologians. Both advocated a super-historical attitude which would be indifferent to success or failure and look beyond history to eternal transcendent values.

This point of view is stated most fully in Nietzsche's early essay on "The Use and Abuse of History" from which I quote the following passage:

Whoever asks his friends whether they would live the last ten or twenty years over again will easily see which of them was born for the "super-historical standpoint": they will answer no, but will give different reasons for their answer. Some will say they have the consolation that the next twenty will be better: they are the men referred to satirically by David Hume:

Who from the dregs of life hope to receive
What the first sprightly running could not give.

We will call them the "historical men." Their vision of the past turns them towards the future, encourages them to persevere with life, and kindles the hope that justice will yet come and happiness is behind the mountain they are climbing. . . .

But that question to which we have heard the first answer, is capable of another; also a "no," but on different grounds. It is the "no" of the "super-historical" man who sees no salvation in evolution, for whom the world is complete and fulfils its aim in every single moment. How could the next ten years teach what the past ten years were not able to teach?

Whether the aim of the teaching be happiness or resignation, virtue or penance, these super-historical men are not agreed; but as against all merely historical ways of

iewing the past, they are unanimous in the theory that
1e past and the present are one and the same, typically
like in all their diversity, and forming together a picture
f eternally present types of unchangeable value and
ignificance.

Now it is important to note that both these writers
vere men who accepted the necessity for a kind of
eligious or transcendent view of history while they
ejected the Christian faith and the Christian hope.
'hey looked back to the ancient Greek view of life,
specially, in Nietzsche's case, to the pre-Socratic
hinkers and poets, above all to Heraclitus. Yet they
ould not entirely ignore their Christian past. They
ook up the Greek tragic view of life with an under-
:urrent of Christian ideas. Burckhardt's criticisms of
he philosophers of history are not unlike those of
Kierkegaard without Kierkegaard's religious convic-
ions, while Nietzsche was driven on in his flight from
history to throw aside all the values of Western culture
and to embark on his attempt to transcend humanity.

To sum up: The "philosophers" of the Enlightenment who created the philosophy of history and the
modern theory of historical progress were not Chris-
ian thinkers. They took for granted that modern
:ivilisation had outgrown Christianity, and they be-
ieved that history and science would provide a satis-
actory answer to the questions that they had inherited from the Christian tradition of the past—what
vas the nature and destiny of man: what were the
rue values of human existence and what was the
meaning of history.

But the writers of whom I have just spoken realised
hat this was a delusion. They saw that history by itself is incapable of leading us to any ultimate truth.
Spiritual reality transcends history, just as it transcends physical science. Yet they continued to accept

almost without discussion the fundamental dogma o
the Enlightenment that Christianity was, if not a
exploded superstition, at least a mode of thought tha
modern civilisation had outgrown. And therefore the
were forced to adopt a negative conclusion, whethe
it took the form of Burckhardt's Stoic resignation o
Nietzsche's ecstatic nihilism and irrationalism.

But to us who are Christians, this century-long con
troversy on the meaning of history must seem the re
sult of a false dilemma. We can accept Burckhardt'
judgment on the failure of the ambitious attempts o
nineteenth-century philosophy to construct an idea
pattern of history out of their own inner consciousnes
or to discover the course of the future of humanity b
the study of its past. But we need not conclude from
this failure that history has no meaning or that mar
lives only in the present. No Christian can accep
these views, for every Christian is a member of a super
temporal society, which has a historical existence and
an eternal significance. In fact the real reason why
Western man has been so preoccupied with the neec
for a philosophic explanation of history and above al
with the idea of progress, that is, the belief that man
kind is continually advancing through the ages and
advancing to some goal, is because Christianity had
first put these ideas into his head and he still clung
to them even when he had lost his faith.

This point becomes very clear when we conside
the original point of departure of the German philoso
phising on history. The first important work and one
that had a profound influence on the thought of the
German Enlightenment was Lessing's essay on *The
Education of the Human Race* published in 1780, and
this is simply a theodicy or a theory of divine revela
tion taken over bodily from Christian sources and
adapted to a rationalist or idealist public.

Seen in this way, Christianity has had an incalculable influence on Western history, because it has formed the minds of the historians—the men who wrote our histories—and the philosophers—the men who reflected on the meaning of history—from St. Augustine and the Venerable Bede to Hegel and Ranke and Acton.

Hegel's Idea of History

HEGEL's *Philosophy of Right* is one of the most seminal books of the nineteenth century. It lies behind Karl Marx and the modern Communist ideology. It inspired the Russian revolutionary intelligentsia before and after Marx. It had a great influence on Fascism, especially on the rationalism of the Fascist state by Gentile. Alone among modern works, it had an equal influence on the conservatives and the revolutionaries, and there is hardly a political movement in modern times that has not been affected by it in some measure. Yet in spite of its international importance, it remains profoundly and characteristically German.

But if the *Philosophy of Right* is the quintessence of Prussianism, how is it that it should have had so powerful an influence on Communism and Liberalism, while National Socialism itself, which by universal agreement is the incarnation of the forces of evil in the German tradition, should have ignored it? In Rosenberg's *Myth of the 20th Century* there are only a couple of references to Hegel, both of them hostile, compared with seventeen references to Kant and a whole chapter devoted to Schopenhauer; whereas in Ruggiero's *History of European Liberalism*, it is Hegel and the disciples of Hegel who occupy the centre of the stage. At first sight this is very surprising when we read the bitter attack on German Liberalism which prefaces the *Philosophy of Right,* but if we read it more closely we find that the Liberalism which

Hegel attacks has a much closer affinity to National Socialism than to Hegel's own doctrine. It is the Liberalism of the first German Youth Movement, of the Wartburg Party Rally, and the emotional appeal to the spirit of the German *Volk* and *Land*. Hence it is difficult to see in Hegel a Nazi or the father of Nazism. But when we come to the question of "Prussianism," the case is different—there was indeed a kind of elective affinity between the Prussian state and the Hegelian philosophy. For the Prussian people, unlike any other people in Europe, had been made by the State and for the State, by a conscious process of military and political organisation.

Such a state was made to appeal to Hegel, who of all the philosophers of his generation—and indeed of all modern philosophers—had the strongest sense of the State and who realised most deeply the importance of the power factor in history and politics. Nevertheless, his idea of the state had little in common with the cold-hearted calculation of Frederick the Great and his pupils. In Hegel's view the state is never a mere political instrument: "As high as mind stands over nature, so high does the state stand over physical life. Man must therefore venerate the state as the Divine upon Earth." "The march of God in the world that is what the state is."

If this is rationalism, it is not the rationalism of the rationalists, and it is derived from very different sources from those of the Prussian tradition of statecraft. Behind the Hegel of the *Philosophy of Right* there is the youth who had once shared with Hölderlin the intoxicating vision of Hyperion—the true city in which man is one with the Gods, where the finite and the infinite are united in the totality of a living community. How far apart their paths had led since those early days! Hölderlin following his vision, like Eurydice, down to the dark underworld of insanity,

Hegel never relinquishing his hold on reality until he had subdued it by the sheer force of thought and incorporated it with all its contradictions and by all its contradictions in the totality of an absolute synthesis. The turning point in Hegel's thought seems to have taken place in 1802–3, at the same time as Hölderlin's tragedy. It was then that Hegel first gave clear expression to all those elements in his thought that we regard as characteristically Prussian: power politics, an anti-democratic conception of government, Machiavellianism, above all the exaltation of war as a necessary and health-giving law of existence.

But in the circumstances of the time in which Hegel wrote, all these ideas were not so much Prussian as Napoleonic. It was the hour of Napoleon's triumph and of Germany's humiliation: not the humiliation of national defeat, as in the years of Austerlitz and Jena, but the humiliation of internal disintegration, when the German princes were fawning on the First Consul for their share in the spoils of confiscated Church lands and the debris of the Holy Empire. In those days Bonaparte rose above the satraps of Germany like a new Alexander, and it was in him and not in the Hohenzollerns or the Hapsburgs that Hegel found the pattern of his World-Historical person in whom the movement of history was embodied and who transcends law and morality by his creative activity.

These ideas were by no means specifically Prussian or German. They were in the mind of an age which had witnessed the French Revolution and had seen the dramatic succession of leaders—Mirabeau, Danton, Robespierre, Hoche, Moreau, Bonaparte—rising and being swept away in turn by the forces they had embodied or created.

If we go on to cast a look at the fate of these World-Historical persons, whose vocation it was to be the agents of the world spirit—we shall find it to have been no happy one. They attained no calm enjoyment; their whole life was labour and trouble; their whole nature was naught else but their master passion. When their object is attained, they fall off like empty husks from the kernel. They die early, like Alexander; they are murdered, like Caesar; transported to St. Helena, like Napoleon.

A World-Historical person is not so unwise as to indulge a variety of wishes to divide his regards. He is devoted to the One Aim, regardless of all else. It is even possible that such men may treat other great, even sacred, interests inconsiderately; conduct which is indeed obnoxious to moral reprehension. But so mighty a form must trample down many an innocent flower—crush to pieces many an object in its path.

These are the words of the philosopher. Now hear the words of a man of action, a member of the Committee of Public Safety, Billaud-Varenne:

The decisions for which we have been reproached we did not wish for the most part two days, a day, or several hours before taking them. It was the crisis alone that produced them. . . . We were *statesmen;* putting the safety of the cause entrusted to us above every other consideration. Do you reproach us with the means we used? But the means made that great cause to triumph. Our eyes were fixed too high to see that the ground on which we trod was covered with blood. Reproach us if you will, but also say: "They did not fail the Republic."

And if we turn to the greatest writer in the opposite camp—to Joseph de Maistre—we find not indeed Machiavellianism, but the same sombre conception of historic destiny and the immanent force of events as well as a far stronger justification of war and the sacrifice of the innocent than anything that Hegel wrote. After all, a generation which had experienced twenty-three years of almost continual war was bound to give war a considerable place in its system of thought, and men who had seen Europe turned upside down and European society transformed by the power of the sword were all more or less believers in power politics. It is not in this that Hegel's originality is to be found, but rather in the stubborn determination with which he maintained his faith in the rationality of history and of the state as the perfect embodiment of spirit— the actuality of the ethical idea. He had deepened the eighteenth-century conception of law and politics by his profound consciousness of the concrete reality of social change and the dialectical movement of history. He saw the state not as a political mechanism but as a moral organism by membership of which alone man can achieve freedom and full moral activity. Man only acquires rights as member of a social system, and this system is not a juridical abstraction, but a concrete living historical organism. History is a process of the construction of such organised systems, and thus it is a second world, a spiritual creation which can be compared to the world of nature in its diversity and organic inter-relation, while it transcends that world by its universal consciousness and its actuality of concrete freedom and ethical order.

Now, according to Hegel, it is in the state that this process of organisation culminates. It is the all-embracing organisation, self-contained, self-conscious, self-determined: an autonomous totality, a complete moral world, the ultimate fruit of the tree of life, the "Divine Idea as it exists on earth." Thus Hegel lays the metaphysical foundation for that cult of the State which has become to an increasing extent the religion of the modern world. It is strange that a man who possessed such a deep and rich sense of history should not have realised that this attribution of absolute and ultimate value to a particular social form limits the movement of history and impoverishes its spiritual value. For it is only in the ancient oriental civilisations, which Hegel terms the first world-historical realm, that the State is a spiritual totality. Elsewhere culture transcends the State not merely ideally but sociologically, so that it is only in a society of states that the cultural whole is to be found. Even the city-state of ancient Greece, which was the source and pattern of Hegel's conception of the State as an ethical totality, was in reality itself a member of a wider society, and it was this society, this Pan-Hellenic world, which was the Whole in which the spirit of Hellenic culture found expression. And this was still more true of Western civilisation, all the typical achievements of which transcended the limits of the State and depended on the fruitful interaction and co-operation of the different European peoples.

Moreover, behind this European community there lies in fact the historical reality of Christendom, the commonwealth of Christian peoples, which did not derive its origin from the State, but was, on the contrary, the spiritual basis which the European State assumed as given and from which its highest values were derived. Hegel's extremely limited view of the nature of religion and the function of the Church made it impossible for him to do justice to these facts. Hegel always declared that he was a Lutheran, and he was in fact in his later years a loyal adherent to the official conception of the Prussian State Church as exemplified in Altenstein's ecclesiastical policy. But it was a very residual and negative Lutheranism in which the Church had become no more than a docile and sentimental *Hausfrau* of a State which itself embodied the spiritual principle in a masculine and objective form.

Hegel was a true Protestant in the sense that he protested with passion and conviction against a Church which claimed to be the objective embodiment of the

Spirit and the representative of Divine Law. But he was no less opposed to the sectarian Protestantism which turned men's minds from the State and from the present world and absorbed them in personal piety. It is characteristic of Hegel's "Lutheranism" that he found "the Hero of Protestantism" not in Gustavus Adolphus or Cromwell, but in Frederick the Great, the man who "had the consciousness of Universality, which is the profoundest depth to which Spirit can attain." What Hegel valued in the Reformation was in fact that it had destroyed the Church as a substantial unity and had restored the unity of human consciousness in one universal objective moral organism: the State. For Hegel's real religion is the Religion of the State: a hybrid growth which owes its external features to the official Lutheranism of the territorial Churches of the German principalities, but which derives its true inspiration from the ideal of the Greek City-State, where, as he remarks, the name of the City "suggests not only a complex of political institutions but no less that Goddess who represented the Spirit of the people and its unity."

To the last, Hegel's glorification of the State as the embodiment of the divine idea—as "this actual God"— retains the traces of the Platonic idealism of his romantic youth when, with Schelling and Hölderlin, he attempted to recapture a lost spiritual world of infinite reality and beauty. But this vision of perfection (like the vision of Blake and Wordsworth and Shelley in England) had no earthly relation with the actual conditions of the modern State, and the *tour de force* by which Hegel identified the two is a typical example of that irrational leap in the dark from Spirit to Nature and from Logic to Reality which is the Hegelian idea. The fact is that Hegel's conception of *Geist* or spirit is profoundly equivocal and covers an infinite gradation of meanings. When the Romantics at the close of the eighteenth century spoke of Spirit, they were using a word that was charged with an immense weight of Christian tradition and mystical depth. And this is no less true of Hegel, who began as a theologian and remained in a sense a theologian to the end. But his identification of Spirit with rational activity—not only the creative activity of the cosmic Logos but also, and no less, the rational activity of the human mind objectifying itself in law and institutions—introduced another element into the conception, which deprived it of its transcendent character and opened the way for the complete secularisation of both the concept and the system by the Hegelians of the Left, culminating in Feuerbach and Marx.

Now the conception of a society which should be the earthly embodiment of the Spirit—a Spirit-created and a Spirit-filled organism—was no invention of the Romantics: It was a common possession of the whole Christian past. Indeed, this society was the spiritual home of European man to a greater degree than the state, and not least in Germany, where the territorial state possessed only the bare bones of political authority and military power without the organic life of a true civil society. Consequently, when Hegel transfers to the State by a *coup d'esprit* the rights and prerogatives of the spiritual community and arrays the grim skeleton of the police state in the royal robe of a Divinity, he is not only denying the Christian doctrine of a supernatural order and a super-political society, he is not even doing justice to the social ideals of the Romantics in which he had once shared. The words which Hölderlin's Hyperion addresses to his friend Alabanda before their parting are a prophetic criticism of the false path his friend was to follow to the misfortune of Germany and of Europe:

You grant the State yet too much power. It should not demand what it cannot compel. For the gift of Love and of the Spirit cannot be forced. Let it leave them untouched, or let men take its law and nail it to the pillory. By Heaven he knows not how he sins who would make the State a moral schoolmaster. Whenever man has sought to make the State his heaven, he has made it Hell. . . .

The State has no jurisdiction over thee. But if it does not hinder thee, thou wilt yet come, thou wilt come with thine almighty glory and raise us above mortality.

This eschatological vision of the descent of "the youngest, fairest daughter of time, the new Church," is almost identical with this vision of the renewal of Christendom with which Novalis concluded his *Europe*, while at the same time in England William Blake was creating a similar apocalypse on a gigantic scale in the series of epics which culminated in Jerusalem. The descent from these cloudy summits of the romantic Sinai to the worship of the Secular State, that Golden Calf in the desert of materialism, is one of the strangest events in the history of European thought, and the philosophy of Hegel remains as a mighty monument and symbol of this spiritual journey into the wilderness.

3

The Trend to Secularism

THE RELIGIOUS HISTORY of the nineteenth century has
yet to be written. The material is too vast and the
workers are too few, so that as yet they are hardly able
to do more than explore the fringes of their subject.
But when it comes to be written, I think there is no
doubt that the personality and genius of Newman will
be seen as a key point of the whole development, as at
once the embodiment and the contradiction of the
spirit of his age.

We are accustomed to regard the nineteenth century as the age when Western culture became completely secularised. Yet at the same time, it was an age
of religious revival—of a renaissance of Christianity,
the importance of which has not yet been fully appreciated. In the eighteenth century the Catholic Church
was a venerable structure which seemed tottering and
decadent. Then came the Revolution, and at its impact the whole edifice of traditional ecclesiasticism
crashed in ruin and destruction. The Gallican Church
was destroyed, the ecclesiastical principalities and the
Holy Roman Empire were secularised, the Pope was
chased out of Rome, and the monasteries and universities of Catholic Europe were dissolved. A hundred
years later, when Leo XIII died, the Church was
stronger than it had been since the seventeenth century, and not only in Catholic Europe but in the
Protestant North, in the new lands beyond the seas,
and in the missionary countries of Asia and Africa,

many of which were first opened to Christian influence at this period. It is clear that Catholicism possessed a principle of life and spiritual development of which the world had been completely unaware, and it was not until the Church was brought into sharp opposition with the spirit of the age and was increasingly threatened by the domination of a completely secular culture that its intrinsic power of regeneration and growth was manifested.

It was the mission of Newman to be the philosopher and interpreter of this Christian renaissance, and he was equally alive to both its positive and its negative aspects. He realised with exceptional keenness of perception and clarity of vision the new dangers which threatened the Christian faith and the whole traditional order of Christian civilisation. And at the same time he discovered and investigated the internal principle of development in the life of the Church by which what is already implicitly contained in Christian faith and tradition is unfolded and applied to meet the needs of the age, so that every new challenge to the Faith becomes an opportunity for the conquest of new truths and reveals unsuspected depths of meaning in truths that are already familiar.

It was only gradually that Newman became aware of the implications of his principles and the direction in which they were to lead him. His thought developed slowly and painfully. Every step was carefully thought out, as though it were an end in itself, and he often deliberately shut his eyes to the step that had to follow,

> Keep Thou my feet; I do not ask to see
> The distant scene—one step enough for me.
> [From Newman's Hymn "Lead Kindly Light"]

Nevertheless, his intellectual pilgrimage was a consistent development of a line of thought which conducted him slowly but undeviatingly to his predestined goal, and his intense meditation on the gradual unfolding of truth in his own mind provided him with a key to the interpretation of the mystery of faith in the history of mankind and the life of the Church.

Newman approached the religious problem of the modern world at an oblique angle, so to speak, to the main current of his generation. He was never subjected, like De Maistre or Lamennais or Lacordaire, to the direct shock of the revolutionary spirit of the age. His mind was formed in the remote and sheltered environment of pre-Victorian Oxford at a time when the University was one of the last strongholds of traditional culture, a celibate society of clerical corporations which had retained their constitution and their privileges almost intact from the Middle Ages. No society could have seemed more remote and secure from the storm centres of the age, and the impact of revolutionary thought reached it only in a muffled and attenuated form. The questions that agitated the University were from the European point of view storms in a very small tea-cup, and its leaders a group of remote and ineffectual dons who were attempting to set back the clock of modern progress. Nevertheless, as Matthew Arnold recognised a generation later, Newman's criticism of the spirit of the age had a far deeper influence than his contemporaries realised, and his name lives and will live when those of the leaders of enlightened thought—the Molesworths and Grotes and Roebucks—are forgotten.

The movement against which Newman directed his criticism and which he termed "Liberalism" was in fact the movement of progressive secularism, which became the dominant force in nineteenth-century civilisation and shaped the world in which we live today. In the form in which he first mentioned it, the ideas of men like Peel and Brougham and Macaulay, it was

neither a revolutionary nor an anti-religious movement. It advocated religious toleration, the diffusion
of useful knowledge, social reform, and economic
progress. Nevertheless, behind the innocuous platitudes of Sir Robert Peel and Dr. Hampden, Newman
felt the steady pressure of the rising tide which was
to submerge, as he said forty years later, "that goodly
framework of society which is the creation of Christianity."

For a thousand years and more, Christianity had
been "the law of the land" in England and in the
West—that is to say, all the conscious moral effort of
society was inspired by Christian ideas and directed to
Christian ends. Now all this was changed. Religion
was no longer the bond of society. A new principle
had taken its place: the principle of utility, the greatest happiness of the greatest number, whether conceived individualistically, as in English Liberalism, or
collectively, as in French and German Socialism.

Christian opinion was slow to realise the implications of this movement. In England, and in the Protestant world generally, religious people shut their eyes
to the fundamental character of the issues, and
evolved that concordat between popular Protestantism and bourgeois capitalism which characterised the
Victorian compromise. In Catholic Europe the issues
were more sharply defined, and there was no mistak-
ing the character of the conflict. Nevertheless, here also
religious people shut their eyes to the inevitability of
the changes that were taking place in modern culture and put their faith in the restoration of the Christian state and the defeat of the revolution by an
alliance with political conservatism. Newman was almost the only Christian thinker who realised the
anti-Christian character of the trend to secularism
without indulging in wishful thinking or identifying
the Church with that of the political reactionaries.

And consequently he was rejected by both sides and was condemned by the leaders of the Catholic revival as a Liberal and compromiser and by the Victorian Liberals as an arch-reactionary who was misusing his brilliant literary and dialectical powers to serve the cause of obscurantism. That was the tragedy of Newman's later life—a real tragedy, since it separated him from his old colleagues and disciples in both camps— from Ward and Faber and Dalgairns, as well as from Whately and Blanco White and Gladstone, and left him isolated with men like Acton and Simpson, who had no real community of thought and aim with him. He was a lonely man because he saw further and deeper than his contemporaries. From a very early stage in his career he had been convinced that "a new cycle of sacred history" was about to begin and that as the old tradition of Christian culture was submerged by the rising tide of secularism, the Church could rely on no external aid but only on the inherent and indefeasible principle of her supernatural life.

But this conviction had nothing in common with that obscurantist spirit which welcomes the separation of Christianity from modern culture because it is itself entirely lacking in appreciation of the gifts of culture and the values of science. Newman's doctrine of development was inspired by an intense faith in the boundless powers of assimilation which the Christian faith possessed and which made it a unitive principle in life and thought. The Church had with her, he wrote, "the very archetypes of which paganism attempted the shadows," and therefore she was able to bring in all the riches of the Gentiles and to enlarge the range of her own teaching by the progressive conquest of new spiritual territory.[1]

Hence, although Newman realised, like Leo XIII,

[1] "Essay on the Idea of Development" (1st ed.) p. 358.

that the modern world was on the verge of a great moral catastrophe, he never accepted the fundamental historical pessimism which is so common today, and which was expressed so powerfully in his own time by his great Protestant contemporary, Kierkegaard. For Newman saw that it was only in history that the divine process of progressive revelation and spiritual renovation could be fulfilled. "The Church," he wrote, "does not teach that human nature is irreclaimable, else wherefore should she be sent? Not that it is to be shattered and reversed but to be extricated, purified, and restored; not that it is a mere mass of hopeless evil, but that it has the promise upon it of great things, and even now, in its present state of disorder and excess, has a virtue and a praise proper to itself. But in the next place, she knows and she preaches that such a restoration, as she aims at effecting in it, must be brought about, not simply through any outward provisions of preaching and teaching, even though it be her own, but from a certain inward spiritual power and grace imparted directly from above and which is in her keeping. She has in charge to rescue human nature from its misery, but not simply by raising it upon its own level, but by lifting it up to a higher level than its own. She recognises in it real moral excellence, though degraded, but she cannot set it free from earth except by exalting it towards heaven." (From *Apologia pro Vita Sua* [pp. 339–40. Oxford edition, ed. W. Ward])

4

The Spiritual Tragedy of Modern Man*

ARTHUR KOESTLER is a writer of great intelligence
and strong convictions, who has for years been carry-
ing on a single-handed fight against that modern mechanical mystery of iniquity, the Totalitarian State.
He fights alone because he is a writer of the Left, even
of the extreme Left, who refuses to accept the myths
and rationalisations of his party and is just as out-
spoken in his condemnation of the totalitarianism of
the Left as he is of the totalitarianism of the Right. He
fights alone, also because he feels acutely the spiritual
tragedy of modern man and the need for spiritual
reintegration, and yet rejects any positive religious
solution of the problem. His diagnosis of the situation
was expressed in *The Yogi and the Commissar*—the
polar opposition of the passive contemplation of the
naked Indian ascetic and the ruthless activism of the
Communist bureaucrat.

No doubt the opposition is psychologically justifiable in terms of the pure introvert and the pure extro-
vert, but I do not feel that it really fits the modern
situation, and particularly that aspect of the situation
to which Koestler devotes so much of the book's argument. For what he is mainly concerned with in *The
Yogi and the Commissar* is not the opposition of action and contemplation, but rather the frustration of
the modern intelligentsia in a world which it has done

* This chapter is adapted from a review of Arthur Koestler's,
"The Yogi and the Commissar," published in *Blackfriars* (1945).

so much to create. The revolutionary intelligentsia created the Marxian ideology, which in turn produced the
Communist State. But something has gone wrong in
the process. The intellectuals believed and taught that
the Dictatorship of the Proletariat would be followed
by the "withering away" of the State. In fact, however,
what has happened has been the development of a
State power more absolute than any absolutism of the
past, and it has been the intelligentsia which has
"withered away." Much of Koestler's work has been a
running commentary on this process by one who has
personally witnessed and shared the slow crucifixion
of the revolutionary intelligentsia in the concentration
camps of Europe, and, as he shows, the process was
not ended with the defeat of Fascism. On the contrary, it has only meant the swallowing up of one
Leviathan by another, and the extermination of the
minorities which had maintained a precarious mar-
ginal existence between the two.

Koestler is very insistent that the elements which
are marked out for extermination or suppression in
the two types of Totalitarian State are precisely the
same. The revolutionary intelligentsia constitute the
first category on both their prescription lists, while
both capitalists and clergymen come in quite a low
category. Thus, in the deportation list for Soviet Lithu-
ania, category No. 1 consisted of "members of the Russian pre-revolutionary parties: Social Revolutionaries,
Mensheviks, Trotskyites, and Anarchists," and it is not
until we come to categories 13 and 14 that we find
"clergymen, aristocrats, landowners, bankers, indus-
trialists, wealthy merchants, hotel keepers, and restau-
rant proprietors."

Needless to say, Yogis did not figure on the list, unless they can be brought into the category which consists of "people who have travelled abroad, Esperant-
ists and Philatelists." For the Yogi has no quarrel with

the Commissar. All that he asks is to be allowed "to live in a fertile country, ruled by a virtuous king (or an efficient Commissar) where he will not be disturbed." The real enemy of the Commissar is not the Yogi, but the idealist who refuses to accept the world as it is, and is consequently a nuisance alike to the party boss who wants everyone to shout the same slogan and to the scientific bureaucrat who wishes to treat mankind as so much material to be organised and conditioned according to the requirements of his large-scale social planning. And this is a bad outlook for humanity, since the Commissar mentality has very little sense of human values and is often incapable of discriminating between the social reformer and the anti-social type, between the idealist and the criminal. In fact the totalitarian state is, by its very nature, intolerant not merely of criticism but of diversity; so that it combines all the intolerances of the past—the intolerance of the absolutist state for the rebel, the intolerance of the orthodox state for the heretic, the intolerance of the police state for the criminal—into a massive weight of social pressure that forces everyone into the same mould of total conformity.

In the past, Western Civilisation was based on the assumption that man had an immortal soul, and however much the state demanded, it admitted, at least in theory, that the destiny of every human being reached beyond the extreme limits of political society, so that human conduct was ultimately governed and judged by super-social laws. The secularisation of Western society did not immediately destroy the consequences of this belief. On the contrary, the more men lost their faith in God, the more desperately did they cling to the belief in the liberty and value of human personality which was the fruit of a thousand years of Christian culture. The present plight of Western culture is due, as Koestler recognised, to the fact that the real values that we are defending against the totalitarian state are values that have been divorced from their religious and metaphysical foundations, and are insofar indefensible, but which remain the highest values which we possess.

No one has done more than Mr. Koestler to bring home to the English and American reader what the loss of the fundamental liberal and humane value entails and how complete is the resultant disintegration of human life. But on the positive side, his treatment is much less satisfactory, since his own mind has been affected by the atmosphere of frustration and scepticism from which it is difficult for a member of the intelligentsia to escape. He does not fully realise how heavy is the responsibility of the intellectuals themselves for the situation he describes in such a masterly way. For the truth is that if the totalitarian state had been constructed by the men of action—soldiers and policemen and politicians and engineers—it would never have become so formidable a threat to man's spiritual freedom. It would have been at least an external threat, like the despotisms of the past. It was the revolutionary intelligentsia which invented the dictatorship of the proletariat, and it was romantic idealists like Nietzsche and Sorel who invented the Fascist mythology of creative violence. And the transformation of the revolutionary idealist into the commissar type took place at a much earlier stage in the development than Mr. Koestler recognises. It is already evident, as far back as 1862, in Turgenev's Bazarov, who more than any of Dostoyevsky's characters represents the real dynamism of the Russian revolutionary tradition. The denial of God by the intelligentsia was the turning point in Western civilisation. From that point the road has led without a turning to the concentration camps and slaughter houses of the totalitarian state. For it is

obvious that any atheistic socialism, whether of the
Left or the Right, can only think in terms of the whole
and not of the individual, and that it will seem as reasonable and just for it to liquidate a class or exterminate a few million of social or racial undesirables as it
is for a surgeon to conduct a major operation for the
health of the organism as a whole. The revolutionary
realist has an unanswerable case against the revolutionary idealist when he accuses the latter of willing
the end and refusing the means on sentimental
grounds, and it is as difficult for a Christian to judge
between them as it was for Alice to make up her
mind between the attitude of the Walrus and that of
the Carpenter towards the oysters.

It is true that the humanitarianism of the modern
intelligentsia cannot be written off as a mere matter of
sentiment. It was based on deep and sincere convictions, with something of the nature of a religious faith,
and there are few movements in history that have had
so great an effect on human life. Nevertheless, it belongs to the age of transition between Christian and
secular culture, and its chief successes were the result
of a working coalition with the forces of organised religion, such as we see in the case of the abolition of
slavery or the factory acts or the movements
against the exploitation of uncivilised peoples. When
humanitarianism is left to its own resources in a purely
secular environment, it tends to wither away like political idealism.

Mr. Koestler is well aware of this fragility of the
intelligentsia and of their work. But he does not fully
recognise their exceptional and unrepresentative position in European culture. After all, "the intelligentsia" is a Russian expression coined to describe the
strange hothouse development of a class without social
roots and political responsibilities, which was the re-

sult of the introduction of Western culture and ideas
into Tzarist Russia. It was a specifically Russian phenomenon for which we can find no true parallel in the
development of the educated classes in Western Europe or even in the student class in the Far East or
India, where the conflict of hereditary and imported
cultures is even sharper.

Now in this vanished world of the pre-revolutionary
Russian intelligentsia, the Yogi and the Commissar
correspond to a real conflict of human types and social ideals. The Russian intellectuals saw on the one
side the German drill sergeant and the Anglo-Saxon
engineer who were bringing an alien efficiency and
method into Russia, while on the other side, the popular tradition still preserved the ideals of the desert
monks, of the ascetics and hermits and "fools for
Christ's sake," whose life had no meaning to the modern mind and no relation to the facts of modern society. The Russian intelligentsia lived in the vacuum
between these two worlds, and the Russian revolutionary tradition arose out of their tension. But in the
West it has not been so. We have had rationalists and
we have had mystics, but we have never had a highly
conscious intellectual class that was separated alike
from popular religious tradition and from political responsibility and control. At no point in its history was
Western civilisation a Yogi civilisation inspired by the
ideal of static contemplation, which characterised the
oriental world. It was a civilisation built by faith on
the solid earth, which maintained the complementary
values of the contemplative and the active life. Western Christendom had been inspired from the beginning by an active missionary spirit, which alone gave
it the power to survive the catastrophes of the barbarian invasions and to initiate the new peoples into the
Christian tradition. But its action did not stop at this

point as did that of Byzantine Christendom. Already
in the Middle Ages it had conceived the specifically
Western idea of the systematic exploration and control of nature by reason and art, and in the following
centuries Western man achieved the immense task of
conquering and transforming the world. And when
Western civilisation lost the faith that formerly inspired it, it did not lose the dynamic character that it
had acquired in these centuries of struggle and
achievement. Indeed, the more it lost its spiritual aim,
the more it clung to its material achievement and the
more fiercely did it concentrate its energies on the
conquest of power. And thus it has come about that
the immense progress of our civilisation in material
resources and in the scientific control of nature and
human life has become a blind movement to destruction, which finds its embodiment in the Frankenstein
monster of the totalitarian state; for dynamism without spiritual purpose or guidance must inevitably be
destructive. And the responsibility for this development rests finally with the intellectuals who are the
brain of society and not with the officials—commissars
or bureaucrats—who are its executive arm. It is true
that at the present time the natural order of the body
of society has been inverted, so that the temporal
power has usurped the functions of the spiritual, and
the scientist and the thinker and the artist have become mere instruments or servants of the men of
power of the commissar or capitalist type. Nevertheless, this perversion of order is itself, in the last resort,
the work of the intellectuals. It is the fruit of a false
philosophy and a false education, which originated
among a small élite of intellectuals and which were
gradually diffused and popularised by the leaders of
"enlightened" and "progressive" opinion. And, as Mr.
Koestler recognises in the last section of his book, the
malady from which our civilisation is suffering can

only be remedied by a reversal of this process, which will restore the true hierarchy of spiritual ends and recognise the autonomy and irreducibility of the higher levels of spiritual reality.

5

Religion and Life

IT IS OFTEN SAID that Christianity is out of touch with life and that it no longer satisfies the needs of the modern world. And these criticisms are symptomatic of a general change of attitude with regard to religious problems. Men today are less interested in the theological and metaphysical assumptions of religion than in its practical results. They are concerned not so much with the truth of Christian doctrine as with the value of the Christian way of life. It is Christian ethics even more than Christian dogma that has become the principal object of attack.

This is not altogether a misfortune, for it shows that people no longer treat religion as something that has no relation to man's daily life. The passive acceptance of religion as something that every respectable citizen takes for granted is no longer possible, and at the same time the self-satisfied bourgeois acceptance of the world as it is, is equally discredited. Today everybody admits that something is wrong with the world, and the critics of Christianity are the very people who feel this most. The most violent attacks on religion come from those who are most anxious to to change the world, and they attack Christianity because they think that it is an obstructive force that stands in the way of a real reform of human life. There has seldom been a time in which men were more dissatisfied with life and more conscious of the need for deliverance, and if they turn away from Christianity it

302   *The Nature and Destiny of Man*

is because they feel that Christianity is a servant of the established order and that it has no real power or will to change the world and to rescue man from his present difficulties. They have lost their faith in the old spiritual traditions that inspired civilisation in the past, and they tend to look for a solution in some external practical remedy such as communism, or the scientific organisation of life; something definite and objective that can be applied to society as a whole.

There is, however, little ground for supposing that the world can be saved by machinery or by any external reform. In fact, the great tragedy of modern civilisation is to be found in the failure of material progress to satisfy human needs. The modern world has more power than any previous age, but it has used its new power for destruction as much as for life; it has more wealth, and yet we are in the throes of a vast economic crisis; it has more knowledge, and yet all our knowledge seems powerless to help us. What our civilisation lacks is not power and wealth and knowledge, but spiritual vitality, and unless it is possible to secure that, nothing can save us from the fate that overtook the civilisation of classical antiquity and so many other civilisations that were brilliant and powerful in their day.

Now this question of spiritual vitality, whether in the case of the individual or society, is the very centre and essence of the religious problem. Religion is not philosophy, or science or ethics, it is nothing more or less than a way of life, whether it be regarded from within as an act of vital communion, or externally, as a system of beliefs and practices by which man brings his life into relation with the powers that rule the life of the universe.

Primitive religion is concerned, as we should expect, primarily with the powers of nature, and it finds its centre in the cult of the powers of fertility and genera-

tion on which the physical life of the earth and man
were alike dependent. All the vital moments in the
life of the tribe or the peasant community were invested with religious significance and sanctified by religious rites, and these rites were not merely magical
in the utilitarian sense, but sacramental and mystical,
since they were the channels by which man attained
contact and communion with the divine powers that
ruled the world. Thus in primitive society there could
be no question of any contradiction or conflict between religion and life, since the two were complementary aspects of the same thing. Religion was the
vital centre of the social organism and governed the
whole economic and political activity of society. Nor
was there any contradiction between the material and
the spiritual, for material things were regarded as the
vehicles of spiritual forces; in fact, to the primitive,
the world is a vast complex of spiritual powers, good,
bad, and indifferent, which affect his life at every turn,
and religion is the trail that he has blazed out for himself through this spiritual jungle.

The coming of the higher religions changed all this.
Religion no longer found its centre in the practical
needs of human life. It became a matter of spiritual
discipline and intellectual contemplation. Man realised the transcendent character of spiritual reality and
freed himself from the terror of the dark and the
power of the sinister forces that lurk in or behind nature. But this higher type of religion, with its clear
realisation of the distinction between matter and
spirit, also contained the seeds of a conflict between
religion and life. There was no room for common humanity on the icy summits to which the path of contemplation led, and yet it was at the same time the
only way to deliverance and spiritual life. This contrast is seen in its most striking and paradoxical form
in Buddhism, for Buddhism is, above all, a direct and

straightforward attempt to solve the problem of human life, and it does this by a radical denial of life itself. The Buddha professed to teach man the secret of happiness and the way of spiritual deliverance, but his noble, ethical teaching has its beginning in the realisation that existence is suffering, and its end in the peace of Nirvana.

This pessimism and turning away from life is characteristic to a greater or less extent of all the great religions of the ancient world; even the Greeks, for all their humanism and appreciation of physical life, did not escape from it. The first word in Greek speculation is the Orphic mysticism, with its yearning for deliverance from the sorrowful circle of birth and death, and its last word is contained in the Neoplatonic doctrine of the evil of matter and the necessity for the soul to escape from the world of sense to the world of pure spirit.

It was to a world dominated by these conceptions, as well as by the decadent remains of the older tradition of nature worship, that Christianity came, and it also brought a message of deliverance and spiritual salvation. But it inherited a different tradition from that of either the Greek or the oriental world, and its dualism was not the dualism of the Indian yogi or that of the Hellenic philosopher. Jewish religion differed from all the rest in the dynamic realism of its conception of God. The God of Israel was no metaphysical abstraction, like the Platonic Idea of the Good, or the universal Brahmin, or the Chinese Tao, "not the God of the philosophers and savants, but the Living God, God of Abraham, God of Isaac, God of Jacob, *Deus meus et Deus vester.*"

This Living God manifested Himself externally by the vital action of His creative Spirit—as the breath of Divine Life that brooded over the primordial chaos and which inspires the prophets with the word of life.

In the Hellenistic language of the Book of Wisdom, it is the power "that reaches from end to end ordering all things sweetly and strongly, which, being one, has power to do all things and remaining in itself renews all things, and from generation to generation passing into holy souls makes men friends of God and prophets."

Thus the Christian idea of salvation was not deliverance from the body and from the sensible world; it was the salvation of the whole man, body and soul, by the coming of a new life. In no other religion is the conception of *life* so central and so characteristic as in Christianity.

From the beginning, Christianity was regarded not as an intellectual gnosis or a new morality, but as a new life: as the communication of a new vital principle, which transformed human nature by raising it to an objectively higher plane of being. In the eyes of the primitive Church, the Christian was a new creature, as different or even more different from the natural "psychic" man as the latter was from the animals. This conception is absolutely fundamental alike to the Pauline and the Johannine theology. To St. Paul, Christ is the second Adam, the first born of the new creation, and it was from the organic and sacramental union between Christ and the Church that the new spiritual humanity was born. And so, too, in the Johannine writings, Jesus is not merely a teacher or a moral exemplar; he is life and the source of life, and the essence of Christianity consists in the grafting of this divine life on the stock of humanity by a vital sacramental act.

This sacramentalism has led many modern critics to compare Christianity to the contemporary mystery religions, which also laid emphasis on the conception of a new birth. But whereas the pagan mysteries were simply the rites of the old nature religions invested with a new metaphysical, or rather, theosophical significance, the sacraments of Christianity are organically connected with its essential nature. The humanity of Jesus is a sacrament, the visible Church is a sacrament, and the vital moments of the Christian life necessarily manifest themselves in sacramental acts. The mystery religions and gnosticism were alike powerless to bridge the gulf between human life and spiritual reality. They were ways of escape from life, not ways of regeneration. Christianity defeated its rivals because it was felt to be a historical and social reality, capable of transforming human life.

Primitive Christianity is instinct with a triumphant sense of spiritual vitality that has no parallel in the history of religion. "Awake thou that sleepest and arise from the dead and Christ will shine upon thee." The new principle of spiritual life that had entered humanity made it possible for men to face the harsh realities of existence with new courage. It did not free from suffering and death, but it subordinated them to vital ends. This is the greatest psychological victory of Christianity: the spiritual reconquest of that great part of life that had hitherto lain under the shadow of death. "Show us miracles," wrote Blake, "can you have greater miracles than these? Men who devote their life's whole comfort to entire scorn and injury and death." The Christian could accept what was unbearable to human nature, because the cross had become the token of life. As St. Paul says, he could rejoice in his sufferings because they were all extension and completion of what Christ had suffered for His body, which is the Church.

This heroic acceptance of suffering is, of course, rare. It is the mark of a saint. But it is only in the saints that the Christian life is completely realised. We cannot judge Christianity by statistics or by striking an average. One saint can do more than a thousand average men, however active and well organised they may be. In this respect Christianity is essentially aristocratic, since the quality of the individual is the only thing that matters. And yet, on the other hand, it is the most democratic of religions, for an uneducated beggar who is a saint counts more than a thousand scholars or organisers. As St. Francis says, the brilliant preacher may congratulate himself on the effects of his sermons, when their success is really due to the prayers of some unknown saint, whose importance is realised neither by himself nor by others.

This is what St. Paul means in his famous panegyric of charity, for charity is nothing else but this mysterious power of spiritual life actuating the will. It is no human power or moral quality, but a supernatural energy that transforms human nature and builds up a new humanity. Nothing gives a more appalling idea of the difference between living and dead religion than the profound degradation that this word has undergone in modern times. It has lost all its vital significance and its mysterious "numinous" quality. It has become identical with the most external and spiritually barren type of social beneficence, and even this beneficence is tainted with the suggestion of social patronage and ethical self-satisfaction. And in the same way that great saying of St. John, "He that loveth not knoweth not God, for God is love," has been degraded from the most profound of spiritual truths into a sentimental platitude.

These are but specimens of the way in which spiritual concepts can become emptied of their vital significance. We have only to compare modern ecclesiastical art with that of the past to feel that the life has gone out of it, and that what was once seen as a living reality has become a dead formula. And this devitalisation of modern religion goes a long way to explain the anti-Christian attitude of writers like Nietzsche and D. H. Lawrence. For there is nothing so repulsive as dead religion; it is the deadest thing there is. As the Gospel says, it is not even good enough for the dunghill.

It cannot be denied that Christianity has often appeared in practice to agree with the attitude of the oriental ascetic or with an equally one-sided ethical puritanism which allows insufficient recognition to the value of the body and the rights of physical life. Nevertheless, Christian asceticism rests in principle, not on the Platonic and oriental dualism, but on the Old Testament principle of a divine law of life that regulated every side of human existence—physical, social, and spiritual. The law was not merely a matter of external ceremonialism. It was a spiritual norm to which man must conform his thoughts and his actions and which made his whole life a liturgical act. And we see in the Psalms how this ideal was incorporated into religious experience and made the foundation of the spiritual life of the individual as well as of the social life of the national Church.

It was on this foundation that the Christian ethic was built, and the Pauline repudiation of the Mosaic law was in no sense a denial of this ideal. The Christian gospel involved the substitution of the power of the spirit—the law of liberty—for the external legalism of the older dispensation. But it was equally comprehensive and universal in purpose. It was, in St. Paul's words, "The law of the spirit of the life in Christ Jesus."

Hence the Christian life is not an ideal for the mind and conscience alone; it is a new life that embraces both body and spirit in a vital synthesis. It is not merely an order of faith; it is the order of charity fulfilled in action.

How can such an order be realised in the circumstances of modern life? We cannot go back to the strict formal asceticism of the past, any more than we can go back to the social law of the Old Testament. But on the other hand, we cannot do without asceticism altogether—that is the fallacy of the Quietist and the sentimentalist. We need a new asceticism suited to the new conditions of the modern world—a strenuous training of body and mind in the new life.

The needs of the new age have already called forth new forms of the religious life. The ascetic ideal no longer expresses itself in the external regulation of life, but has become so intimately fused with the religious vocation that it finds its own spontaneous expression in the life of the community. It is, however, easier for the religious to solve this problem, since his whole life is ordered to a religious end, and he is not distracted by a division of aims. The position of the layman is inevitably more difficult, since the external forms of life are determined by economic forces which take small account of religious considerations. And not only is religion confined to the inner life, but that life itself is also exposed to multiple distractions. Now even the poorest has opportunities for diversion, which surpass anything that even the privileged classes knew in former ages. It seems almost absurd to expect people to bring the spirit of Galilee and Assisi into the environment of Hollywood and Chicago. No Christian can deny that it is possible. But it involves something more than pious platitudes and ethical idealism. It calls for a heroic effort, like that which converted the Roman Empire. I believe myself that the need produces the man, and that the coming age of the Church will see a new out-pouring of spiritual energy manifested in the Christian life. But that does not acquit us of responsibility. It is not enough for us to sit still and wait for an apocalyptic solution of our problems. The saint, like every other great man, is the organ of a social purpose, and the

success of his mission depends on the reserves of faith
and spiritual will that have been accumulated by the
anonymous activity of ordinary, imperfect men and
women, each of whom has made an individual contribution, however minute it may be, to a new order
of Christian life.

6

The Dark Mirror

WHAT IS MAN'S essential religious need, judging by the experience of the past? There is an extraordinary degree of unanimity in the response, although, of course, it is not complete. One answer is God, the supernatural, the transcendent; the other answer is deliverance, salvation, eternal life. And both these elements are represented in some form or other in any given religion. The religion of ancient Israel, for example, may seem to concentrate entirely on the first of these two elements—the reality of God—and to have nothing to say about the immortality of the soul and the idea of eternal life. Yet the teaching of the prophets is essentially a doctrine of salvation—a social and earthly salvation, it is true, but nevertheless a salvation which is essentially religious and related to the eternal life of God. Again, Buddhism seems to leave no room for God and to put the whole emphasis of its teaching on the second element—deliverance. Nevertheless, it is based, as much as any religion can be, on the idea of Transcendence. Indeed, it is an exaggerated sense of transcendence which led to its negative attitude towards the ideas of God and the Soul. "We affirm something of God, in order not to affirm nothing," says the Catholic theologian. The Buddhist went a step farther on the *via negativa* and preferred to say nothing.

Now, a concentration on these two specifically religious needs produces an attitude to life totally op-

posed to the practical utilitarian outlook of the ordinary man. The latter regards the world of man—the
world of sensible experience and social activity—as the
one reality, and is sceptical of anything that lies beyond, whether in the region of pure thought or of
spiritual experience, not to speak of religious faith.
The religious man, on the contrary, turns his scepticism against the world of man. He is conscious of the
existence of another and greater world of spiritual
reality in which we live and move and have our being,
though it is hidden from us by the veil of sensible
things. He may even think, like Newman, that the
knowledge of the senses has a merely symbolic value;
that "the whole series of impressions made on us by
the senses may be but a Divine economy suited to our
need, and the token of realities distinct from them,
and such as might be revealed to us, nay, more perfectly, by other senses as different from our existing
ones as they are from one another."[1]

Thus the whole universe is, as it were, the shadow
of God and has its being in the contemplation or reflection of the Being of God. The spiritual nature reflects the Divine consciously, while the animal nature
is a passive and unconscious mirror. Nevertheless,
even the life of the animal is a living manifestation
of the Divine, and the flight of the hawk or the power
of the bull is an unconscious prayer. Man alone stands
between these two kingdoms in the strange twilight
world of rational consciousness. He possesses a kind
of knowledge which transcends the sensible without
reaching the intuition of the Divine.

It is only the mystic who can escape from this twilight world. But the mystic is not the normal man;
he is one who has transcended, at least momentarily,
the natural limits of human knowledge. The ordinary

[1] *University Sermons*, p. 350.

man is by his nature immersed in the world of sense, and uses his reason in order to subjugate the material world to his own ends, to satisfy his appetites, and to assert his will. He lives on the animal plane with a more than animal consciousness and purpose and, insofar, he is less religious than the animal. The life of pure spirit is religious, and the life of the animal is also religious, since it is wholly united with the life-force that is its highest capacity of being. Only man is capable of separating himself alike from God and from Nature, of making himself his last end and living a purely self-regarding and irreligious existence.

And yet the man who deliberately regards self-assertion and sensual enjoyment as his sole ends, and finds complete satisfaction in them—the pure materialist—is not typical; he is almost as rare as the mystic. The normal man has an obscure sense of the existence of a spiritual reality and a consciousness of the evil and misery of an existence which is the slave of sensual impulse and self-interest, and which must inevitably end in physical suffering and death. But how is he to escape from the wheel to which he is bound by the accumulated weight of his own acts and desires? How is he to bring his life into vital relation with that spiritual reality of which he is but dimly conscious and which transcends all the categories of his thought and the conditions of human experience? This is the fundamental religious problem which has perplexed and baffled the mind of man from the beginning, and is, in a sense, inherent in his nature.

I have intentionally stated the problem in its fullest and most classical form, as it has been formulated by the great minds of our own civilisation, since the highest expression of an idea is usually also the most explicit and the most intelligible. But there is nothing specifically Christian about it. It is common to Christianity and to Platonism and to the religious traditions of the ancient East. It is the universal attitude of the *anima naturaliter Christiana,* of that nature which the mediaeval mystics term "noble," because it is incapable of resting satisfied with a finite or sensible good. It is "natural religion" not, indeed, after the manner of the religion of naturalism, but in the true sense of the word.

It is, of course, obvious that such conceptions of spiritual reality presuppose a high level of intellectual development and that we cannot expect to find them in a pre-philosophic stage of civilisation. Nevertheless, however far back we go in history, and however primitive is the type of culture, we do find evidence for the existence of specifically religious needs and ideas of the supernatural, which are the primitive prototypes or analogues of the conceptions which we have just described.

Primitive man believes no less firmly than the religious man of the higher civilisations in the existence of a spiritual world upon which the visible world and the life of man are dependent. Indeed, this spiritual world is often more intensely realised and more constantly present to his mind than is the case with civilised man. He has not attained to the conception of an autonomous natural order, and, consequently, supernatural forces are liable to interpose themselves at every moment of his existence. At first sight the natural and the supernatural, the material and the spiritual, seem inextricably confused. Nevertheless, even in primitive nature-worship, the object of religious emotion and worship is never the natural phenomenon as such, but always the supernatural power, which is obscurely felt to be present in and working through the natural object.

To us, agriculture is merely a depressed industry which provides the raw material of our dinners, and so we assume that a religion which is largely concerned with agriculture must have been a sordid materialistic business. But this is entirely to misconceive primitive man's attitude to Nature. To him, agriculture was not a sordid occupation; it was one of the supreme mysteries of life, and he surrounded it with religious rites because he believed that the fertility of the soil and the mystery of generation could only be ensured through the co-operation of higher powers. Primitive agriculture was, in fact, a kind of liturgy.

For us Nature has lost this religious atmosphere because the latter has been transferred elsewhere. Civilisation did not create the religious attitude or the essential nature of the religious experience, but it gave them new modes of expression and a new intellectual interpretation. This was the achievement of the great religions or religious philosophies which arose in all the main centres of ancient civilisation about the middle of the first millennium B.C. They attained to the two fundamental concepts of metaphysical being and ethical order, which have been the foundation of religious thought and the framework of religious experience ever since. Some of these movements of thought, such as Brahmanism, Taoism, and the Eleatic philosophy, concentrated their attention on the idea of Being, while others, such as Buddhism, Confucianism, Zoroastrianism, and the philosophy of Heraclitus, emphasised the idea of moral order, but all of them agreed in identifying the cosmic principle, the power behind the world, with a spiritual principle, conceived either as the source of being or the source of ethical order. Primitive man had already found the transcendent immanent in and working through Nature as the supernatural. The new religions found it in thought and the supreme Reality and in ethics as the Eternal Law. And, consequently, while the former still saw the spiritual world diffused and confused with the

world of matter, the latter isolated it and set it over
against the world of human experience, as Eternity
against Time, as the Absolute against the Contingent,
as Reality against Appearance, and as the Spiritual
against the Sensible.

This was indeed the discovery of a new world for
the religious consciousness. It was thereby liberated
from the power of the nature daimons and the dark
forces of magic and translated to a higher sphere—
to the Brahma world—"where there is not darkness,
nor day nor night, nor being nor not-being, but the
Eternal alone, the source of the ancient wisdom," to
the Kingdom of Ahura and the Six Immortal Holy
Ones, to the world of the Eternal Forms, the true
home of the soul. And this involved a corresponding
change in the religious attitude. The religious life was
no longer bound up with irrational myths and non-
moral tabus; it was a process of spiritual discipline
directed towards the purification of the mind and the
will—a conversion of the soul from the life of the
senses to spiritual reality. The religious experience of
primitive man had become obscured by magic and
diabolism, and the visions and trances of the Shaman
belong rather to the phenomena of Spiritualism than
of mysticism. The new type of religious experience,
on the other hand, had reached a higher plane. It consisted in an intuition that was essentially spiritual and
found its highest realisation in the vision of the mystic.

Thus each of the new religio-philosophic traditions
—Brahmanism, Buddhism, Taoism, and Platonism—ultimately transcends philosophy and culminates in mysticism. They are not satisfied with the demonstration
of the Absolute; they demand the experience of the
Absolute also, whether it be the vision of the Essential Good and the Essential Beauty, through which the
soul is made deiform, or that intuition of the nothing-

ness and illusion inherent in all contingent being which renders a man *jivana mukti,* "delivered alive." But how is such an experience conceivable? It seems to be a contradiction in terms—to know the Unknowable, to grasp the Incomprehensible, to receive the Infinite. Certainly it transcends the categories of human thought and the normal conditions of human experience. Yet it has remained for thousands of years as the goal—whether attainable or unattainable—of the religious life, and no religion which ignores this aspiration can prove permanently satisfying to man's spiritual needs. The whole religious experience of mankind—indeed, the very existence of religion itself —testifies not only to a sense of the Transcendent, but to an appetite for the Transcendent which can only be satisfied by immediate contact—by a vision of the supreme Reality. It is the goal of the intellect as well as of the will.

A religion which remains on the rational level and denies the possibility of any real relation with a higher order of spiritual reality fails in its most essential function and, ultimately, like Deism, ceases to be a religion at all. It may perhaps be objected that this view involves the identification of religion with mysticism, and that it would place a philosophy of intuition like that of the Vedanta higher than a religion of faith and supernatural revelation, like Christianity. In reality, however, Christian insistence on the necessity of faith and revelation implies an even higher conception of transcendence than that of the Oriental religions. Faith transcends the sphere of rational knowledge even more than metaphysical intuition, and brings the mind into closer contact with superintelligible reality. Yet faith also, at least when it is joined with spiritual intelligence, is itself a kind of obscure intuition—a foretaste of the unseen, and it also has its culmination in the mystical experience by which these obscure spiritual realities are realised experimentally and intuitively.

Thus Christianity is in agreement with the great oriental religions and with Platonism in its goal of spiritual intuition, though it places the full realisation of that goal at a further and higher stage of spiritual development than the rest. For all of them, religion is not an affair of the emotions, but of the intelligence. Religious knowledge is the highest kind of knowledge, the end and coronation of the whole process of man's intellectual development. Herein they all differ profoundly from the conceptions of religion and religious experience which have been developed by modern European thinkers. For the modern mind no longer admits the possibility or the objective value of spiritual knowledge. The whole tendency of Western thought since the Renaissance, and still more since the eighteenth century, has been to deny the existence of any real knowledge except that of rational demonstration founded upon sensible experience. Intuition, whether metaphysical or mystical, is regarded as an irrational emotional conviction, and religion is reduced to subjective feeling and moral activity. Such a religion, however, can have no intellectual authority, and in consequence it also loses its social authority and even its moral influence. Civilisation becomes completely rationalised and secularised, as may be seen from the last two centuries of European history. Nevertheless, man cannot live by reason alone. His spiritual life, and even his physical instincts, are starved in the narrow and arid territory of purely rational consciousness. He is driven to take refuge in the non-rational, whether it be the irrational blend of spirituality and emotionalism that is termed romanticism, or, as is increasingly the case today, in the frankly sub-rational sphere of pure sensationalism and sexual impulse.

The mediaeval mystics base their whole theory of mysticism on the doctrine of the knowledge of God essentially present in the human soul. Underneath the surface of our ordinary consciousness, the sphere of the discursive reason, there is a deeper psychological level, "the ground of the soul," to which sensible images and the activity of the discursive reason cannot penetrate. This is the domain of the spiritual intuition, "the summit of the mind," and the spiritual will, which is naturally directed towards God. Here the soul is in immediate contact with God, who is present to it as its cause and the principle of its activity. It is, in fact, a mirror which has only to be cleansed and turned towards its object to reflect the image of God. In the words of Ruysbroek: "In the most noble part of the soul, the domain of our spiritual powers, we are constituted in the form of a living and eternal mirror of God; we bear in it the imprint of His eternal image, and no other image can ever enter there."

According to this view, every man naturally possesses an immediate contact with God in the deepest part of his soul; but he remains, as a rule, without the realisation and the enjoyment of it.

His soul is turned outwards to the things of sense, and his will is directed to temporal goods. It is the work of grace to reconstitute this divine image, to bring a man back to his essential nature, to cleanse the mirror of his soul so that it once more receives the divine light. Nevertheless, even apart from grace, the divine image remains present in the depths of the soul, and whenever the mind withdraws itself from its surface activity and momentarily concentrates itself within itself, it is capable of an obscure consciousness of the presence of God and of its contact with divine reality.

The religious attitude is only possible in the presence of the eternal and the transcendent. Any object that falls short of this fails to inspire the sense of awe and self-surrender which is essential to true religion. Man cannot worship himself, nor can he adore a Time God which is the creation of his own mind. As soon as he recognises its fictitious character, such an idea loses its religious power. And for the same reason, every attempt to create a new religion on purely rational and human foundations is inevitably doomed to failure.

7

The Hope of the World

A HUNDRED YEARS is a relatively short period. It does not even exceed the span of a single human life. Yet the last hundred years have changed human life more completely than any period in the history of the world. It is as though the stream of time had been transformed from a slow-flowing river to a roaring cataract. A hundred years ago the greater part of the human race was still living as it had always lived. The Far East was still a closed world, as remote in thought from Europe as though it had been a different planet, while the Far West was still empty, and tropical Africa still unknown. In the space of three generations the whole world has been opened up, brought together, and changed. There has been a breathless advance in population, wealth, and knowledge. The cities have not only increased in numbers and size; they have drawn the world together into a single society. The time is approaching when the cities become one city —a Babylon which sets its mark on the mind of every man and woman and imposes the same pattern of behaviour on every human activity.

Yet in the last generation the evils which the nineteenth century thought that it had banished forever— proscription and persecution, torture and slavery, and the fear of sudden death—have returned, and with them new terrors which the past did not know. We have discovered that evil too is a progressive force and that the modern world provides unlimited prospects for its development.

Thus it is no accident that the period that has seen the culmination of the modern development of scientific and economic power should have brought Western civilisation to the brink of ruin. For it is our power that is our destruction, and the world is drunk and poisoned with power, as primitive peoples have been poisoned by the gin and germs and gunpowder of a more advanced civilisation.

There is in fact an even wider gulf between the external conditions of our life and those of our ancestors a century ago than there was between the civilisation of the Spanish Conquistadors and that of the natives of the New World. The motor car and the aeroplane represent far more revolutionary changes in the relation of man to his environment than the coming of the armoured horseman who destroyed the civilisation of Mexico and Peru. But the change has been too sudden for men to adapt themselves to the new conditions. Human nature changes slowly, and the men who have conquered time and space and acquired almost unlimited material power are no more super-men than were their great-grandfathers of 1840. Yet they have been made super-men in spite of themselves—they have been taken from the plough and the cobbler's bench and have been given power which even the deified autocrats of the Old World empires never possessed.

These are the conditions that have led to the rise of the totalitarian state. It is an attempt to solve the problem of mass power by force, and thus it produces a new series of tensions and conflicts, which intensify the destructive character of the crisis. The problems of power cannot be solved by power alone, nor can they be solved by science, since science has become the servant of power. Liberty and reason are being destroyed by the powers that they created, and humanity is slipping blindly and helplessly towards the abyss, for humanity cannot save itself by its own efforts. When it is left to itself it perishes, and the greater its power and material resources, the more complete is the catastrophe.

That is the truth which was recognised by every civilisation that the world has known but which has been forgotten or denied by modern man in the intoxication of his newly acquired power. Nevertheless, it has not been left without a witness. Throughout the last hundred years the Church has not ceased to maintain the principle of the dependence of human society and human law on an order which transcends politics and economics, and to warn men of the inevitable catastrophe that must result from the attempt to create a civilisation which knew no law but man's own needs and ambitions. To Christians, therefore, the shock and the disillusionment should be less severe than to those who have put their faith in the nineteenth-century gospel of secular progress. For the Christian faith never minimised the reality of the forces of evil in history and society, as well as in the life of the individual, and it has prepared men's minds to face the extreme consequences of the external triumph of evil and the apparent defeat of good. Yet nonetheless it is no defeatist philosophy; it is a triumphant affirmation of life—of eternal life victorious over death, of the kingdom of God prevailing over the rulers of this world of darkness.

Fifteen centuries ago the ancient world was faced with a crisis that threatened civilisation with destruction almost at the moment when the Church had won the victory over paganism. For one thousand years the Mediterranean world had lived securely in the light of Hellenic culture. Now its sun had set, and the darkness and cold of the barbarous North descended on

the world. The East German warrior peoples driven
from South Russia and the Danube, by the advance
of the Mongol hordes from beyond the Volga, broke
through the defences of the Empire and wrecked the
imposing fabric of Roman order. Yet St. Augustine had
his answer. He could stand above the conflict because
though he was a loyal Roman and a scholar who realised the value of Greek thought, he regarded these
things as temporary and accidental. He lived not by the
light of Athens and Alexandria, but by a new light that
had suddenly dawned on the world from the East
only a few centuries earlier. Imperial Rome was, after
all, the daughter of Babylon, the incarnation of human
pride and material wealth, the persecutor of the saints,
and the oppressor of the poor. Man's true destinies
were realised elsewhere, in Jerusalem, the City of
God, which was being built up through all the ruin
and destruction of human kingdoms and empires by
the irresistible momentum of a divine purpose.

But for us today, the answer is far more difficult.
For the civilisation which has been undermined, and
is now threatened by total subversion, is a Christian
civilisation, built on the spiritual values and religious
ideals of St. Augustine and his like; and its adversary
is not the simple barbarism of alien peoples who
stand on a lower cultural level, but new powers armed
with all the resources of modern scientific technique,
which are inspired by a ruthless will to power that
recognises no law save that of their own strength. This
is almost a reversal of the situation envisaged by St.
Augustine. In his day the world was falling, and the
gates of the Church stood open as a city of refuge for
a defeated humanity. Today the world is strong, and
it has no pity for weakness and suffering. It has no
use for Christianity, which it despises as the most dangerous form of escapism and defeatism. It has its own
religion—a religion which reverses the Christian moral

values, which says, "Blessed are the strong, for they shall possess the earth," but which, no less than Christianity, demands unlimited sacrifices and an undivided allegiance of the whole man. Thus the situation that Christians have to face today has more in common with that described by the author of the Apocalypse than with the age of St. Augustine. The world is strong, and it has evil masters. But these masters are not vicious autocrats like Nero or Domitian. They are the engineers of the mechanism of world power, a mechanism that is more formidable than anything the ancient world knew, because it is not confined to external means, like the despotisms of the past, but uses all the resources of modern psychology to make the human soul the motor of its dynamic purpose.

Hence, while the fundamental Augustinian principles of the Two Loves and the Two Cities retain their validity, they have assumed a new form in these times, unlike anything in the previous experience of the Church. For today a deliberate attempt is being made to unify and energize human society from its lower depths: to bring Jerusalem—the spirit of man as the vessel of the spirit of God—into servitude to Babylon—the spirit of man degraded into the blind instrument of a demonic will to power. There is no room here to discuss the origin and development of this evil. It is sufficient to say that the revolutionary tendencies in modern civilisation which were originally inspired by a positive humanitarian optimism have become perverted into a "Revolution of Destruction." And the main cause of this, as Nietzsche pointed out, has been the loss of the Christian moral values, which "prevented man from despising himself as man, from turning against life, and from being driven to despair by knowledge."

For when once morality has been deprived of its religious and metaphysical foundations, it inevitably becomes subordinated to lower ends; and when these ends are negative, as in revolution and war, the whole scale of moral values becomes reversed. It is possible to understand how this moral nihilism may be combined with a kind of fanatical idealism in a subterranean revolutionary movement. But it becomes a much more evil thing when it is adopted as the creed of a government and is used by the ruling power to defend violence and injustice, when the revolutionary terrorism of the secret society blends with the repressive terrorism of the secret police to produce a new totalitarian technique of government by force and by fear, which undermines the psychological foundations of moral freedom.

From the Christian point of view, the most serious feature of the situation is that evil has become, as it were, de-personalised, separated from individual passion and appetite, and exalted above humanity into a sphere in which all moral values are confused and transformed. The great terrorists from Robespierre and St. Just to Dzershinski have not been immoral men, but rigid puritans who did evil coldly, by principle, without any thought of personal advantage; while the new mass dictatorships associate the highest and lowest qualities of human nature—self-sacrifice and boundless devotion, as well as unlimited violence and vindictiveness—in the assertion of their will to power.

This is the new evil that has spread from Russia, westward, into the very heart of Europe. It is no longer necessarily associated with Communism. On the contrary, it spreads by opposition, even more than by imitation. As soon as men decide that all means are permitted to fight an evil, then their good becomes indistinguishable from the evil that they set out to destroy. The subordination of morals to politics, the reign of terror, and the techniques of propaganda and psychological aggression can be used by any power or party that is bold enough to abandon moral scruples and plunge into the abyss.

The disintegration of Western culture under the moral and economic strain of wars is not a danger that can be lightly dismissed. Nor can it be accepted by Christians in the same spirit in which they accepted the fall of the Roman Empire, for that was an external disaster, which left the sources of spiritual vitality unimpaired, while this is a spiritual catastrophe, which strikes directly at the moral foundations of our society and destroys not the outward form of civilisation but the soul of man, which is the beginning and the end of all human culture.

8

A Universal Spiritual Society

Two ESSENTIAL CHARACTERISTICS distinguish the Christian faith and the Catholic Church: uniqueness and universality. Each of these can be extended by a number of associated features. The uniqueness of Christianity is related to its divine origin, its historic revelation, and its sacred or supernatural character. Its universality is related to its unity, its character as a visible society, and its sacramental nature. These characteristics are summed up in the traditional doctrine of the four notes of the Church—unity, sanctity, catholicity, and apostolicity—as we find in the statement of the creeds, "I believe in one Holy, Catholic, and Apostolic Church," and this definition underlies all the later developments of theological doctrine.

Against this Catholic conception of the Church as the universal spiritual society, there have always been two opposing views—so far opposed to one another that Catholicism stands midway between them. These are Sectarianism and Humanitarianism.

Sectarianism represents a rigorist or puritan tendency which has always been strong among Christians from the days of Tertullian to the Jansenists. It exalts the note of *holiness* above that of universality. The Church was seen as the society of the elect, the saints, to the exclusion of sinners. This was the cause of a whole series of early schisms—the Montanists and Tertullianists, the Novatians and the Donatists—all of whom held that there could be no forgiveness for those who had once fallen away from the Church, especially in times of persecution. Again with the Reformation, many Reformers, and especially the Calvinists, emphasised the idea of the Church as the society of the elect—an invisible Church to which the different visible or local churches belong in varying degrees. So too, Calvin's emphasis on the doctrine of predestination tended to limit the Church to a relatively small number of Christians who possess an assurance of their salvation. Thus the Church is not so much a universal society as a select society, and its mission is not to save the world but to separate a chosen remnant from the condemned mass of mankind.

There has, however, been an opposite tendency, which I have termed Humanitarianism, to criticise the Catholic conception of the Church as too narrow and to go beyond it towards the ideal of a universal Christian or natural religion—not limited to any particular form of belief or system of organisation—an all-inclusive spiritual society of all men of good will. According to this view, the Churches are simply voluntary associations of men for religious worship, and the less they claim to be exclusive, the better. This liberal, humanist, or relativist view of the Church became very prevalent from the eighteenth century onwards, and it has contributed no less than the Puritan view to form the religious pattern of the modern world. It is, however, political as well as religious; for since the French Revolution, the concept of the Church as the universal society has been replaced by Rousseau's ideal of the democratic state as a spiritual community, or the religion of humanity, which has taken many different forms and has been a powerful force in modern times.

Here it is clear that Catholicism stands or falls with the belief in a universal visible spiritual community. It is a very simple idea at first sight, and one which is neither mysterious nor hard to understand; yet everything depends on it, and every aspect of Catholicism illustrates it in one way or another.

This insistence on the unity and universality of the Church goes back before the beginning of Christianity, for the Church was the New Israel and had inherited the promises and the vocation of that very distinct and unique society. The fact that it had been transformed by the coming of the Messiah and extended by the vocation of the Gentiles did not destroy its sense of corporate identity. On the contrary, it strengthened it by raising it to a higher plane of cosmic significance. For the Church is the organ of human salvation, through which the redemptive work of Christ is transmitted to mankind. As Christ is the New Adam, the Church, which is the Body of Christ, is to be the new humanity in which the broken fragments of fallen humanity are brought back to unity and restored to the life of God. Thus the Church must be one, because Christ is one, and it must be universal, because it extends to the whole of the human race: indeed, it is the whole human race, insofar as humanity recovers its spiritual nature and returns to the divine fellowship.

So the Incarnation and the Church form one whole. They are the two aspects of a single process, and they are bound together not only by faith but also by the sacraments, which provide the organic link between the Head and the Body—between the life of Christ and the life of the Church. The Church therefore is not a voluntary religious association formed by the coming together of individual believers, but a supernatural divine organism which transmits the gift of eternal life to mankind.

These truths have always been accepted in some sense by all Christians everywhere insofar as they have accepted the teachings of the New Testament.

But we know only too well that there have been differences and discussions among Christians as to the interpretation of these principles. The thousand sects of Christendom, present and past, bear a very discordant witness to the one body. Some of them have staked everything on a particular interpretation of a particular doctrine, while others have gone into the wilderness in pursuit of a mirage of perfection which separated them from their fellow Christians. But the mark of the Catholic Church has always been its undeviating insistence on its universal mission. As Matthew Arnold wrote in one of his critical essays, it differs from all other religious bodies because it does not represent any particular type of man or school of thought, but is as wide as humanity. If the Christian Church was predestined from its foundation to be a universal society, it was necessary for it to be an international society, and this the Catholic Church has achieved on a scale of time and space wider than that of any other Christian body. The remarkable thing is that it has transcended national frontiers without destroying or weakening national individuality and sentiment, so that the most nationalistic peoples—Irish, Poles, Spaniards—are often the most ardent Catholics.

Even more important is the way in which Catholicism has succeeded in reconciling its universality with the claims of the individual soul. For the Catholic Church, in spite of its elaborate hierarchical organisation, its world-wide extension, and its authoritarian claims, has never lost contact with its individual members. The men of power and the men of learning have quarrelled with the Church, but the little men and women of all ages have made it their home. For the relationship of the individual Christian to the Church is never external or legalistic: every Christian has a direct access to the heart of the mystery, and his importance does not depend on his social or ecclesiastical position but on his personal participation in the life of the spirit by which the Church is animated. Thus we see how an uneducated peasant girl like Bernadette Soubirous played an important part in the religious life, not only of her country, but of the whole Catholic world, so that today she is far more widely known than contemporary ecclesiastical politicians like Cardinal Antonelli, or theologians like Cardinal Franzelin. In this way Catholicism depends, and has always depended, on the spiritual contributions of its individual members. It is a charismatic as well as a hierarchical society, and its universal mission is carried on not only by the organising work of the great religious orders and congregations, but by the unpredictable intervention of saints like Bernadette of Lourdes or Jean-Baptiste Vianney of Ars, who are the representatives of the common Christian people—the *Plebs Christi*.

These are the two poles of the Church's life, and the closer the communion between them, the more flourishing is its condition, whereas if they become in any way disconnected or dislocated, everything tends to go wrong, as in the fifteenth century, when the hierarchical Church condemned and burned St. Joan of Arc and Savonarola. The Catholic recovery in the following century was due not merely to the ecclesiastical and disciplinary reforms of the Council of Trent but no less to the appearance of so many great spiritual figures—like St. Ignatius Loyola, St. Philip Neri, St. Francis Xavier, St. Teresa, and St. John of the Cross, who reopened the paths of Christian perfection, restored the ideals of Christian life, and renewed the patterns of Christian sanctity.

The view has become widespread in modern times that the essential difference between Catholicism and Protestantism is due to the former being predominantly priestly or sacerdotal and the latter mainly prophetic. In the fourteenth century, however, when the sacerdotalism of Catholicism was more highly developed than ever before by the Avignon Papacy, the prophetic element was at the same moment most strongly asserted, as by the two great women mystics, SS. Bridget of Sweden and Catherine of Siena. In this case the connection between the mystical and the prophetic seems clear. But can we extend this to mysticism in general? Are the mystical and the prophetic elements equivalent?

Mysticism was of central importance to mediaeval Catholicism, and this raises the point of the relation between mysticism (with its prophetic element) and the priestly aspect. More broadly speaking, it is clear that in mediaeval Catholicism the mystical element is part of the larger notion of the saint. The cult of the saint is most important in Catholic culture. In fact, the very idea of a saint as a charismatic individual, definitely belonging to the prophetic type rather than the sacerdotal, has always been characteristic of the Catholic rather than the Protestant tradition.

The idea of the saint comprises three elements: (1) The numinous or supernatural element. (2) The democratic element, since it is always the voice of the people that counts. In distinction from the hierarchical character of the Church, recognition of saints comes from the laity; the popular cult precedes the Church's recognition. (3) The moral or mystical element. The saints are seen as mirrors of the holy, patterns of the perfect Christian life; of this aspect St. Francis is an outstanding example.

Surely we may question the assertion that Protestantism is predominantly prophetic? Can it not be said that the characteristic element of modern Protestantism is intellectual and social? In the past, no doubt, the Puritans, Quakers, and Baptists were strongly prophetic. In these cases, however, the pro-

phetic element was related to the mystical, though the
Protestant mystic was not the same type as the Catholic. Certainly the strong prophetic character in Protestantism led to the formation of new sects. I am, however, increasingly convinced that the mystical and
prophetic elements are *different* aspects of the same
thing. And about the relation between them there has
been little discussion. Von Hügel, for example, ana-
lyses religion into three categories: the institutional,
the intellectual, and the mystical. He does not mention
the prophetic.

For Protestants the problem presents a special difficulty. For Lutherans, Luther was himself such a
unique and outstanding figure. Few others of mystic
or prophetic type are known. Luther, moreover, was
very hostile to the ideal of sanctity expressed in mediaeval Catholicism. He regarded these Catholic saints
as representatives of the doctrine of good works, em-
bodiments of human perfection—both notions which
he, of course, rejected.

The seventeenth-century German Pietist movement,
which has in the past been regarded as having a mystical character, is now a highly controversial subject.
Many modern Lutheran scholars deny that this was
the case.

It is easier to study and parallel mysticism in Calvinism and Puritanism. In the Church of England, Anglican piety is well represented by George Herbert,
who exercised a lasting influence on Anglican devotion, even to the time of John Keble in the nineteenth
century.

Today the study of mysticism is overshadowed by
the influence of existentialism and the emphasis given
to the prophetic. The new religious type of personality, such as Kierkegaard, is not representative of
either Catholic or Protestant spirituality.

In Catholicism the mystical tradition (with its

prophetic and philosophic elements) is inseparable from the tradition of the saint, the cult of the saint. Too sharp a distinction is therefore unjustified between the sacerdotal and the prophetic, either in themselves or as representing the essential characteristics of Catholicism and Protestantism.

Co-ordination of the common ecclesiastical order and the individual quest for spiritual perfection is, I think, one of the characteristic notes of Catholicism and one of the secrets of its strength. For it is not the case elsewhere. In other religious bodies the two movements rarely coincide, so that each renewal of spiritual life involves the creation of a new sect or denomination. We see a striking example of this in England in the eighteenth century. John Wesley was no rebel. He was a thoroughly loyal son of the Church of England in the traditional sense. Yet the ecclesiastical organisation could not find room for him or his work. The new wine burst the old bottles, and he was driven into schism against his will and his principles.

If we attempt to look deeper into the causes of this combination of universality and individuality which lies at the heart of Catholicism, I think we shall find it in the economy of the sacraments. It is evident from the history of Catholicism that the development of the ecclesiastical polity, the growth of canon law, and all the other forms of external organisation, have been accompanied *pari passu* by a development of the sacramental system, which brought the whole ecclesiastical order into immediate contact with the psychological experience of the individual. Thus in the patristic period, the greatest public act of the Church, which still survives in the Paschal liturgy of the Roman rite, was the annual or bi-annual ceremony of the blessing of the font and the communal baptism of catechumens. Here the Church is seen not as a ruler, lawgiver, or guardian of orthodox tradition but as the

mother of a reborn humanity, each member of which
is the heir of the divine promises, recipient of the gift
of the spirit.

Similarly in modern times, the increase in ecclesiastical centralisation has been accompanied by an increasing emphasis on the participation of the individual Christian, daily if possible, in the sacrament of
unity. For the sacramental system brings home to the
believer the psychological dimensions of the changes
in human nature involved in the construction of the
universal spiritual society. Without the spiritual rebirth of the individual there can be no restoration of
humanity, and unless the new man has an immediate
access to the source of divine life, he cannot remain a
living cell of the new divine organism. All this is ex-
plicitly stated in the Fourth Gospel and in the teachings of St. Paul, and it remains the theological and
moral and psychological centre of Catholicism.

But if Catholicism means a universal spiritual society, so that the Church is the organ by which
mankind as a whole is spiritually transformed and re-
created, how comes it that the Catholic Church remains such a limited and incomplete society, so that
there are great masses of humanity to which it has
barely penetrated, if at all, and then only in the last
few centuries? This has always been an obvious difficulty, common to all forms of Christianity. The Scandal of the Church is inseparable from the Scandal of
the Cross. If it is difficult to believe that this particular
historical society is the form of a new humanity and
the organ of the renewal of the universal human race,
it is also difficult to believe that this individual Person is the Incarnate Word of God and that his ignomini-
ous death is the source of the redemption of humanity.

However we look at it, there is no avoiding this scandal or paradox, which is central to the Christian faith,
and which St. Paul insisted must always be unaccept-

able to the wisdom of the world and its princes. For it is only accessible to Revelation, that is to say, the knowledge that God has chosen particular means, which human reason could not have discovered, to realise his purposes for man, which equally transcend the limits of human knowledge and reasoning. But if we once accept the principle of a divine intervention in history, so that particular events, personalities, and social traditions may be used as the vehicles of divine purpose, the idea of a universal spiritual society, which is the medium for the realisation of these purposes, is not only conceivable but necessary and inevitable. For then the Church can be accepted as an integral part of the supernatural economy of salvation —that economy which St. Paul calls "the Mystery" par excellence.

Even a writer who accepts wholeheartedly the ideal of a universal spiritual society as the goal of history, Dr. Toynbee, cannot bring himself to admit that the hope of the world should be committed to a spiritual tradition and prefers to put his faith in a consensus of the great world religions, East and West. Catholicism, however, does not rest on a consensus of human wisdom—even on its highest and most spiritual plane—but upon a divine revelation which is also an act of creation. And since creation in itself transcends human reason, how much more must this be so with the act of spiritual creation or regeneration which brings the human animal into immediate relation and communion with the divine nature. It is, however, a rational presupposition to suppose that this cannot be brought about by the cumulative labours of human reason—by adding philosophy to philosophy and religion to religion. It must come *a parte Dei*, not *a parte hominis* —from God, not man. And this is what all Christians confess by their faith in the Incarnation and the work of Christ—a particular person who lived in a remote corner of the Roman Empire at a particular moment of history. It is therefore entirely consistent that this work should be carried on and fulfilled in a particular society which develops throughout the whole course of human history bearing the seed of a new world and a new humanity.

Thus apart from the continuity of Catholic tradition there are ample historical reasons for insisting on the dogma of the visible unity of the Catholic Church. We must, however, bear in mind that this doctrine has a dual aspect. In the past much has been written about the distinction between the soul and the body of the Church. Most modern theologians reject this terminology because it suggests a duality in the membership of the Church and those who belong to its soul. If, however, the distinction is referred to the two aspects of the one visible Catholic Church, such objections do not arise, and there is much to be said in its favour. Thus if we are asked, "What is the Catholic Church?," the obvious answer is, There it is before your eyes: an enormous visible social institution which is as much a part of our daily experience as our own country. We all, or most of us, know something of its organisation —Pope, cardinals, bishops, priests, religious orders, and so on—and of the influence it exerts over its members by its hierarchical authority and its code of ecclesiastical law. But all this is only the *body* of the Church, and anyone who knows this alone knows very little about Catholicism. For the Church is also a society founded on faith and animated by the Spirit. This is the *soul* of the Church, without which it could not exist and upon which the spiritual life of the individual Catholic depends. Both these aspects, however, are necessary to one another—the body cannot exist without the soul that animates it; the soul cannot *be* a soul without the body it animates.

To understand the Catholic idea of a universal spiritual society, it is above all necessary to understand this unity of the two elements that comprise the spiritual organism, for this is the entire Catholic system. At every stage and in every activity these two elements coexist and interpenetrate. As humanity is one, the Church must be one, because the Church is humanity restored to Christ. The principle of unity is the person of Christ, but there must also be an external organisation of unity and of institutions in which this internal unity finds its contemporary forms. Otherwise the unity of the spiritual society would be lost among the multiplicity of sects, in the same way as the unity of humanity has been lost in the Babel of mutually incomprehensible languages and cultures. The *raison d'être* of the Church is to heal this division by bringing back the nations—the *gentes* or Gentiles—into spiritual unity. For, as St. Thomas has said, the union of men with God is the union of men with one another —*conjunctio hominum cum Deo est conjunctio hominum inter sese*. On the other hand, if Christianity were to lead the nations still farther apart from one another into spiritual disunity, it would defeat the central purpose of the Church's institution.

Epilogue:
The Future Life

THE BELIEF IN THE FUTURE LIFE has accompanied human society from its origins to modern times, and has had an immense and incalculable influence on the development both of religion and of culture. Today, perhaps for the first time in human history, this belief is no longer taken for granted by the ordinary man. Doubts and difficulties that were formerly confined to the few have become the property of the many. The progress of modern secular civilisation, with its increasing demands on men's time and energies and its increasing opportunities for diversion, all tend to push the thought of death, and the hope and fear of what comes after death, into the background.

To some extent this has even affected religion. Modern religion has tended to lose its "otherworldly" character—to become more concerned with social problems and responsibilities and less preoccupied with the thought of death and judgment. No one will regret the disappearance of the eschatological sensationalism which was one of the most repellent features of popular Protestantism in the last century. Unfortunately, the growth of religious humanity and liberality has been accompanied by a certain loss of objectivity.

Hope has taken the place not only of fear but also of faith, and the firm outlines that marked the traditional Christian doctrine of the future life have tended to disappear in a haze of sentiment. There is a characteristic example of this in Maeterlinck's play,

The Blue Bird, which solves the agonising problem of
human mortality with a high-sounding aphorism—
"there is no death." Nothing could be further removed
from this than the traditional Christian attitude, with
its awful consciousness of death and judgment and its
objective faith in a real deliverance. It is the product
not of a facile idealism but of a hard-won struggle in
which more than human forces were involved. The
mystery of death, which has always lain so heavy on
the human race—the despair of Ecclesiastes before the
emptiness of life, the agony of Job in face of the apparent injustice of God—find their solution in the yet
more profound mystery of the Cross, in the darkness
of Calvary, not in the light of human philosophy and
science.

Thus the Catholic faith in "the resurrection of the
body and the life of the world to come" is much more
than a belief in the survival of the individual soul. It
is the acceptance of an organic world of spiritual realities into which man obtains entry not of his own
right, but by "grace"—that is to say, by a creative act
of divine initiative. The Christian is one who has "already tasted the powers of the world to come" and
who has become a member of a society that is trans-
human and transmortal. The Church is the visible,
historical organ of this new world and this new society, or rather, to speak more correctly, the Church
is itself this society, the body of restored humanity,
and what we usually call the Church is only that small
part of it which moves and acts in the world of men—
the Church Militant.

This is why Catholicism attaches such immense importance to the doctrine of the Communion of Saints,
the solidarity of the living and the dead in the common life of the One Body. All those beliefs and practices with regard to the future life which are most

distinctively Catholic—the invocation of saints, prayers and Masses for the dead, indulgences and the doctrine of the treasury of merits—all of them depend on this conception of a community which transcends the limits of mortality, a society which possesses a common principle of life and whose activity is not stopped or even weakened by the barriers of death. The dead still share in the organic life of the Church; they help and are helped by the living, so that the life of the world to come is already actualised in this vital communion. Thus to the Catholic, death may be only the gate to a wider and more intense form of social activity, as with St. Therese of Lisieux, who used to say that her real work for others would begin when her earthly life was finished.

This conception answers to a profound need of the human soul, a need that expresses itself in all those manifold practices and beliefs connected with the cult of the dead that played so large a part in primitive religion and that contributed so much to the classical idea of "piety." Yet it cannot be regarded as due to the survival of such primitive ideas or to the infiltration of alien religious elements. It has its true *raison d'être* in the very nature of Christianity and in the central doctrines of the faith. We see in the art of the catacombs how prominent a part the cult of the dead held in the primitive Church, and how every device of symbolism and imagery was employed to bring home to the spectator the great fact of the triumph of life over death, a triumph which proceeds without interruption from its beginning in the sacramental mystery of Regeneration to its consummation in the mystery of the Resurrection. For the keynote of the Christian doctrine of future life is not Immortality, but Resurrection; not the survival of an immaterial principle, but the vital restitution of human nature in its

integrity. The goal of the process of redemption is not
the perfection of the individual, it is a universal, cosmic change—the life of the world to come.

It is indeed difficult for the human mind to accept
the possibility of so vast a change—not because the belief is in itself irrational, but because it so far surpasses
the limits of our knowledge and experience. Yet it is
of the very nature of a mystery that it should so transcend our experience and the reasoning that is based
on experience. Yet if we reject the idea of mystery, the
religious point of view itself becomes impossible. A
mystery is not contrary to reason or without relation
to reality. It forms part of a system of reality, but not
of that system which is familiar to our experience. As
Newman says somewhere, it is like an island which
seems lost in a world of waters, but which is really a
peak of a hidden range of mountains. So it is with the
mystery of the Resurrection. If the cosmic process is a
mechanical one and human consciousness is nothing
but the accidental and transitory outcome of blind,
material forces, then indeed the hope of a resurrection
is as vain as all the rest of man's hopes and beliefs.

But if mind is the key to reality and the cosmic process has a spiritual significance, then we should expect
that the most permanent things in the world would
be not atoms or elements, but persons, and there
would be nothing shocking to the reason in the belief
that the goal of the cosmic process was to be found
in an order which restored and preserved that which
was spiritually valuable in the present world. The human animal is no more capable of comprehending
the purpose of the world by the light of his practical
experience than the ant that crawls on the pylon of a
wireless station is capable of understanding the meaning of radio-telegraphy. And the world to come—

saeculum venturum—may be no less different from the world of our sensible experience than is a symphony of Beethoven from the complicated mechanism which has been framed to transmit it.

Appendix

Sources and the dates of writing or publication of material used in each of the chapters of this volume:

Chapter 8   Chapter III, *The Movement of World Revolution*, 1959.

Chapter 9   Chapters III and IV, *The Gods of Revolution* (published posthumously), 1972.

Chapter 10 Chapter I, *The Modern Dilemma*, 1932.

Chapter 11 Chapter IV, *Religion and the Modern State*, 1935.

Chapter 12 Chapter III, *The Modern Dilemma*, 1932.

PART THREE: THE NATURE AND DESTINY OF MAN

Introduction: Chapter I, *The Historic Reality of Christian Culture*, 1960.

Chapter 1   Harvard Lectures, 1958–62.

Chapter 2   *Dublin Review*, October 1943.

Chapter 3   *The Tablet*, August 5, 1972 (posthumous).

Chapter 4   *Blackfriars*, October 1945.

Chapter 5   *Dublin Review*, January 1933.

Chapter 6   *Dublin Review*, October 1930.

Chapter 7   Chapter I, *The Judgment of the Nations*, 1943.

Chapter 8   Chapter XIX, *The Formation of Christendom*, 1967.

Epilogue: *The Spectator*, December 15, 1933.

Index of Proper Names

OTHER IMAGE BOOKS

THE IMITATION OF CHRIST – Thomas à Kempis. Edited with an Introduction by Harold C. Gardiner, S.J. (D17) – $1.75

SAINT THOMAS AQUINAS – G. K. Chesterton (D36) – $1.45

ST. FRANCIS OF ASSISI – G. K. Chesterton (D50) – $1.45

VIPER'S TANGLE – François Mauriac. A novel of evil and redemption (D51) – 95¢

THE CITY OF GOD – St. Augustine. Edited by Vernon J. Bourke. Introduction by Étienne Gilson. Specially abridged (D59) – $2.95

RELIGION AND THE RISE OF WESTERN CULTURE – Christopher Dawson (D64) – $1.95

THE LITTLE FLOWERS OF ST. FRANCIS – Translated by Raphael Brown (D69) – $1.95

DARK NIGHT OF THE SOUL – St. John of the Cross. Edited and translated by E. Allison Peers (D78) – $1.45

THE CONFESSIONS OF ST. AUGUSTINE – Translated with an Introduction by John K. Ryan (D101) – $1.75

A HISTORY OF PHILOSOPHY: VOLUME 1 – GREECE AND ROME (2 Parts) – Frederick Copleston, S.J. (D134a, D134b) – $1.75 ea.

A HISTORY OF PHILOSOPHY: VOLUME 2 – MEDIAEVAL PHILOSOPHY (2 Parts) – Frederick Copleston, S.J. Part I – Augustine to Bonaventure. Part II – Albert the Great to Duns Scotus (D135a, D135b) – Pt. I, $1.95; Pt. II, $1.75

A HISTORY OF PHILOSOPHY: VOLUME 3 – LATE MEDIAEVAL AND RENAISSANCE PHILOSOPHY (2 Parts) – Frederick Copleston, S.J. Part I – Ockham to the Speculative Mystics. Part II – The Revival of Platonism to Suárez (D136a, D136b) – Pt. I, $1.75; Pt. II, $1.45

A HISTORY OF PHILOSOPHY: VOLUME 4 – MODERN PHILOSOPHY: Descartes to Leibniz – Frederick Copleston, S.J. (D137) – $1.75

A HISTORY OF PHILOSOPHY: VOLUME 5 – MODERN PHILOSOPHY: The British Philosophers, Hobbes to Hume (2 Parts) – Frederick Copleston, S.J. Part I – Hobbes to Paley (D138a) – $1.45. Part II – Berkeley to Hume (D138b) – $1.75

A HISTORY OF PHILOSOPHY: VOLUME 6 – MODERN PHILOSOPHY (2 Parts) – Frederick Copleston, S.J. Part I – The French Enlightenment to Kant (D139a, D139b) – $1.45 ea.

A HISTORY OF PHILOSOPHY: VOLUME 7 – MODERN PHILOSOPHY (2 Parts) – Frederick Copleston, S.J. Part I – Fichte to Hegel. Part II – Schopenhauer to Nietzsche (D140a, D140b) – $1.75 ea.

These prices subject to change without notice

OTHER IMAGE BOOKS

These prices subject to change without notice

OTHER IMAGE BOOKS

These prices subject to change without notice

OTHER IMAGE BOOKS

These prices subject to change without notice

B 75–4

Q27